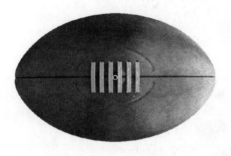

LEGENDS
IN BLACK

*New Zealand Rugby Greats
on Why We Win*

TOM JOHNSON

WITH ANDY MARTIN, GEOFF WATSON AND MARGOT BUTCHER

PENGUIN BOOKS

PENGUIN BOOKS

Published by the Penguin Group
Penguin Group (NZ), 67 Apollo Drive, Rosedale,
Auckland 0632, New Zealand (a division of Penguin New Zealand Pty Ltd)
Penguin Group (USA) Inc., 375 Hudson Street,
New York, New York 10014, USA
Penguin Group (Canada), 90 Eglinton Avenue East, Suite 700, Toronto,
Ontario, M4P 2Y3, Canada (a division of Penguin Canada Books Inc.)
Penguin Books Ltd, 80 Strand, London, WC2R 0RL, England
Penguin Ireland, 25 St Stephen's Green,
Dublin 2, Ireland (a division of Penguin Books Ltd)
Penguin Group (Australia), 707 Collins Street, Melbourne,
Victoria 3008, Australia (a division of Penguin Australia Pty Ltd)
Penguin Books India Pvt Ltd, 11, Community Centre,
Panchsheel Park, New Delhi – 110 017, India
Penguin Books (South Africa) (Pty) Ltd, Block D, Rosebank Office Park,
181 Jan Smuts Avenue, Parktown North, Gauteng 2193, South Africa
Penguin (Beijing) Ltd, 7F, Tower B, Jiaming Center, 27 East Third Ring Road North,
Chaoyang District, Beijing 100020, China

Penguin Books Ltd, Registered Offices: 80 Strand, London, WC2R 0RL, England

First published by Penguin Group (NZ), 2014
10 9 8 7 6 5 4 3 2 1

Copyright © Tom Johnson, Andy Martin and Geoff Watson, 2014

The right of Tom Johnson, Andy Martin, Geoff Watson and Margot Butcher to be identified as
the authors of this work in terms of section 96 of the Copyright Act 1994 is hereby asserted.

Design © Penguin Group (NZ)
Rugby ball graphic and background texture from iStockphoto.com
Photographs on pages 36, 52, 72, 86, 104, 120, 132 and colour pages 1 (with Stan Meads
and Kel Tremain), 2, 3 (with Frank Oliver), 4, 5 (with Zinzan Brooke), 7 (with Tana Umaga),
8 by Peter Bush
Photographs on pages 148, 172, 188, 204 and colour page 6 by Photosport
Photograph on page 8 from Tom Johnson
Prepress by Image Centre Ltd
Printed and bound in Australia by Griffin Press, an Accredited ISO AS/NZS 14001
Environmental Management Systems Printer

ISBN 978-0-143-57180-3

A catalogue record for this book is available
from the National Library of New Zealand.

www.penguin.co.nz

CONTENTS

INTRODUCTION

A WINNING CULTURE

Winning isn't everything; it's the only thing
– Vince Lombardi, coach of the Green Bay Packers

The final whistle cuts the night air and men in black rugby kit suddenly relax and, if it was more than the usual intense, graunching test, sink to the ground in exhausted relief. It's a ritual so familiar to any New Zealand rugby supporter, raised from the cradle on the staunchness of All Blacks rugby, that it's almost taken for granted that the All Blacks will win a rugby test more often than not.

The winning record of the All Blacks stands out as truly remarkable – not only within the context of international rugby, but in the entire world of sports teams. Since their first official international match in 1903, the All Blacks have won a massive 75 per cent of all their test matches. That places them among the most successful sports teams in history. Football's five-time world champions Brazil, for example, have an overall winning record of 62 per cent in international matches. And while some American sports franchises, such as the Chicago Bulls and San Francisco 49ers, have had periods of success, unlike the All Blacks they have not been able to sustain that over such a lengthy period.[1]

Something special must be at play for an ever-changing group of men, generation after generation pulling on their revered black jerseys, to keep up such an imposing winning record. The big question then – something perhaps every other sports team on the planet would love to know – is what is that x-factor that makes the All Blacks winners? That's what we wanted to know, too.

The All Blacks' success and legacy over 110 years certainly makes them a compelling case study of a winning team. For New Zealanders, great All Blacks teams have a significance beyond the immediate sporting arena; they form part of New Zealand's wider history and culture.

And, teams such as the 1905 'Originals', which won 30 of their 31 matches, scoring 976 points and conceding only 59; and the 1924 All Blacks side aptly referred to as the 'Invincibles', which won all 32 of their matches, have an enduring place in both New Zealand and international rugby history.

For much of the period covered by this book, South Africa was the supreme opponent – the fierce rivalry between the two countries having started with drawn series in New Zealand in 1921 and South Africa in 1928. Then, in their 1937 and 1949 encounters, South Africa began a period of domination that lasted until 1956 – when the All Blacks were victorious for the first time in a series in New Zealand. To this day, that series is put up in lights and discussed by rugby cognoscenti. It took another 40 years for the All Blacks to win a series in South Africa, having lost series in 1960, 1970 and 1976, yet the All Blacks sustained their overall winning record regardless.

As the one-on-one interviews with the rugby legends in this book reveal, All Blacks teams are acutely aware of their history. It has been a powerful, undeniable source of motivation. The respect for this tradition and history is succinctly summed up by former All Blacks captain Sean Fitzpatrick:

> Those traditions within the All Blacks that have remained, whether they be songs or sayings, processes or protocol, serve to connect us back through all the players that have shared them with us, all the way back to James Allan – All Black number one – in 1884 . . . An adidas advert summed it up brilliantly when it said of the All Blacks jersey, 'The legacy is more intimidating than any opposition.'[2]

Legends in Black is, we hope, an insightful examination of those traditions. How they have come about, how they have evolved over the years and, ultimately, how they have cultivated and inspired generations of winning All Blacks.

Tom's first chapter 'A Life of Rugby' introduces our passion for the game, then we sit down with some of the greats – Sir John Graham, Sir Colin Meads, Sir Brian Lochore and Ian Kirkpatrick ('A Winning Legacy'); Andy Haden, Andy Dalton, Wayne 'Buck' Shelford and John Hart ('Winning the World Cup'); Laurie Mains, Wayne Smith and Sir Graham Henry ('Winning the World Cup Twice'). Our final section ('A Study of Winning') digs a little deeper, reflecting on the key themes of the interviews and presenting an absorbing analysis of the game. Finally we look at the evolution of the sport and its culture as women began to pull on a black jersey and run with the ball. Farah Palmer, who steered the Black Ferns to three successive World Cup victories, tells that fascinating story from the inside.

What emerges is a rich and varied portrait of commitment to success, passion for the game, dedication to one's teammates, an ability to be constantly challenging the status quo, and a collective strategy for success that has ensured the All Blacks remain world rugby leaders. There is no other team quite like them.

CHAPTER ONE
A LIFE OF RUGBY

DR TOM JOHNSON

Aim to win. If you do win, park it quickly. If you don't, use the failure. Take a positive out of it wherever you can. Reframe it not as a failure, but as feedback, as a necessary part of the process of winning.[1]
— Sean Fitzpatrick

For the 55,000 rugby enthusiasts who had managed to gain tickets to the 2011 Rugby World Cup final at Eden Park, the dying minutes were a nail-biter to say the least. For the greater audience sitting in front of television sets both in New Zealand and abroad, the term 'nail-biter' would be an understatement of the strained emotions that were being confronted. Painful memories of the All Blacks' 2007 Rugby World Cup quarterfinal loss to France lingered. People turned away, unable to watch the struggle of the last seconds of play as the All Blacks ground up the field in a series of rucks from well within their own half of the field. *Five . . . four . . . three . . . two:* the ball was moved through to the pack and punted out as the final hooter sounded. Suddenly the tension dissolved into tears. Screams and cheers resounded in every hollow. The final score, an 8–7 victory to the All Blacks over France, was the win that had eluded the men in black and their silver fern since claiming the inaugural World Cup of 1987.

How is it that a small country like New Zealand can produce such a noteworthy rugby team? The story is essentially off-field and behind the scenes. In order to tell it, considerable research involving All Blacks coaches and captains has been undertaken. This research examined past and present activities and highlights specific matters that are deemed to directly contribute to the All Blacks' success, along the way building an understanding of how the likes of cultural diversity, history, organisational culture, leadership and professionalism intertwine to contribute to the All Blacks' accomplishments.

In telling their part of the story, the shared perspectives provide an information and knowledge base about the sports team with the legendary record. Whilst winning or losing a sports game essentially reflects the combined abilities (including skill execution) of those on the field on the day and the tactical decisions made, we need the ability to understand what has gone on behind the scenes as a lead-up to the event in question. If we are able do this, then we can have a more rational explanation and assessment of an outcome, rather than only some emotional reaction after the final whistle. Can a game's lessons truly be sustained and maintained into the future? The answer lies in the degree of comfort any new information provides in terms of its fit with our existing knowledge, and our own ability to allow new information to become second nature – if a fit is possible.

A LIFETIME OF RUGBY

It is because of my lifelong involvement with rugby that I have such a passionate interest in the welfare of the national game – a desire to see the success of the All Blacks maintained, as well as the game continuing to be promoted as an enjoyable sport and recreation for all New Zealanders. The period I had in rugby gave me valuable experience in how to try to be an inspirational leader, with a sound knowledge and understanding of the strategies and tactics necessary to be successful. It made me conscious of the need to plan adequately, and how to motivate your fellow players.

Leadership is a challenge because you are usually thrust into the role without really knowing why you have been selected for the job, but experiential learning and success builds confidence. In my case, my rugby experience helped me in the various leadership roles I held in senior management and lecturing positions later on in my working life. When I began my academic studies (ironically at the same time as two of my sons were attending university), I realised how much I would have benefited earlier in my business career had I gone to university at a younger age. I know I could have done a much better job in company restructuring, for example, had I had the understanding I have now of organisational culture. This combination of a love for rugby, experiential interest in leadership and theoretical exploration of organisational culture motivated me to undertake research and ultimately write this book.

A LEGACY OF WINNING – 1940S TO 1950S: GROWING UP WITH THE RUGBY CULTURE

My earliest recollections of rugby begin when I was growing up in a state house during the war, and immediately thereafter, in Latham Street, Marewa, Napier.

I remember listening to the All Blacks playing Australia in 1946 and South Africa in 1949 through the scratchy static of our radio, and I vividly recall sitting up listening in the early hours of the morning during that 1949 tour when goal-kicking prop Aaron 'Okey' Geffin kicked five penalties to win the first test for the 'Boks' – after the All Blacks had deserved to win by scoring the tries. I listened to them all, and repeated the process in 1960, before the advent of TV in New Zealand.

The result of that 1949 test series, which New Zealand lost 4–nil, on top of the South Africans' 2–1 win in the 1937 series, actually gave the Springboks an advantage in the win/loss ratio until 1956. It only served to inflame the rivalry. The 1956 tour by coach Danie Craven's team was a pivotal one from a New Zealand perspective. New Zealand won the series 3–1, after some titanic battles. Such was the widespread pride in that All Blacks team that many of the incidents have become part of New Zealand rugby folklore: the feats of Kevin Skinner, who dealt with the South African front row in the third test in Christchurch; Peter Jones's try in the final test in Auckland; and the dominating effect of 'DB' Clarke in the same tests.

As a fourth-generation European New Zealander and a product of the World War II era, many of my personal values were established in this period. Having a father away at the war, knowing the deprivation and hardship of shortages and rationing, and fear about the future all helped instil a work ethic. There was 'no such thing as a free lunch' and there was a palpable national pride in New Zealand having proved itself both in successive wars and on the rugby fields. The egalitarian ethos associated with the image of New Zealand society was symbolically mirrored in rugby, which was promoted as a game for all (all males, at least) – regardless of ethnicity, social background, size or skill level. Rugby was the legacy from New Zealand's colonial past that made a lasting impression on me.

My early playing memories are of scrag-type rugby on the fields by my school and becoming aware that my father, Bill, had been a very good player who had broken his ankle playing for Hawke's Bay against the Springboks in 1937. That game had been one of the big events in Napier during that era, and the memories of it stayed relatively fresh through the wartime years. My father had scored a try and the general consensus was that, had he not been carted off with a broken ankle – and Hawke's Bay therefore forced to play a man short – they could have beaten the 'Boks' in what was generally conceded to be the toughest game they had on tour, outside the tests. One of my father's good mates, Doug Dalton, had played in the test series and had given my father the Springboks jersey of Jan Lotz. So, to a degree, I was raised on the aura of

All Blacks versus Springboks rugby tests as the ultimate in sporting endeavour in New Zealand. Although little was said about it, I also became aware that my grandfather, Joe, and his brother Crawford had played for Hawke's Bay back in the 1890s.

Organised rugby started for me in Hamilton, at Forest Lake Primary School – before there was any organised Saturday-morning rugby for kids. I had two years playing for both the Hamilton Primary School Reps and the Waikato Roller Mills teams before I went to Hamilton Boys' High School, where I played in the First XV for two years. For some inexplicable reason I ended up captain of all these teams. Then, as a 17-year-old in 1956, I began my senior rugby career playing for Ardmore Teachers' Training College in the Counties senior competition the same year. Our team won. In those days I would also travel from Hamilton to Auckland at four in the morning to get into Eden Park and then sit all day on the terraces to watch test rugby. The atmosphere was electrifying. Don Clarke's prodigious kick at goal from just inside the All Blacks' 10-yard mark had a hugely demoralising effect on the Springboks team – even though it just missed! Then Ron Hemi made a break from the front of a lineout and had Peter Jones flash through to collect the ball, run 30 yards and score the try. That sent the crowd into a delirious frenzy – such was the importance of rugby to the national psyche. It remains one of my most memorable moments in a lifetime of playing and watching rugby in New Zealand.

Our Ardmore team had 12 players who played representative rugby then or thereafter, so it was a team with some ability playing a glorified First XV style of rugby. As a 17-year-old it just seemed too easy, as from number 8 I scored a try in each of the first five games of the season, but then what I love about rugby is its ability to bring you back to earth. An injured ankle kept me out for the rest of the season. However, the following year I played the last two games of the season for Counties, thus starting my representative career. In the first match against Poverty Bay, which we drew 11–all, the game was remarkable for the fact that Sonny Rutene, who had scored all 11 of the points for Poverty Bay, did so by using all the means at his disposal – a try, a conversion, a penalty and a dropped goal, and I started my first match with a try myself.

By 1958 I was teaching at Rangiriri School and playing for Hamilton Old Boys in the Hamilton competition – a most enjoyable year. I made the Waikato team, which was a real thrill as the team had the great 'DB' Clarke, his brother Ian Clarke, Wilson Whineray and very good players from the team that had beaten the Springboks in 1956 – Rex Pickering, Bryce Cowley and Malcolm McDonald. It was a wonderful learning curve for me going on a South Island tour with such experienced players, who taught me much about the game. My first match was against Wellington at Athletic Park, before the erection of the Millard stand, where I experienced the oratory of Waikato selector-coach Bill Corby at a team talk for the first time. It was rousing stuff, in the Billy Graham mould, and something new to me.

People already talked in that era of a national culture in New Zealand of 'rugby, racing and beer'. It was a generalisation, of course, but there was certainly an element of truth in the assessment. New Zealand had come through a depression and world war that had made people conscious of deprivation and the need for hard work. It was very much a patriarchal society in the sense that men were expected to be the income earners, head of the household; and women to be mothers and look after the household and the children.

Rugby was part of the fabric and culture of the country,[2] which suited the social needs and formed the value patterns of the new frontier.[3] Amateur ideals of playing the sport for enjoyment and 'mateship' also fitted the egalitarian ideals of the still-young country. It is from this beginning and ingrained set of values and beliefs that a New Zealand culture of that era was formed, with rugby holding an undeniably powerful place both in local and national society. The importance of this history to the culturalisation processes is endorsed by anthropologist Sahlins, who argued that one cannot really understand a phenomenon like organisational culture without first understanding historical events and the cultural meanings attributed to them.[4]

Our interviews with All Blacks captains and coaches highlight the legacy of winning, which goes back to the 1905 side, and the subsequent perceived need to preserve the record. This theme of winning and success is one of two historical threads that consistently appear in most analyses of the position of rugby in New Zealand society. The other is a sense of national identity. Unquestionably, success on the world stage helped shape a New Zealand national identity – the awareness growing that here was something at which we were, for whatever mix of reasons, inherently more successful than other nations.

1960S: PLAYING RUGBY, ALL BLACKS TRIALS, PLAYING AGAINST SOUTH AFRICA FOR HAWKE'S BAY

It is interesting to compare rugby in the 1950s and 1960s, the fiercely amateur period in which I played, with the professional-era rugby of today.

From 1957 to 1968 I was fortunate enough to play 116 games for Counties, Waikato, Hawke's Bay and Auckland, as well as representing the North Island on two occasions. It may surprise people that the most striking difference to me is not the payment of players, or player size and fitness levels, but the improved condition of the grounds. Today, even in wet conditions the grounds do not 'cut up' – providing a platform for attractive, running rugby. This seemingly mundane point emphasises the role of technology in sport. Coaches and players have all embraced and accepted the benefits of improved scientific technology, whether it be advanced physical conditioning methods, nutritional requirements for athletes, sports medicine, recovery techniques, aerodynamic footballs, innovative new gear or boots. A stark reminder of the difference between the eras is that, in spite of playing representative rugby for 12 years, I was never even provided with a free pair of boots, let alone money!

When I returned home to Napier in 1959 I became the third generation of my family to represent the province. Not a happy year, as it turned out, with the thrashing from the British Lions and then suffering from a stress fracture of the hip, which curtailed my season. It was also marred by media flak for our poor performance against the Lions under my captaincy. I swore it would never happen again. I had begun my association with Colin Le Quesne, aka 'The Führer', our selector-coach who should have become a New Zealand selector. Astute team selection was his forte. However, his abrupt, abrasive approach denied him support outside the province.

Looking back in recent years, I have come to understand some of Colin's visionary abilities in those days. We became a good combination by introducing physical fitness training, using Bryan Wilson – a New Zealand Junior sprint champion – as our fitness coach. Our planning, tactical and strategic approach was taken into our play, targeting the key games we wished to focus on. Bryan had spent hours analysing and timing the amount of aerobic and anaerobic running the players did in every position, and then designed fitness programmes for each; we were ahead of our time.

Our Ranfurly Shield game against Auckland in 1961 was a turning point for the province, lifting the standards of our play. Although beaten 5–3, all the points had been scored in the first 10 minutes of the game – and our tactic of planning everything we did from the first kick-off to the final whistle had worked pretty well. In fact, a double backline defence system and superior fitness had very nearly won the Shield for us as, in the final seconds, with an open goal-line ahead, it was only when Bill Davis was ankle-tapped that he failed to score what would have been the match-winning try.

In 1963 we beat England 22–5, with five-eighths Ian MacRae scoring three of our four tries. That was followed later in the season by a 3–all draw in the Ranfurly Shield match with the great Auckland side of that era. I would rate it as the most memorable game I played in, for the atmosphere: it was the largest midweek crowd ever seen in New Zealand at that stage. Auckland had had to repel the challenge in order to beat Hawke's Bay's record number of defences, which dated from the 1920s.

That was probably the greatest game I ever saw Kelvin Tremain play, too, and that is really saying something. He was dynamic, a terrific All Black of his time. As I said at the after-match function, 'The Shield match in 1961 had re-ignited the fires of Hawke's Bay rugby and if today's match had not fanned it into a burning flame, at least we had had our flickering moments.'

In 1966 we drew 11–all with the British Lions, in a match to which we could apply boxing manager Joe Jacobs' oft-quoted line, 'We wuz robbed' – with justification. Billy Davis scored what should have been the match-winning try, but it was disallowed because Mike Gibson had screamed obstruction to the referee – obstruction which had never occurred.

It was not until the end of the 1966 season that Hawke's Bay won back the Ranfurly Shield – then we retained it until 1969, successfully defending it for 21 games until losing to Canterbury. The Ranfurly Shield period had some memorable games, but I was on the injured list for much of it and, although I played in the game that initially claimed it, the Shield therefore didn't mean as much to me as it did for those who took the field. The role of assistant coach in the last year of the Shield defences was an interesting one, however, and was an area I would far rather have got into than administration. Little did we all know that it would be some 44 years until the Ranfurly Shield would go back to the Bay, albeit briefly, in 2013!

My first All Blacks trial came in 1959, in a regional trial held in Napier. To be honest it was a non-event, so I consider my first 'real' trial to have been in 1961, when I had started to establish myself. I then played in the 1962 trials in Palmerston North and had a very good game, scoring a couple of tries. I came into the final trial match after Victor Yates, the All Blacks' number 8, withdrew. I had another very good game, probably best summed up in an article by Clarrie Gibbons in Wellington's *Sports Post*: 'With luck Hawke's Bay could have supplied two more members in the team . . . Johnson played not one, but two blinders and revealed himself as being the most skilful loose forward with hands and feet on show at the trials. To that I would add "and head, too" because a player cannot side-step, swerve and dummy while travelling at top speed unless he has a cool and quick thinking brain to call the moves. Johnson just about has everything and at 24 is certain to be called into the big time before long.'[5]

It wasn't to be, however. After a good game for North Island at the trials in 1962, I blew any chance I had with the way I played in the same match the following year.

To play against South Africa was the ultimate for a New Zealand rugby player – something you will find reflected again and again in the interviews with captains and coaches of this era. In 1965, I experienced the challenge and enjoyment of playing against the Springboks for Hawke's Bay. Even now, reflecting on the events that led up to the 1981 Springbok Tour and the subsequent outcomes, my views have scarcely changed at all. For most rugby players, playing South Africa was never about endorsing apartheid, which was always morally indefensible, but about the rights of an individual within the law to play sport with whomever one chose, free from political interference.

1970S: ADMINISTRATION, MANAGEMENT, LEADERSHIP AND GOLDEN OLDIES

My interest in rugby and the management of the game has never waned. For over 30 years I have been a member of the Barbarians Rugby Football Club and have witnessed nearly all the test matches played at Auckland and Wellington. The experience of captaining Hawke's Bay on 50 occasions, then coaching for a season, were leadership roles that were helpful in preparing me for the role of chairman of the Hawke's Bay Rugby Union in 1972. The following year, I transferred to Wellington and was elected to the Council of the New Zealand Rugby Football Union (NZRFU), ultimately spending 12 years in national administration prior to retiring in 1986.

My initial involvement in administration happened by accident – in Hawke's Bay, becoming chairman of the union without having ever been on the committee previously. I stood for the position on the retirement of long-serving chairman Wallace Bramwell because I was asked to, and because I was concerned about the debilitating parochial conflict between Napier and Hastings. After a challenging and enjoyable year, it was then that I was promoted to Wellington by the oil company I worked for and was asked to stand for the NZRFU council.

Much to my surprise – and in something of a boil-over – at the 1973 annual general meeting (AGM), Russ Thomas, Bill Freeman and I were elected. Brian F. O'Brien of *Sports Digest* reported: 'The ascension of Freeman and Johnson to rugby's Olympus might be the portent of a new era in New Zealand rugby administration.'[6] High hopes, but no cigar in reality! Being considerably younger than most of my peers on the council (I was 34 when first elected), I was probably more conscious of the social changes taking place in our society than many of them. At the 1972 AGM a year earlier, I had criticised the union's opposition to television coverage of test matches as being partly responsible for the union's poor public image. I had given a detailed cost analysis of the impact on gates around New Zealand from radio coverage alone, and put forward the proposition that rugby had the capacity to organise itself so that loss of revenue could be eliminated. I received a verbal baton charge at the time from chairman Jack Sullivan, but it was probably these actions that got me elected the following year.

The issues which led to the Springbok controversy in New Zealand were both moral and political but were issues, in my opinion, for which only politicians could resolve and accept responsibility. Prime Minister Norman Kirk attempted to do so – although to his detriment – in 1973. One of the interesting anecdotes from my involvement there was hearing Jack, our chairman, recounting to NZRFU executive members his meeting with Kirk about the proposed cancellation of the 1973 tour. Kirk probably believed, when he invited Jack to the meeting at Parliament, that it would be relatively easy to get him to see reason and call off the tour. After all, Kirk was an ex-stationary engine driver who had successfully risen through the Labour Party ranks to become prime minister of New Zealand. Jack, on the other hand, had been an oil company tank wagon driver who had successfully risen through the ranks of Caltex Oil to become their managing director in New Zealand. The meeting was in the company of Grey Nelson, Kirk's secretary. When Kirk asked Jack to call it off, he refused on the grounds that he didn't have the authority to do so as NZRFU chairman – representing 26 provincial rugby unions that had all indicated their unanimous support for the tour. Jack claimed that Nelson had told him that, after he left the room, Kirk had turned to Nelson and said, 'I have just lost the next election.'

Living in a democracy and playing amateur sport, I believed I had every right to pursue my own personal desires provided they were within the law, and fought for that right of players to play rugby against South Africa. In those years prior to World Cups and professional rugby it represented the ultimate challenge. So in 1976, despite anti-tour opposition, the All Blacks went on tour. Without exception, all the rugby players I have interviewed expressed that their decision to play was not because of any support for apartheid, even tacitly. The hypocrisy of selective morality, however, was an issue – as the same standards of morality were never applied to the numerous nations with appalling human rights records.

After the tour was over, I believed we should have then told the South African board that – due to the disruption to the game in New Zealand – until South Africa got its house in order and resolved the issue of apartheid, regrettably, that we should postpone further rugby contact. I was interviewed by David Yardley for one of the Sunday papers and my views made the front page, not my intention, but something that was inevitable. At the next meeting of the council, at which Jack announced his retirement as chairman, he spent an hour in a closed session berating me for those views. I was called a scab on the union, to a hushed room where no councillor spoke in my defence. I told Jack at various stages that I took exception to his remarks and at the lunch break I had a number of councillors say how they wouldn't have taken the insults, and would have 'planted him'. Jack was a typical bully – it was all done behind closed doors, where the press could neither see nor listen.

Sick of the continual controversy and the hassles it brought – and well aware of the anti-rugby views of many feminist schoolteachers – I believed New Zealand rugby needed a break from this type of conflict. I probably should have ended my council involvement at that point, as I was conscious of the conflict ahead with the proposed 1981 tour, but I didn't anticipate the violence that would occur. I was also deeply involved with getting Golden Oldies rugby off the ground, so I continued, not really expecting to be re-elected.

The 1976 boycott of the Montreal Olympic Games by 24 countries over New Zealand's sporting contacts with South Africa ushered in something of a political norm thereafter. The USA boycotted the 1980 Moscow Olympics to protest the 1979 invasion of Afghanistan by the Soviet Union. That boycott included 64 other nations. In 1984, a revenge boycott led by the Soviet Union depleted the fields in certain events at the Los Angeles Olympics, although a record 140 nations still took part. The tragedy of these boycotts is that little was achieved other than depriving athletes of participation.

Over the years, a Mexican standoff situation developed between the opposing factions of anti-tour protesters and rugby supporters as their respective views became entrenched. Rugby players were aware of the issues and conscious of the inconsistent application of political redress. Overall one of the undesirable factors to emerge from the whole South African rugby debacle was that the separation of sport and politics in New Zealand was now regarded as no longer possible.

Around 1975, as a member of the NZRFU, I had become increasingly conscious of the quite dramatic social changes that were taking place in New Zealand society, impacting on the national game. The social-liberal movements of the 1970s, the rapid rise of feminism and Springbok tour opposition were all drivers of change. Rugby was being played less in schools, partly due to changing attitudes, but also because of an increasing ratio of female teachers to their male counterparts. The NZRFU at the time had a poor understanding of these social changes but, for obvious reasons, did recognise a need to focus on the recruitment and coaching of young players.

I decided to do something about it and wrote a 1977 booklet for the Asian and Pacific Nations Congress in Christchurch. My little publication, glibly titled *The Three Ps of Rugby – Promotion, Publicity and PR*, had a section on recreational rugby, with a plea to provincial unions and clubs to provide opportunities for the recreational player in their clubs, as well as grades for the gladiators.

My concern was the dropout rate (substantiated by recreational research at the time) of players over 25 years of age. The principal reasons were family or business and work commitments – but very often those players were then lost to the game for good. It was hoped that clubs would look to a variety of other activities that would be attractive to wives, partners or girlfriends, thus reducing the pressure to go elsewhere. The Golden Oldies project with which I had become involved in 1977 was very much related to this social change. A success story, it was ultimately an example of responding to the social forces of the macro environment.

In 1987 Auckland Mayor Dame Cath Tizard spoke at a spectacular opening ceremony for the Auckland Festival at Eden Park and commented: 'Tom Johnson, in starting off Golden Oldies at its first festival in 1979, would have had no conception as to how popular the event would become.' Well, in truth I never doubted the Golden Oldies concept would be successful – mainly because of the rugby mates who became involved and who would be instrumental in making it successful. However, as they say in maternity circles, the conception was easy, the birth complicated and difficult.

Pivotal to the ultimate success of the movement was the involvement of Professor Emeritus Dr Dale Toohey, an Australian academic living in California and working at California State University, Long Beach. I had first met Dale in 1974 at the Asian and Pacific Rugby Congress in Sydney and maintained contact with him thereafter – as I also did with Bob Elder, who was to become president of the Canada Rugby Union, and who was a prime mover for change in world rugby during his period in administration. It was from discussions with both these men that the idea of an inaugural tournament in New Zealand was born.

The first festival, as they would become known, was attended by 17 teams (one international team, USA; the rest were local). That mushroomed to 49 at Long Beach, California two years later, but it was the third festival in Sydney at which Golden Oldies really came of age – due to some superb organisation by the former treasurer of the Australian Rugby Union, John Howard; a willing band of Randwick Rugby Club helpers (some 500 in number); the participation of 118 teams; and support from government and local authority people. A sobering reality for me was the realisation that we had attracted more participants than the Commonwealth Games the previous year in Brisbane, and more even than the 1956 Olympic Games in Melbourne. The event captured the imagination of the Australian media who, with some illuminating television clips and colourful newspaper articles (with headlines like, 'It's Bigger Than Ben Hur'), truly 'got' the spirit of the event.

In London in 1985, the participating teams increased to 165 and, following a spectacular opening ceremony at Twickenham, the final dinner had to be held at a facility at the London docks where, in an area the size of three rugby fields placed end to end, 6500 Golden Oldies sat down to cap off their outstanding experience.

The initial couple of years getting the concept off the ground had indeed been difficult, however, and were spent encouraging Barbarians-type clubs to field a team of their 'oldies'. I am indebted to my former representative player friends who responded. After securing sponsorship in 1977, I was able to run short matches as curtain-raisers to the Lions' tour matches at some venues. The games were short enough to be not too demanding on the players, and long enough to provide some interest and nostalgia for the public. It also confirmed to me that all the participants genuinely enjoyed taking part. For the final curtain-raiser in Auckland I was turned down by some prominent former All Blacks, but on the Friday preceding the Saturday test a match played between New Zealand Barbarians and a group of past international players from the United Kingdom, all tour supporters, was played at North Shore's Onewa Domain. Five thousand people turned out to watch. Whilst the Brits had, at that stage, some comparatively young ex-internationals, like Andy Ripley and Nigel Starmer-Smith, what was quite remarkable to me was that John Tanner, an All Black in 1950 against the Lions (and, one would imagine, well into his fifties) played, displaying a level of fitness that was impressive in itself, plus many of the skills of yore. I knew that day we were onto a winner.

Also playing in our Barbarians team were a couple of rugby mates who were to become key figures in the Golden Oldies movement, Bryan Craies and Barry 'Tank' Herring. Both are larger-than-life characters – like 'Louie the Lip' and 'Big Jule', neither would be out of place in one of Damon Runyon's short stories about New York and the prohibition era. More importantly, they had both devoted a lifetime to rugby as players, coaches, club men and representative selectors. Their efforts in establishing the first festival in Auckland, together with other key people, were critical in getting the whole idea off the ground. Thus the concept of 'Fun, Friendship and Fraternity' was born, with the object of keeping older players in rugby, encouraging better fitness and providing wives and girlfriends with the opportunity of travelling overseas and enjoying themselves.

In the age of amateur sport, the hard part was how to fund the infrastructure needed to sustain the concept. I mention this point because it highlights, quite graphically, the difference between the amateur and professional eras. It was logical to approach an airline that would benefit from marketing the event as part of an international travel destination – bums on plane seats for them. I approached Allan Dumbleton at Air New Zealand and he accepted the concept – realising that if it were to take off in rugby, it could be applied successfully to other sporting codes as well: potentially a huge sports tourism market. Paul Gleeson, who later became leading worldwide agency International Management Group's representative in New Zealand, gave the movement a more polished and professional image, but initially it was the things we could do utilising the wonderful amateur rugby fraternity that deserve a special mention.

For instance, at the proposed Long Beach festival venue there were no rugby goalposts at the ground – so the Forestry Service in Taupo milled and supplied six or eight sets for free. Sir Russell Pettigrew, through his Freightways organisation, transported the goalposts to Long Beach at no cost. This is the legacy of the amateur era that members hold dearly. The Golden Oldies logo, which also perfectly encapsulates the ethos of rugby in an amateur era, was drawn by Malcolm Evans for nothing, using a hirsute Bryan Craies as his model while sitting around his kitchen table. The rest is history.

1980S: THE FLOUR BOMB TEST, THE 1981 AND 1985/86 SPRINGBOK TOURS

Most rugby fans are familiar with what happened in the third and final test between the Springboks and All Blacks at Eden Park in 1981. The match decided the series, the game won by the All Blacks 25–22, thanks to an injury-time penalty slotted by Allan Hewson. However, that's not why it is remembered so broadly. Instead, the bizarre circumstances in which the match was played have embedded themselves in our collective knowledge.

During the match I was responsible for ground security as the NZRFU's police liaison officer, and therefore for any decision to call off the match if the occasion arose. The game was overshadowed by off-field events. Outside the ground, all hell broke loose between police and protesters. Fighting erupted in the streets surrounding Eden Park, where the police were pelted with rocks and missiles.

The security around the ground had been the tightest of the whole controversial tour, but here the battle was unexpectedly taken to the sky above

Eden Park, by Marx Jones and Grant Cole in their hired Cessna aeroplane. The sight of the dive-bombing plane is one of the abiding memories I have of the game. Making numerous raids while the match was in progress, they dropped flour bombs and pamphlets in an effort to stop the test. At times the plane flew below the level of the goalposts – an extremely dangerous proposition with over 40,000 spectators at the game. One of the flour bombs hit All Blacks prop Gary Knight on the head. I knew him well and said to him afterwards, 'It was a good thing it hit you on the head, Axle, because if it had hit you anywhere else it would probably have hurt!' He had a very suitable reply about my parentage. Nevertheless, we got through to the end of the game without too much disruption, and it wasn't until the day afterwards when one of the South African press, Daan Retief, asked me how close I had come to calling off the match that I realised the thought had never entered my mind.

Opposition to sporting contacts with South Africa, fuelled by the activism overseas of protesters like Peter Hain, and tours of Britain and Australia (not just rugby tours; touring South African cricket and rugby tours attracted protest), had in turn fuelled the protest movement in this country. New Zealand historian Sir Keith Sinclair called the 1905 test match with Wales 'The Gallipoli of New Zealand sport'[7], but stated that the result of the 1981 tour was 'the worst scenes of disorder and violence since the Anglo-Maori wars of the 1860s'.[8]

Most of the tour critics have been historians and academics who understandably took a moral stance that apartheid was abhorrent, and any contact with South Africa an endorsement of their racial policies. Without exception, they were highly critical of the role of rugby and the NZRFU. The issues surrounding the tour (that had built up over a 10-year period) have been accurately covered by Trevor Richards, the founder of HART (Halt All Racist Tours), formed in 1971. He stated that it pitted internationalist 1960s idealism against values shaped by two world wars and depression, by rugby and isolation. Between the late 1960s and the mid-1980s, the confrontation wrote a significant chapter in New Zealand's social and political history.

Despite the protest opposition, rugby had a resilience that helped it survive the fierce controversy. The NZRFU annual accounts from 1981 to 1984 show that income was not adversely affected in the period immediately after the Springbok Tour. Whilst sections of the New Zealand school teaching fraternity were very vocal in their opposition – and some withdrew their support as coaches – quantified information received from the New Zealand Secondary Schools Rugby Union told a different story. In 1977 there were 280 school teams in Auckland and – consistent with falling school rolls – 226 in 1984. Auckland Grammar School, which had 19 teams in 1977, had 22 in 1984. There were many similar examples from around New Zealand, so the claims that the tour was a disaster for rugby have to be balanced with the facts. Despite the problems, rugby had survived quite well for its supporters.

Nevertheless, sporting contact with South Africa divided the rugby community, as the interview with Sir John Graham and autobiographies of former players demonstrate. Chris Laidlaw, a former race relations conciliator and diplomat as well as an All Blacks captain and Rhodes Scholar, makes these pertinent comments on the South African conflict: 'When apartheid reared its serpentine head, rugby became the meat in a racist sandwich and divided a nation possibly more than at any time in the history of sport . . . a division that astonished social scientists and forced the people of New Zealand to take a long hard look at themselves . . . the wounds have largely healed . . . the lingering message is that the excessive devotion to sport at the expense of wider social or political considerations is the mark of a pretty dumb society.'[9]

All Blacks and their attitude to playing the Springboks varied, with some choosing whether to play or not based on their personal values, motives and political viewpoint. Graham Mourie, in his book *Graham Mourie Captain*, encapsulated what it was like to make a decision not to play against South Africa – and how this was regarded in the rugby fraternity: 'Today (November 17) I announced that I would not play against South Africa . . . I believe the tour is wrong – for morality, for rugby because of the controversy, and the effects of the tour will be bad for the game . . . Ces Blazey (Chairman NZRFU) was understanding and tolerant of my decision, a gentleman as always . . . there was a type like (Auckland Rugby chairman) Ron Don, seeing me as a misinformed, misguided youngster, attempting to return me to the fold by supplying me with information supporting his own views . . . My club mates at Opunake didn't question my decision, although I have no doubt they were all in favour of the tour.'[10]

Mourie also referred to the support he received from disparate groups such as cabinet ministers, diplomats, anti-tour protesters and the general public, who thought he was: 'Courageous, crazy, communistic, thoughtful, stupid, scared and sometimes all of these at once.'[11]

Probably the most bizarre experience I had came with a summons of the NZRFU council to Parliament by Prime Minister David Lange, ostensibly for him to tell us to call off the proposed 1985 tour to South Africa. In the aftermath of 1981, I most certainly had hoped that a face-saving compromise could be negotiated, one that would postpone the tour and allow New Zealand rugby to get back to normal. In the presence of Laidlaw, whose career in Foreign Affairs saw him become New Zealand's Consul General to Southern Africa, we had the meeting. It was a disaster. Lange was both nervous and ill prepared. After Ces Blazey had explained the NZRFU's position, David Lange gave a virtuoso performance of 'shooting from the lip' – the only way I can describe it, in a series of one-line quips that antagonised all in attendance. As he went out the door Lange made the remark, 'I am now telling you – you can't go.'

The result was inevitable. An incensed and insulted council rejected the Prime Minister's demand not to tour, voting to proceed. This brought about an action in the New Zealand High Court by two lawyers who sued the NZRFU, claiming such a tour would breach the NZRFU's own constitution. They were successful – but an unofficial tour did take place in 1986 by a team that included the majority of the All Blacks who had been selected for the previous year's cancelled tour. This was of course the New Zealand Cavaliers, an unauthorised team which resulted in its players being declared ineligible for two tests in 1986 against France.

The council was a highly conservative and traditional organisation that had a 'status quo' mentality, not uncommon in amateur sport, business and government administration of those times. When I look back on my years there, I often use a phrase from Cervantes' 1605 novel *Don Qujxote de la Mancha* to describe my involvement. It is where the eponymous hero imagines himself fighting giants as he attacks windmills – the phrase 'tilting at windmills' has come to describe an act of futility. Despite the union at the time probably being New Zealand's most efficient sporting body, as well as its most financially wealthy, it had a very poor public image. It was not a proactive or innovative body, and I believe much of what I was involved in was tilting at windmills. It was seen by many as remote and autocratic – this could have been easily improved by showing greater transparency, by having considerably more of its meetings open to the media. It should have communicated much better with the rugby public and supporters in general through greater media contact and openness. It should have involved its public more in issues such as the instigation of a World Cup and better national competitions.

Former Auckland Rugby Union chairman Ron Don, then in his mid-eighties, talked to me once about modern rugby management and leadership compared to our day. He said, 'You know, it is an indictment of you and me (and by inference, our other councillors) that we didn't do enough to bring about realistic change.' I agreed with Ron, but pointed out that it was easier said than done in the political system of our times. 'Think back to the days when the Auckland Rugby Union, year after year, submitted notices of motion on invariably very sensible changes for New Zealand rugby,' I reminded him, 'only to have them thrown out at the AGM because of parochialism.'

However, by altering tactics – only bringing up key issues in 'general business', thus preventing organised opposition, we were eventually able to bring about a number of beneficial changes. These included the establishment of a marketing committee, the introduction of a national coaching system and the requirement that potential New Zealand selectors had to have gone through a successful provincial coaching apprenticeship and a much more focused selection process. In my first year on council I had found myself voting for the three All Black selector-coaches – arguably the most important job I had to do, and yet there were only three nominations for the three positions! There was no competition. It was a pitiful state of affairs, which thankfully we changed.

WINNING OVER THE WORLD – 1980S: RUGBY WORLD CUP

While rugby was administered efficiently and conscientiously by the administrators of the time, they lacked vision and innovation. The process was more important than the outcome. Ces Blazey was highly principled and hard-working, and had stoically led the union through its South African turmoil. In behavioural terms he was a perfect example of the administrative man. Despite his conservatism, it was during his period of leadership that the 1987 Rugby World Cup was successfully introduced, driven by both New Zealand and Australia. Some of the alterations were due to the changing rugby environment with non-IRB countries clamouring for recognition and increasing pressure from players for payment.

At the 1985 Asian and Pacific Nations Rugby Congress in Canada, John Howard, as treasurer of the Australian Rugby Union, and I were keynote speakers. John spoke about the inevitability of the professionalisation of rugby, while I spoke about the desirability of a World Cup with which international rugby could promote the game worldwide. The Asian and Pacific congresses (perceived as being more inclusive of non-IRB countries) had been started in 1974 by the Australians to celebrate the centenary of New South Wales rugby, which I attended with our president at the time, Frank O'Connor. They were to become a catalyst for change in rugby during the late 1970s and 1980s, but the three members of the IRB in attendance in 1985 politely dismissed the key points of our talks as never likely to happen. They did, however, become more and more conscious of the attitudes and desires of the smaller rugby nations as the week wore on. Within two years the World Cup was a reality, and by 1995 rugby had professionalised – so much for their visionary capabilities.

At an NZRFU council meeting in Auckland in late 1985, prior to the annual meeting of the IRB, the subject of the World Cup came up as an item on the IRB agenda. Chairing the meeting, Ces Blazey commented that of course it didn't have 'a hope in hell' of being agreed to. I challenged Ces on this, saying I hoped he wasn't going to express that as the opinion of the bulk of rugby people in New Zealand, as they would strongly support the introduction of such a worldwide contest. Predictably, however, the IRB wiped the move and in an interview with one of our weekly sports papers I condemned the IRB for its ignorance, lack of reality and inability to provide for the needs of its support base.

Ces used to stop off in Hawai'i at the Ilika'i Hotel on the way home and write up his copious notes and reports on the IRB meeting. Don Cameron of *The New Zealand Herald* rang Ces and read the headlines and content of my interview to Ces over the phone. Whatever annoyance Ces may have felt over the article, it stirred up considerable support for the concept and the NZRFU duly appointed a committee of Dick Littlejohn, Ivan Vodanovich and me to become the New Zealand representatives or negotiators for it. We subsequently met in Sydney with our Australian counterparts – the original World Cup committee – with two other New Zealanders and three Australians. We recognised the difficulties of dual control and offered the Aussies support to run the show on their own, knowing full well they did not have the capacity to do so. What we were hoping was that they would then turn to us and support us to run it on our own. However, it quickly became evident that we needed to work together to first be able to convince other international board members of the need for a World Cup in the first place. Dick established a very good working relationship with Australian co-chairman Sir Nicholas Shehadie, and that proved instrumental in making the 1987 Rugby World Cup a reality.

Graham Mourie was working at the time for sports promotion firm West Nally. I had bumped into him at a Golden Oldies meeting in London and on my return to Wellington I was able to arrange for West Nally to do a presentation on the sponsorship funding of the Rugby World Cup event. My introduction of Patrick Nally to our combined group in Sydney initially raised the hackles of Nick Shehadie, until he heard the presentation and realised such involvement would solve all the funding issues. Because of the association I had with Paul Gleeson of IMG, which was a pioneer in its field, I was able to arrange a presentation by them as well. In all the years I had on the NZRFU, the only responsible position I was given was to chair the marketing committee of the World Cup. It was surely indicative of either my lack of ability, in which case I should not have been elected, or of the fact that mavericks are isolated on boards and committees if they don't follow the 'party' line. That aside, it was evident in the bids by both

West Nally and IMG that, whatever the final decision, the funding of the World Cup would not be a problem.

Once the World Cup was a reality, it was inevitable that the pressure to go fully professional would intensify. It had been a great success, particularly with the All Blacks deservedly winning the inaugural trophy. Whilst the organisation and the promotion was primitive compared to later events, I believed it was always going to be a success because once the matches started, the rugby would take over – and here at last was a showcase bringing together all the world's best.

WINNING A WORLD CUP TWICE – 1990S: PROFESSIONALISM, 'KILLING THE GOOSE THAT LAID THE GOLDEN EGG?'

As far as the professionalisation of rugby was concerned, it was not difficult to predict that New Zealand – with its comparative lack of critical mass – would never be able to compete financially with England, France, Australia and probably South Africa, once the game went professional in 1995. A drover's dog, to use a euphemism from an Australian political campaign, could have shown management the likely problems that would arise.

Joseph Romanos and Paul Thomas, two of New Zealand's award-winning journalists and sports authors, have both written thought-provoking books on the state of New Zealand rugby and how the transition from amateurism to professionalism was managed. Romanos, in *The Judas Game*, was quite scathing in his criticism, calling professionalisation the betrayal of New Zealand rugby.[12] He also believed the game at that time was in serious trouble, racially divided and fatally dislocated from the average club player. Thomas, in *A Whole New Ball Game*, confronted what he called, 'the myths and realities of New Zealand rugby'. He wrote: 'When amateurism was mercifully put to sleep, few in the New Zealand rugby community spared it a thought beyond good riddance . . . the first flush of professionalism is like a lottery winner coming to the painful realisation that being an instant millionaire isn't all it is cracked up to be.'[13] The reality is that many clubs, unions and other rugby participants weren't able to cope with the change.

Both authors quote some of the iconic figures of the game to substantiate their case. Thomas cites Fred Allen's trenchant comments: 'The All Blacks aren't a sports team, they are a commodity that everybody is using in some way to get rich . . . The All Blacks are out there playing for money now. They say they are out there playing for pride, but I don't see the same tremendous feeling that former All Blacks had when they pulled on the black jersey.'[14]

That money in rugby would change the ethos of the sport forever was to be expected. You didn't have to be a rocket scientist or a Rhodes Scholar to know it was inevitable. The move initially alienated many of the old rugby players and supporters who saw the modern player as egocentric and disloyal to a sport they loved. There was a time when you played for your country and the pride of representing it, but this appears to be a very secondary consideration today, with some notable exceptions. Our current All Blacks coaches say this is not the case, but there is no question when the choice is for money or New Zealand rugby, money wins hands down, as shown by the exodus of players overseas each year.

I don't begrudge players making the choice of earning big money and going, but in doing so there should be a price to pay. If not, they will 'kill the goose that laid the golden egg'. The status of being an All Black is the one major factor in getting premium payments. If the status of the All Blacks declines because of future failure to win test matches, then the payment expectations of the players will decline also. What I find inexplicable is the fact that the NZRU gets no payment or transfer fee out of each player and coach being paid to go overseas. Rectifying this would mean an injection of capital back into the game here, compensating for leeching off New Zealand's intellectual capital. In my opinion, this should apply to coaches as well; after all, they have acquired their positions through their experiences gained in New Zealand, just as much as through their abilities.

Today, the number of New Zealanders playing in Japan, the United Kingdom and France has reached epidemic proportions – over 1000 Kiwis play rugby overseas. If players earn an average NZ$200,000, this amounts to $200 million – a tidy sum. If the transfer fee was 20 per cent, it would mean the NZRU would get a fee of $40 million. The principle is important, even if my knowledge of the actual amounts being paid today may not be accurate. There is considerable money that would assist the New Zealand union to promote rugby at home, compensation for establishing the players and coaches in the first place.

The management leadership of the NZRU could be described like a Clint Eastwood movie, *The Good, the Bad and the Ugly*. The good has been the periods of enlightenment that saw the introduction of the 1987 World Cup and the efforts of Jock Hobbs and Chris Moller in successfully winning the hosting rights for 2011. The bad has been the periods that lacked imagination, innovation and resulted in a poor public image. The ugly was the loss of RWC hosting rights in 2003 – described as the worst mismanagement fiasco in New Zealand's sporting history, partly through arrogant and incompetent management.[15]

The failure to win the World Cup after the initial 1987 success meant no mercy shown for the coaches of the various campaigns who failed – some of whom were treated abysmally by the New Zealand rugby public. Leaders will always be confronted with problems to solve, so I do not think the game is 'fatally dislocated from the average club player and fan'[16], as Romanos claimed, but rather more like Thomas found, 'transformed often for the better, but facing serious challenges to its traditional place'.[17] Because of its traditional resilience as the national sport, rugby in New Zealand has quickly rebounded from past adverse results and the prophets of doom.

2000s: COLLECTIVE LEADERSHIP

I have had a personal interest in leadership theory and its practical application because I have had leadership roles in rugby right throughout my playing days and in senior management positions in business. Why are you selected or appointed to these positions? What do people see in your abilities that means selection or appointment over somebody else? In rugby I played under captains like Whineray, Tremain and Bob Graham, all of whom exhibited different strengths and abilities. In business I have had a mixture of the occasional exceptional leader like my oil company boss Bill McNee, to an array of totally incompetent, sometimes narcissistic, micro-managers without any man-management skills, vision or objectivity, but invariably ambitious despite their lack of ability. It's a learning curve we all go through.

Our interviews with Sir John 'DJ' Graham, Sir Brian 'BJ' Lochore through to Sir Graham Henry reaffirmed something I have always said: nobody provides you with a manual on leadership when you are 'thrown to the lions' and expected not only to survive, but to flourish. Knowledge comes through experiential learning and socialisation processes. Former All Blacks captain Graham Mourie said of the captain's role: 'It is a difficult art about which little has ever been satisfactorily said . . . certainly there was never any captain's manual thrust into my hand.'[18] The reality, successful captains grow into the role through experiential learning.

As a 20-year-old I had captained Hawke's Bay against the British Lions and suffered a 52–12 hiding that is still humiliating for me today. The fact that I had captained sides from the Waikato primary school reps through to the Hamilton Boys' High School First XV and club rugby scarcely prepared me for the later roles in rugby or business.

Leadership is a fascinating subject that has spawned thousands upon thousands of academic articles and theories, without ever generating agreement as to one best form. New Zealand rugby has had a number of exceptional captains like Whineray, Lochore, Mourie and McCaw, and many exceptional players in every era. One of the other fascinations for me, in assessing coaches as leaders, was finding that it was a myth that New Zealand rugby players have always been well coached.

Every top player from my era whom I asked to name an outstanding coach (from our own era) had difficulty. Sir Colin Meads said it was difficult to name even one, with the exception of Sir Fred Allen. This was not to say there weren't many dedicated rugby men who looked after teams – there were. However, the knowledge requirements for success have increased year by year, as have the leadership requirements. The previous All Blacks coaching panel (2004–11) and the present one (2012–14) are light years ahead of many of their predecessors. Today's All Blacks coaches would not make the mistake of selecting two left wingers for a test, as happened in the second test against the 1959 Lions. Nor would Sir John Graham's story from the third test against the Springboks in 1960 happen today. Asking the coach who would play at the end of the lineout – after both he and Dick 'Red' Conway, two end-of-the-lineout players, had both been selected – he was told, 'Whoever gets there last.'

However, if 'quality leadership' was not always apparent in formal roles such as coach or captain, another part of the All Blacks organisation assumed leadership responsibility. If the coaching was poor, the players stepped up. Alternatively, if there were player misdemeanours, the coach stood up, and if hard decisions had to be made, the administrators/board made them. What mattered in the end was that the All Blacks organisation continued to be successful, and that someone (individual or collective) fronted up to ensure that was maintained.

The development and introduction of the collective leadership style and approach of the 2004–11 management group came after considerable research, investigation and analysis, and was backed up by the in-depth collective experience of those involved (Sir Brian Lochore, Sir Graham Henry, Wayne Smith and Steve Hansen), and the academic theory and expertise of specialists in education and psychology with whom they consulted. Selecting the collective management group because of their specialist skills, knowledge or experience endorsed the collective leadership theories of Denis, Lamothe and Langley; and Lemay.[19] Whilst there is not one easy, common definition, it is about embracing and marshalling human, cultural and technological resources, where group members are motivated by a common purpose, and build relationships with each other that are genuinely respectful and focused on achieving optimal results. It is about co-constructed, shared purpose and work – relationships in action that trust shared wisdom and the liberation of individual ability, reinforced by ongoing self and team analysis and critiquing.

'Once cultures exist, they determine the criteria for leadership . . . and thus determine who will or will not be leader.'[20] When cultures become unsuccessful or dysfunctional, leaders are invariably replaced so that the organisation can survive and adjust to a changing environment. New Zealand's failure, until 2011, to win the Rugby World Cup since 1987, is such an example. In all instances, except 2007, the current coaches retired, resigned or were unceremoniously discarded by the governing body (the NZRFU), perhaps due in part to the negative press and public reaction to losing in what is now considered the pinnacle global event for rugby. The press, for instance, kept up a barrage of vitriol after the All Blacks' failure in 2007. *New Zealand Herald* sports columnist Chris Rattue stirred up a hornet's nest with his assertion that he would not support any team coached by Graham Henry – which contemporarily meant the current All Blacks.[21] All Blacks captains associated with losing World Cup squads have also had to deal with media attention, public disappointment and criticism of their leadership abilities. Rugby and, more specifically, success at the elite, high-performance level of All Blacks rugby, clearly matters for many New Zealanders.

PART I

A WINNING LEGACY

When amateurism was mercifully put to sleep, few in the New
Zealand rugby community spared it a thought beyond good
riddance.
– *Paul Thomas in* A Whole New Ball Game[1]

THE AMATEUR ERA

Underpinning any particular strategy or tactics used by the All Blacks across their long amateur history was the basic value present since its inception: the winning ethos. Does that mean winning at any cost, or accepting losses as they unfolded?

Doing what it took to win, the early All Blacks presented generally younger and stronger players than their British or European counterparts were able to muster at the time. The hard work in the 'colony' that continued over time, the building of team spirit, personal pride and general overall physical fitness served as the basic foundation points in terms of both strategy and tactics. During the amateur period, various coaches and captains did the basics very well in most cases, not only because of personal commitment, but also because they were drawn from the same stock and background as the players themselves. It could never be said that they were overloaded with information, as might be suggested of today's coaching brigade – some of whom might suffer from over-analysis or even paralysis as a direct result of the tumult of video analysis that's now available. Some coaches may have watched other teams and noticed what they did differently, as long as they were in close proximity. Of course, not every team had a Don Clarke in their ranks to whom the ball could be passed and booted downfield while at the same time releasing the backs for attack.

In the early days of the game, there was limited knowledge of strategy and tactics as such, despite considerable effort being devoted to practice and defence. At the same time, there was certainly an intention to make the system in place work for the team and their ultimate goal – to win. This commitment of team and coaches, and some coaches' preparedness to try new things, supported the competitive advantage at various points in time.

One important ritual to emerge during this amateur era was the phenomenon known as the *back of the bus*. While this will be discussed in more detail in our section on professionalism, suffice to say that the *back of the bus* was introduced as an induction system by senior players that literally occurred at the back of the team bus. It is important to note not only the involvement of those senior players, with their collective experience and know-how, but also the fact that the process advised new players what was expected of them on-field in the match to follow. In no way was this system seen to contravene or undermine coaching efforts. Rather, it fostered the notion of team spirit, commitment and experience by setting values and rules of behaviour outside of the influence of team management. It provided stability, and contributed to the preservation of All Blacks traditions.

The following chapters offer more detailed comment on aspects that influenced the culture of the All Blacks, whether it was artefacts like the jersey and silver fern, the rituals of the haka and the team's leadership, or the perceived values of the team and their deeply embedded assumptions.

CHAPTER TWO
JOHN 'DJ' GRAHAM

S ir David John Graham was born 9 January 1935 in Stratford. 'DJ', as he is widely known, played 22 tests as a loose forward between 1958 and 1964, including three as captain. Relatively small by today's standards for a flanker – he was under six feet (1.83 metres) tall and his maximum playing weight was 83 kilos – his distinguishing qualities as a player were his speed, wholehearted commitment and his capacity to think 'faster, more accurately and more scientifically about the possibilities of loose forward play than almost any man of his time'.[1]

Eminent rugby scribe Sir Terry McLean characterised him as a 'natural leader of men', particularly in rugby where he was 'a strong and ruthless captain . . . He had a withering tongue for the foolish and instant commendation for the man who had done a thing well, and, in the captaincy of a province like Canterbury, the South Island or, as required, the All Blacks, he set and demanded the highest standards of performance.'[2]

Off the field he gained a Master's degree in history and his leadership abilities were highly visible in the realm of education. He was a schoolteacher in Christchurch and later headmaster of Auckland Grammar School from 1973 to 1993. Later, as manager of the New Zealand men's cricket team (the Black Caps) from 1997 to 1999, he also earned the respect of leading cricketers for his forthright manner and sage, compassionate counsel. The University of Auckland's Chancellor from 1999 to 2004, he was also elected president of the NZRFU in April 2005 and led a government review into the funding of sport. Graham was knighted in 2011 for services to education and the community.

PRIDE IN SELECTION

I heard of my selection over the radio. My wife Sheila went to pick up the paper in the morning. She brought me a cup of tea in bed and we opened the paper and my name was there as an All Black. The feeling was exceptional. I never ever envisaged being an All Black – it was not something that I grew up assuming would happen – because you didn't in those days. Youngsters didn't grow up and say, 'I want to be an All Black!' You felt lucky if you got into a senior club side, blessed if you got into a provincial side because that meant people had noticed you as someone who had a bit of ability, then if you were chosen to play in the national sport of this country, that was very special.

It wasn't something I aspired to until I got picked for the Rest of New Zealand (a trial team for the All Blacks made up of those players on the fringe of selection) in 1958 and you felt that's not far away from the next one. So I just felt fortunate – saw it as a privilege and hoped above all that I could play to the level that was expected of anybody who was to wear the silver fern. That was really the sort of emotions I had, and there was some doubt as to whether I could achieve.

I suppose the key feeling I had, when I thought about it, was to be grateful for the players I played with over the years in Auckland and in Canterbury at club level. I look back at my coach, [John] 'JJ' Stewart. He started me off in the game and intellectualised it to me. He made me think about where I was playing and what I was doing. He was only one of two coaches that did that in the rest of my career – nobody else did that apart from Neil McPhail, to a lesser extent. So I was grateful for that type of support, and not only from players, but from my colleagues as a schoolteacher. They realised that when I got into the Canterbury side that perhaps it could happen. I used to say, 'Oh, don't be daft. It's not like I'll make the All Blacks – don't be ridiculous, too small, too light!'

So I just felt honoured and blessed. It was a bonus – a huge, massive bonus. It wasn't until you got there that you realised, because people looked at you, which again was unusual. They didn't look at me as much as they looked at Colin Meads and Don Clarke, but you were admired as somebody who had achieved something special in this country.

RITES AND RITUALS
The haka

Graham notes a change in significance of the importance of the haka to the team in the professional era, compared to his own playing days.

Sadly, it was an extra with which I could have done without. I did not understand its significance. I found the actions difficult; it wasn't a natural thing for me to do. I couldn't roll my eyes, didn't poke my tongue out and I did the haka very badly, as most of my colleagues did. I still have some doubts about the haka as now it's a showpiece, and I believe the current All Blacks see it as a very important part of their build-up and part of their emotional output in preparing for a game.

I wouldn't say we treated it as a joke. We didn't, because we did it as best we could. However, as we had no training and never, ever practised it, it was badly done. It really didn't mean a great deal to me – which is sad in some ways looking back, because I can see now that it has become something special to a lot of our sportspeople. The All Blacks' haka has gone beyond the All Blacks and into the wider culture of the country – and therefore unquestionably I accept it now.

The back seat of the bus

I never wanted to be in the back seat and wasn't. That wasn't something I saw as a necessary requirement. I had limited regard for those who considered themselves special and wanted to sit in the back seat. There was no way I had ever been invited. I wasn't a 'back seat boy' in terms of my make-up and beliefs and behaviour.

I didn't despise them – I just saw it as a bit of a joke, really. It went too far in some teams, I think. During the Whineray era, we didn't really need those sorts of disciplines anyway. Standards were set by the manager, coach and skipper, and while there were some outstanding All Blacks who were seen as senior players, they were part of the team. There were no 'celebrities' in the teams that I played in; everybody was seen as equals. The skipper set the standards and we were blessed with somebody who had huge ability. So, I had no induction whatsoever. You just got in the team and the guys said, 'Congratulations John' (because 'DJ' hadn't started, at that stage – that came later) and that was it. Certainly no one looked after me. You came in and were expected to perform, full stop. Every other guy was doing his job, getting himself set up for the game without worrying about DJ Graham.

VALUES AND BELIEFS
Pride in winning

I never, ever thought about losing. It never entered my head that we would lose – and that was ingrained. That was the heritage you picked up from the past. I mean, coaches were good at that sort of thing. 'You've inherited something special' was a common statement they made. That got into your system. Those who've gone before have passed on this wonderful heritage of the fern on the black jersey and New Zealand rugby and the New Zealand psyche. You're honoured to be here, privileged to be here and I felt that, really felt that.

I only played in two losing tests out of 22, so that speaks for itself – both to Australia, by the way. It was the same in the Canterbury side, but different in Auckland. Quite different. We didn't like losing in Auckland, but it wasn't the end of the world. When you wore the red and black for Canterbury, you were expected to win and if you didn't win you were told not only by your coach, but also by the public – there was absolutely no doubt about that expectation there. It was there even when I played for Christchurch's Old Boys club – and we never won a championship in all the years I played. Every time we went out, there was always the assumption that we'd win, even if we were playing against the top team. There's no point in going out and not wanting to win. I was a hugely competitive person and it was part of my psyche that came out in the rugby environment. It's still the same now.

LEADERSHIP
Coaching
I got no instructions from anybody about how to play the game. I wasn't told why I was picked. In the first test in the loose forward grid, we survived. I don't know how the hell we did, because there had been no debate about who was going to take who at the end of the lineout. In the second test I played [in 1958], that came home to roost: we got well stuffed by the Aussies at the back of the lineout. I got dropped after that game. I got the blame for it, but my colleagues who were senior to me had given no advice whatsoever, so you were on your own.

I was determined after that. If I got back in again – and I was desperate to get back in again, having got there – I didn't want to be a 'two-match dropped All Black' for the rest of my life. That would have been unacceptable to me personally. When I got back in, I never ever went into a game with the All Blacks without knowing what each one of us was going to do in scrums and lineouts: in those core positions and set plays. We worked it out ourselves, amongst the three of us. Although Peter Jones was in the first two tests and he didn't have much to say to me at all.

Bob Stuart was a former All Black who had captained the All Blacks on their 1953/54 tour to the United Kingdom and France, and also acted as a forwards coach to the All Blacks during the 1956 series against South Africa.

Kel Tremain, Hugh Burry and myself were the three Canterbury loose forwards. We were coached by Bob Stuart in those days – he was a number 8 himself, so we had our jobs perfectly spelled out to us. All three of us had reasonable brains and we talked a lot together about how we were playing and what we were doing, so we knew exactly what we were going to do. That was what was so mystifying to me when I got up into higher professionalism: there was no personal guidance to me as to what was required.

In the third test in South Africa they picked 'Red' Conway. We were both 'tail gunners'; both of us wanted to play off the end. So I went up to Jack Sullivan, who was the coach, and said, 'Who is playing off the end?' His answer was, 'Whoever gets there last.' Now that was, quite frankly, a bizarre statement. It just did not make sense that the coach didn't understand that there was a totally different requirement for seven and eight. That's what happened to me in that test and that third test against Australia in 1958. I got taken out the whole time by Des Connor. He would run at me and I had to stop because no one was looking after him, and so the five-eighths had a free run. Quite rightly I got dropped, because I never got anywhere near him. That's just one example of the amazing lack of detail in the coaching which you had to pick up yourself.

Graham feels the best coaches are part of the modern professional era:

The coaches whom I experienced *believed* they were coaches – but by and large it was a team talk that they were responsible for, the selection process which they got involved in, and they would have developed a basic procedure with players. It wasn't individualised. The individual approach right now is just remarkable compared to what we had. As I have indicated, I got told very little at any stage as to what to do when I was playing for the All Blacks, particularly when I first got in, but right through to 1962/63 when Neil McPhail took over. His information to me was pretty basic: 'DJ, make sure you get your defensive areas right – scrum defence, lineout defence, back defence in terms of covering. Get those things right, 100 per cent accurate, the rest – bonus. Got it?'

That was what happened in most team talks that I was involved with and at training there was very little talk to any of us about exactly where the lines were. 'You're getting too direct on the five-eighths,

John, get a bit wider. If you look at the last game you were too straight at him. Did you take note of play when he passed? We'd rather have you on your feet getting into the second and centre; they've got the ball rather than being taken out of play.' You had to work that out for yourself.

Certainly in the 1990s, when I was coaching with Graham Henry, I would say those things to Mark Carter and Michael Jones. Carter picked it up straight away. Jones, 'Yeah, yeah, yeah, DJ, okay.' He was a different person, a wonderful player, hugely instinctive, but he was not easy to coach. You had to leave him alone.

Captaincy

I'd had considerable experience in captaining sides and most of the sides I'd captained were successful, though not necessarily because of my leadership. When I captained the Canterbury side, we had some great years. We were unbeaten one year, which was unusual for any provincial side. I'd captained sides from my school days right through to Canterbury University. Again, I don't know why I was picked as captain. At Auckland University I was made captain. Trying to define captaincy is extremely difficult.

You do have to be confident in your own position, and be seen by your team members as being worthy of a place in the team. There is nothing worse than playing with a captain who is lucky to be there – that can't work in any team. So I assume that they believed I was good enough to hold down my place and then also assumed that I could handle the pressure; that I would be able to handle the team collectively. Half-time team talks had to be given by the skipper [because coaches were not then allowed on the field to talk to teams] so there were a number of things that you had to be able to do in order to be the captain.

No coach ever got too close to any of the All Blacks sides I played in: so the assumption was that at that level you could do the off-field stuff competently. Essentially they could see you as being a person that the rest of the side would look up to, that they'd accept you as a skipper and that you could do the job.

I had the privilege of holding a very special record as captain; the third test against Australia was the All Blacks' biggest loss in the team's history! [5–20 versus Australia in 1964]. I wasn't captain again! In my case, Wilson Whineray had stood down following the end of the 1963/64 tour and they had had to find somebody to captain the side. I was picked, and was honoured to be picked. There was no question about that, it was an honour. It wasn't a great experience, though, because I was filling in for Wilson, our outstanding long-term skipper.

I had said to Neil McPhail before that Australian game, 'Have you got a decent team talk for today? Because I'll tell you what, the side's not ready to play a test match.'

I knew. I just knew. Attitude and mental focus before you start is just as important as anything during the match and at half-time. I had the challenge of trying to get that side up to scratch. We were obviously struggling. We got beaten by 15 points, whereas we'd beaten them 17–3 a week beforehand. They'd lost to Canterbury midweek, so I found that extremely difficult. This is probably a very personal statement, but of the three tests we played, I think I played best in that test because I sensed that it wasn't right and I just wasn't able to fix it. That was by far and away the most challenging situation I ever faced in my career.

It was such a short period. I'd had six to seven years of playing for the All Blacks and I had huge confidence in this group of guys to be on the job and to give their best. After the 1963/64 tour most of us had had a gutsful of rugby and the reason Wilson didn't play [during the 1964 season in New Zealand] was that he was tired after a long, long tour where he had been the key man. After every game he had had to give a speech, 36 games. It's a huge responsibility and he deserved a rest, quite frankly.

I had one special coach and that was McPhail. He was a Christchurch Old Boys member so I knew him. I think one or two guys always felt that I was blessed because I came from his club. That was never said to me, but it was an unfair statement. He was a returned soldier and therefore had mana as a person. He'd been a prisoner of war, so he'd been through experiences that none of us had to go through, and because of what he'd done we were in strong, reliable hands.

Neil's key values were outstanding: integrity, honesty, commitment, strength, good faith, morality and discipline, which were crucial in any human institution. All of those values are essential if the group is going to be viable and survive under pressure. All Blacks sides are under pressure every time they assemble to show those qualities and Neil stood for most of those things.

Frank Kilby was a manager in that side. He was an acidy little guy and a good man. I enjoyed him immensely and those two together, particularly Neil.

I had a very good club coach in the Auckland University senior side, Neil Lawrence, who had the same types of skills as JJ Stewart. He made me think about defence on the side of the scrum. We didn't play openside flanker in those days, we played on set sides, and so he taught me through all that and would talk about lines off the lineouts. He was another man that I admired – a very, very good businessman, and a successful human being, so I could look up to his values, integrity and honesty and discipline.

Disciplining a university side was not easy. One Saturday guys turned up after capping week in their dress suits from the university ball for one game, with their bow ties still on. So that was the good humour side of it – but he could handle that. He handled it because I remember him saying to two of them, 'Okay, you'd better play well, you two guys. There are no replacements. If you get on the paddock you've got to stay on and you'd better perform. The rest of the guys are here already.'

Those guys allowed you to have good fun, enjoy yourself and relax – providing it was done within policy and was never over the top. If you were having a few beers, and you might have them in excess, or some of them might drink too much, it would be done in privacy, not in public. You never did that in public bars.

Our Sunday sessions in 1963/64 and in 1960 were great days when you relaxed. Sundays were a lot of fun. At the end of the day, Colin Meads used to run those sessions and he always said, 'OK. Go and have a shower, get dressed, put some decent clothes on, get down to the dining room and behave yourselves. No stupidity, no noise.' So all of those things were looked after, and I don't think we ever had any trouble.

Communication and strategy in the All Blacks

The coach would tell us aspects of our game that were not up to scratch, like perhaps the lineouts or scrum or second phase. Neil would talk about needing to do bits and pieces there which would improve things, but most of it was done on the training field – and it was limited even then as to what was tactical. In fact, there was a game in South Africa for which I was asked to captain the side and I said, 'I'll do it if you let me organise the tactics' – and they agreed. The game was against Transvaal and we won, and it was basically very simple: inside our half, any ball we won went back to DB Clarke and he kicked it down the ground and out of play. The ball went out to our backs only in the opposition half. It was extremely successful, and became part of the concept of how to play in South Africa. Then I said to Wilson Whineray, 'You can't keep playing this all the time. It will catch up with us.'

Despite his other great qualities, 'Clarkey' wasn't the sharpest in terms of his mobility, and this showed up in the third test so tactically we were actually pretty limited. We had far more discussion in North versus South Island games tactically, and even in trial games where you captained the side, where you were allowed to sort out how you were going to handle things.

I still remember going to play in the so-called 'Springbok trials' [for the All Blacks' 1960 tour of South Africa] in Wellington. There was a massive wind blowing straight down the ground. Our coach Jack Finlay came and said, 'John, there's a big wind, if you win the toss and play with it, you can run up a big score. They won't catch you in the second half.' Simple advice, but good tactics.

I won the toss and we were up 26–0 at half-time. I said to the guys, 'Look, if we hammer this side, most of us will be in the team.' We won 37–16 – a big score, and I think 12 of us did get into the touring team and to this day we put that selection down to Jack Finlay's advice.

I think it's easy to clone the modern player. When you have the same scrum coach going around all of the unions in the country, saying, ' This is how you scrum', no one's going to become elevated in the scrum technique. You've got to be careful that you don't hide and control individual skills. Individual players were great, like Grahame Thorne and those sorts of guys in our time; they were just treasures and you've got to try and use the great skills of those players. Meads was an individual and had really great individual skills. And then there's the question of where to play your best player. Do you put him in at lock, or do you put him in at number 8? Good question.

CHANGE TO PROFESSIONALISM

Well, it couldn't be avoided. It had to happen. It got to the stage where if we hadn't gone into the professional era, we would have lost our players – they would have bolted. They were bolting anyway and so they would have gone out on their own and the whole structure of the game would've gone so, by default, we simply had to allow it to happen. It's taken a long time for it to settle in properly and I don't think it's been resolved completely yet.

We don't know yet what will happen to the majority of those who retire, and what they'll do. The experience of a number of them is that they stay in the game, rather than go out and earn an 'honest day's living'. To me it's a very one-dimensional experience, 24/7 rugby. They're not grounded in the real world. I don't know what time they get up in the morning, or whether they're disciplined in terms of the way they look often unshaven, with weird hairstyles – different to my era when I could never look scruffy.

I'm not blaming the guys at all, but the environment is such that they've got no concept of what it means to work an eight-hour day and be bored in some aspects of what you do. Everything is turned on for them. They don't have to think, certainly about clothes, accommodation, travel and so on at All Blacks' level anyway, so it's a very sheltered experience. I can best sum it up by saying that they didn't have the life that we had, and there's sadness about that. I don't think they get the experience of getting to know their mates that they play against, which gives you lifelong satisfaction. They're not very interested in the countries into which they go to play because they're playing test after test after test, so there's no relaxation for them. It really has serious challenges.

All unions claim that they attempt to get their youngsters out into the real world, but it's just a token thing as the majority of them don't want to do that. When I was managing the New Zealand cricket team I tried desperately to get those guys to get out and do something outside their cricket, like study some part-time subjects for those who were intellectually inclined. One or two did it, but it was difficult and as soon as the team disbanded, they stopped doing those things because there was no one pushing them. The same occurs with the All Blacks. I don't know what they do in the 'rest time'. I mean, it's all right them turning up to fundraising things, visiting schools, that's not work – that's just a bit of tokenism really. While the kids like it, it doesn't do a hell of a lot for the individual.

So how do you get them to finish their professional career as 'whole' men is the real test? That is the real fighting test. Tana Umaga was the first 'big' All Black to retire and look what he's doing. He went and played again as a player-coach over in France; he can't get out of the game. He's doing some good things for his Counties team [with Tana as coach in 2013, Counties won the Ranfurly Shield for the first time in history]. I was at a function to raise money for The Rugby Foundation, of which I'm president, looking after injured players at the Spinal Unit in Otara, Auckland. Tana was good enough to turn up and people loved him being there. But the overall picture for these players is my concern.

Other changes? Coming off playing against Southland in Southland on a wet day – I mean, you couldn't recognise each other! You were completely covered in mud from top to toe. You had great big heavy boots with leather sprigs so that you could track in the mud. The facilities were much poorer then, so all those parts of the game are now superb, and far superior to our day.

Crowds don't turn up as much as they did in the past, so professionalism is not the panacea of all ills. There isn't the interest in it, possibly because there's too much rugby on show now.

When we played, there were no videos – players and coaches just had to try and remember what had happened. If a team got some advantages through outstanding coaches, it used to take the opposition some time to work out exactly what was being done because they couldn't see it on video. There can be a sameness about the coaching now, because you can look at all teams at provincial level right through to the All Blacks' level and all the professional rugby teams can look at other sides, can look at themselves in instant detail – so the game is sanitised now. However, there is some strength in it because we've seen some wonderful rugby by our teams, but we've also seen a lot of sameness about tactics and patterns. Rules are complex and the game is not easy to referee especially at second phase.

The university set-up doesn't encourage rugby the way it did in my time, so a lot of intelligent players can't play the game now, or don't play. The fact that guys who were highly intelligent could go to university and still be rugby players in the amateur era meant that you had a pretty intelligent group of guys overall – Ken Gray, Dennis Young, Wilson Whineray: that was our front row. Whineray got a degree and postgraduate qualifications, Ken Gray was a highly intelligent prop. Allan Stewart was a lock with a degree, I had a degree, Earle Kirton had a degree, Chris Laidlaw was a Rhodes Scholar. None of those sorts of guys now play for the All Blacks. If they exist, they'd have gone straight into academies and then straight into the All Blacks, so we don't notice. One or two All Blacks like Conrad Smith have got degrees, and I admire them for this hugely – they've done something really special, and that's an interesting aspect to me.

I notice you don't get any top rugby players teaching now. I had a number at Auckland Grammar: Graham Henry as a coach at Grammar, Steve Watt who played front row for Auckland, Dave Syms played for Auckland, so I had school coaches who were playing top rugby, plus coaching teams and the best junior kids. That doesn't happen today so there's a loss to coaching because of the change in the environment – again, they're going to academies and straight on into professionalism, if they're good enough.

POLITICAL INFLUENCE
South Africa

In 1960, not long before we went overseas, there was the killing of 60-odd people, shot by the police in Sharpeville. I witnessed concerned New Zealanders being dragged off the playing fields of Athletic Park. I got on the field at half-time and that concerned me, seeing that happen, but I wasn't strong enough, brave enough or informed enough to say, 'Well, I'm going to make a political stand here.'

It took 1981 for me to do that. I didn't go to the games. It was a silent protest. I didn't publicise that, but as a player, politics hadn't affected me and I really don't think it affected the teams particularly. At the time of the 1960 tour rugby was the dominant game in the country, 1981 had not occurred, the feminist movement was still to come, and the anti-feminist group which still exists in rugby was strong.

SOCIETY AND CULTURE
Alcohol

Sadly, that has got worse. The social climate in this country, in terms of discipline and the right things to do, has deteriorated markedly. Binge drinking amongst young people now is almost endemic – it is a real issue for society to control that and the fact that young women are now involved in those sorts of activities. You get both males and females being much looser in their social activities and therefore vulnerable. That has a real impact on amateur rugby, as well as on the whole of New

Zealand society, and this is reflected in some of our All Blacks players – until they get into the All Blacks and are told, categorically, that if you don't behave you're not going to stay.

Maori players

Looking back, I never saw them specifically as 'Maori players' in my day: they were just good guys for whom I had a huge regard. They were very good players, they had the same incentives that I had, did an honest day's work and came to footy training and trained and played with us. I grew up on a farm and we had a Maori boy there who worked for Mum and Dad, lovely bloke; he taught me all sorts of beaut things like horse-riding and climbing trees and bird-nesting, shooting hares and rabbits. He was a great guy. I didn't see him as 'a Maori' at all, I just saw him as a good joker, a good man. When you mention [Pat] Walsh, [Waka] Nathan, [Alby] Pryor and [Maunga] Emery – there are many others that you could name – they were just good New Zealanders who had the same joys and pleasures we had. I knew Alby's boys, his wife and his family, and he was special. His boys came to Auckland Grammar School. Whenever I see Maunga Emery, we always recognise each other and say, 'Fancy seeing you', which is lovely. For me there is no differentiation between a 'Maori player' and Dan Carter – they're just two New Zealanders playing for their country and doing their best as individuals.

Polynesian players

In this part of the world Polynesian influence in the game is a big physical problem, a big challenge. That's a societal change which certainly wasn't there in my time. I went and watched the Auckland Under-20 side play Canterbury Under-20 one Saturday and there were two white boys in the Auckland side and 13 white boys in the Canterbury side: the social change is right there. Large numbers of young boys who would have played rugby, particularly in the northern part of New Zealand, don't play because their mothers don't want them to play the game against larger boys, they don't like it. The 1981 tour fallout highlighted or exacerbated that markedly, I believe.

Many of the Polynesian players are superb athletes, absolutely. We lose dozens and dozens of them because they don't go on with it.

What made players like Umaga and Keven Mealamu see it through? That's what we must ask. Mealamu is a good footballer – and also, what a superb person. There are some wonderful kids coming through and you don't want to lose those boys, but it has an impact on the skinny, white boy who wants to play first five-eighths, who's got all the skills, but just gets knocked out of it by the physical differences in contact.

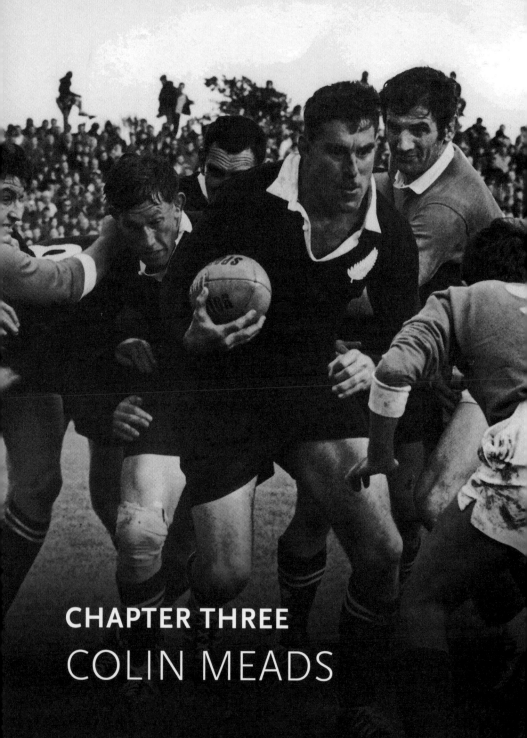

CHAPTER THREE
COLIN MEADS

S ir Colin Earl Meads' reputation is such that there are few rugby aficionados who do not know something of his legendary stature in the game – both physical (at 1.92 metres tall) and metaphorical. He was born on 3 June 1936 in Cambridge and played his first game for his home province of King Country in 1955 as a strapping, farm-bred 19-year-old. Nicknamed 'Pinetree', between 1957 and 1971 he played 133 games, including 55 test matches, for the All Blacks, most frequently in the lock position. His blond-haired brother, Stan, played 30 matches for the All Blacks, including 15 tests between 1961 and 1966, also mostly as a lock. Colin captained the All Blacks a number of times, although never regularly, initially in 1960 and finally in 1971.

Author and sports journalist Alex Veysey, quoting DJ Graham, shed some light on Meads' informal leadership of this era in his 1974 biography, *Colin Meads, All Black*: 'The side to Meads' greatness, which many perhaps do not quite appreciate, is the contribution he makes in a side's corporate welfare. Colin Meads is a humble man, a man of action rather than a talker about his actions, yet he is always the unofficial adviser, guide, assistant, leader of any All Blacks party outside the official leaders of the side . . . Meads does not seek this position, the rest of the team simply place him in it.'[1]

In 1986 Meads was elected to the national selection panel, but sacked later in the year for acting as coach to the unauthorised New Zealand Cavaliers tour of apartheid South Africa.

Meads is widely considered one of the greatest players in All Blacks history. He was named Player of the Century at the New Zealand Rugby Awards in 1999, and was knighted in 2009. One of the trophies contested in the Heartland Championship, which comprises teams formerly in Divisions Two and Three of the National Provincial Championship, is named the Meads Cup in his honour, and he has remained a regular go-to man for New Zealand media seeking comment on rugby matters.

PRIDE IN SELECTION

I played through the trials in 1956. A lot of people said, 'Oh, you'll get picked', but you don't believe them. You have this doubt until you hear your name called out. On first being picked [in 1957], it was the greatest thing that had happened to me. Of course, you get married and have family things in your life too, but from a sporting point of view it was the greatest thing that ever happened to me.

For this shy, country boy to be named in the All Blacks – I reckon I was in shock for two days; certainly for that night after it was announced. It was in Athletic Park under the stand there, a great place for announcements. You were told to go to one of the dressing rooms, and you did what you were told.

I was rooming with Nev McEwan at the time. He was a Wellington boy and, the trial being in Wellington, he had his gear all packed up and was out partying up somewhere. They all seemed to go off to functions, everyone else, and no one asked me to go. I was left there at the bar just drinking on my own in shock and trying to hide from everyone. We were told early the next morning that we had to be ready for a medical. I thought, 'What, a medical? Now what are they going to put us through?'

Being named was a culture shock for the boy from Te Kuiti, who didn't know many of the players. I knew Whineray, but he was in a different trial team to me. I knew one or two others, but very few. While I'd been at the trials in 1956, once the Springbok tour was over they didn't want to recognise you, you were a Lone Star Ranger from Te Kuiti in the King Country.

We were told we were leaving for Australia in about two and a half weeks after this trial, but in the meantime we had to play club football. Everyone played club football in those days. I was worried as I had read about other players being picked for the All Blacks, but had never played – they'd got injured. Well, I played a couple of club games down here and tried to do nothing, and that's the worst thing that you can do.

Then we assembled and were away to Australia. It was marvellous! I remember Dick Everest was coach and our first game was against Sydney, which was one of the top sides. Outside the test, it was the biggest game we were to have. We arrived there on a Sunday or Monday, and on the Tuesday he arranged a game down in Wollongong that I was picked for. I can remember sitting all night – I was scared to move in case I tripped over, slipped and broke my leg before I got out on that field. We played that game and it wasn't even classed as a first-class game. It wasn't anywhere on the schedule, either: just an extra game – and here's me thinking I'd played my first official game for the All Blacks.

It was a relief all the same to put that jersey on and get out and do the haka and be part of the whole scene. Also, there was tremendous inner pride, something that's unique.

RITES AND RITUALS
The haka

Meads reflects on how the emphasis and importance of the haka changed from his era to that of the first Rugby World Cup, and then up to the most recent decade:

There wasn't a great deal of emphasis put on the haka in our day – we never did it in New Zealand in those early days. The haka was a lot different to what it is now. We all had to jump up in the air with our arms out, legs bent. The big worry was if you missed the jump, because that was the moment they took the photographs which appeared in every paper. If anyone missed the jump, he was fined at the next court session and my biggest worry was that I got the jump timed right so that I didn't get caught out.

Wayne 'Buck' Shelford is the one who's got to be thanked for saying, 'If we're going to do the haka, let's do it properly.' But that came later. A lot of the things we did in our day were so different to now. Ours was just all in one line, everyone jumped at the finish and a lot of noise. It was virtually the 'Ka Mate' haka, but it was different.

It surprised me in 2006, when the All Blacks did the haka in their dressing room while in Cardiff. The Welsh had wanted to sing their anthem after our haka – it was their centenary that year, but the haka is always meant to be the last thing that's done. There had been a dispute and the All Blacks said, 'Oh well, we won't do the haka at all.' So the All Blacks ended up doing the haka in their dressing room, and people got upset about that.

A year later, when we lost the Rugby World Cup quarterfinal to France, I got a phone call after the game from an English lady who is mad on rugby. Her husband used to be on the English Rugby Union, he was one of the old farts in Will Carling's day. Well, she rung up and said, 'Serves you right, you arrogant, rude people.'

I said, 'Why?'

'Because you wouldn't do the haka for us last year. It serves you right.' Again, I said, 'Why?'

'Oh,' she said, 'people love the haka. We go to see it and you didn't do it for us and that was sheer arrogance.'

It made me stop and think that the haka, as a tradition, is tremendous and something unique to New Zealand. Nothing compares to a New Zealand haka, if it's done properly.

The back seat of the bus

When we were there, it was an agreement, the rite of the back seat – but you had to fight your way into it. You had to achieve it. Somebody either got dropped and then you got in there before somebody else, or there was a dispute over it that was usually sorted out between the players concerned.

When I went back as a manager, it was done on seniority in the team, and they all had their rituals. The captain had to sit down the front and the back seat was Zinzan Brooke, Mike Brewer and Richard Loe, because they were the oldest All Blacks.

When we went away in 1960, we had a Catholic player in the back seat – so that set a tradition. We ended up with Earle Kirton, and because he was the only Catholic in the team in 1967 we also ended up with him in the back seat and he loved it. So there were traditions, but they weren't the same from era to era or anything. The traditions changed over time.

It was usually the 'elderly' players that were in there, but there was always a challenge for it. Kel Tremain and I were in there for years – I went in there at a very young age. I wasn't in there in my first year, but we had a little bit of a tutu and one or two disputes! We were on our way to a flash dinner after a game, and another player (who shall be nameless) and I, we'd ripped our shirts a fair bit. When we got there old Bill Craddock (and old Bill, a former chairman and long-time member of the NZRFU, was the most jovial, good-humoured old guy) said, 'Get a taxi – you'd better go back and get dressed up again and put another shirt on together.'

I didn't go into the back seat, but this guy was in the back seat and I thought, 'When we get back from this taxi, before we get changed, we should sort this out.' He didn't want a bar of it and so I thought, 'Well I've had a victory here.' I felt pretty good at that.

Induction

You were all sat down in a room and were given a few lectures about the rights and wrongs of life and your social behaviour and those types of things, usually by the chairman or people in high-profile positions in rugby. Alan 'Ponty' Reid was my first captain, he had a little bit to say. Tom Morrison, who had long since turned from playing to administration, gave us a lecture on one or two things. Then they got round to punctuality. You got given a few lectures, but 90 per cent of it the players knew from their provincial set-ups.

Back in King Country, we never trained – if we had two or three training runs a year, that'd be it. We just played and you felt your way as you went. The senior players led you into everything, even guiding where you sat in the dressing room, i.e. the two locks sat together.

Now the players all come from a franchise, the Chiefs, the Hurricanes and so on, so it would be different. They would be more experienced in that sort of protocol than we ever were. The modern-day player has got so much more experience before he becomes an All Black than we had, even though some of us had played a lot of games for the province. They're more organised now than we ever were, with modern techniques for injuries, and doctors and medical staff on hand.

In Meads' day, there was a gulf between playing for King Country and the All Blacks:

I played trials in 1956 and then played back in King Country. They had a training run a week or so later and the whole team sat down and said, 'Well, what did you learn?' Even the coach was asking me, 'So what did you learn?'

You learnt to try and impart what you'd heard them talk about at training and what they did in the games. What Ron Hemi did as a hooker, the way he packed in the scrum and the way they threw the ball into you in the lineouts. King Country back in those days didn't even have lineout calls – they just threw it where the halfbacks stood. I was so young, only about 19 or 20 when I was playing those trials, but I was immediately entrusted into giving knowledge to King Country: 'What are you going to tell us?'

It made me stop and think about the game, and about what makes this game tick. Why are South Island players better 'ruckers' than North Islanders, as they always tell us?

The 'dirt-trackers'

There was also a distinction between being a 'dirt-tracker' (players who played in midweek games) on tour and being a member of the test team.

It must have been hard to be a dirt-tracker, if you're a dedicated one, but you just couldn't quite make it. Some of the dirt-trackers got led into thinking, 'Oh well, that's my lot.' They had a marvellous social tour, but their rugby didn't come on, it went off.

We played Newport on the 1963/64 tour. For Earle Kirton and BJ Lochore, it was their first game and we got beaten (neither Lochore nor Kirton were picked again until the seventh game of the tour). BJ was in panic mode, training like mad; he was rooming with me and would say, 'Well, what have I got to do to get a game?' Then he'd room with DJ Graham and he'd talk to him. We'd all say, 'You just keep training. Don't get sucked into the social life.'

Dirt-trackers were permitted to go a lot of the places where the playing team didn't go, but they had to train extra hard. BJ got the eighth or ninth game (I wouldn't know which one it was) and by about the twelfth game he was in the test team. In the end he went from being a real dirt-tracker to a test player just by Waka Nathan breaking his jaw and having a couple of good games (he had come back and played well when he did get the opportunity). It was between him and Keith Nelson as to who got the job; he got it and never looked back.

VALUES AND BELIEFS
Pride in winning
Meads comments on the significance of winning but, more importantly, the reaction to losing:

When we lost in our days, it was a 'national tragedy', a national disaster and you got, not abused, but scorned by people. In 1964 Stan and I were right in the middle of lambing, and we had bought a lot of extra land so the old man was under stress at home. We said we'd come home after the game on Saturday night. There was a train leaving at 7.30 or 8 p.m., they used to call it the 'Limited'. It used to get through home at five in the morning, so the old man would pick us up off the railway station and we could spend Sunday at home working. Well, we got a taxi from the hotel and the taxi driver abused us. We got onto the train, we had a sleeper and you had the guards there. The guard on the train reckoned, 'We shouldn't give you a bed. You fellows don't deserve one because you've just been beaten by the Aussies down there.'

The attitude of New Zealand [towards winning] will not change because it's our national sport – and people say we've got to learn to accept that [as players]. I don't think we do. The moment we do, we're going to lose something – and it's not a fear of losing; it's a fear of letting your country down, more than anything. You get politicians speaking about elections being won and lost on test series. Isn't that carrying it too far? Politics shouldn't interfere with sport, yet politicians say that. [Former Prime Minister Sir Robert] Muldoon and others created an image where if the All Blacks go well, everything goes well in the country. It's a great tribute to have as All Blacks, but we are a bit over the top at times.

Memorable wins

One of the greatest games I played in was the second test against the Springboks in Cape Town. To win over in South Africa in those days was unbelievable, because of the problem with referees. They probably had the same problem here in New Zealand when they came out in 1956. In 1960, we were a pretty good side. We were very young and I was a young captain. I don't know why they played me at number 8. I hadn't played number 8 all the tour. I got a try and it was a game where things went right, but we also did some things wrong. Don Clarke arrived with only one boot. He put on one of Tremain's boots, which were lightweight ones. It was a left boot. He drop-kicked a goal with Tremain's boot on. He couldn't do a thing wrong is what I'm saying.

Memorable losses

The 1965 series against the Springboks was as complete a team as we had, so we shouldn't have lost the one we did at Christchurch. It's too easy to be flippant about it, but Pat Murphy was the referee and went off at half-time. We were winning 16–5 at that stage and lost 19–16. So there was something there, but also one or two backs let us down badly by missing tackles, and their centre Johnny Gainsford cut us to ribbons. He scored two tries just in the second half. There was Gainsford and that little winger Syd Nomis, but we still should have won four tests and it was in many ways sad that we didn't. It would have been repaying them for 1949. We all thought we'd let that side down, but it was still a great team and good to play in, because we had the same forward pack for the whole four tests.

The next year they changed only one and that was Jack Hazlett for Whineray, so everyone knew one another. Stan and I used to just fall into place and 'Bunny' Tremain and I played together for so long. We were all captains, I suppose. We all yakked and talked and the poor Springboks didn't know what was going on at times. We never had the brilliance of the South Africans, but we had a good, steady backline and they kept it pretty simple and pretty straight up.

Nineteen sixty-three was a great team. We drew one test, won the others so we didn't get a Grand Slam, and then lost to Newport, but it was the most enjoyable experience you could have had – and one of the happiest teams I've ever been in. A great side.

LEADERSHIP
Coaching

They've all got different attributes and they all approach things differently. Neil McPhail was a great army man, not a great coach. Whineray had as much to do with coaching that team as anyone – that's when he became a great captain. Fred Allen was the 'dictatorial dictator', wanting to spin the ball, and he convinced us that it was the way to go. He got onside with the players to get what he wanted, but Fred never gave some of the players a second opportunity. If you let him down, say socially, Fred never went back to you. You were cast out, you were gone, whereas other coaches would get around that and say, 'Come on, we need you back in this team. You've got to pull your horns in.'

Dick Everest was a very astute coach, but not well liked by the rugby union. I don't know what that was about. Jack Sullivan was a great player, but not a great coach – just a selector, administrator and probably an old bully in his day. You grew to like them. You got to know them through playing with them. It wasn't until we got Fred Allen that we really got coaching, such as, 'This is what you do and this is how we do it.' Once you went onto that field, it was BJ who ran the cutter. Fred was a great man for playing running rugby. We'd played in an era where there wasn't too much running – well, we didn't think there was, but if you go back another 10 years before that, there was not a lot of running at all.

Ponty Reid was one of the worst halfbacks I ever played with as an All Black, but the best tactician. He knew where every forward should be – and this was before video analysis. After a test match over in Aussie, I was playing as a loose forward and he said, 'When the Aussies scored that try, where were you?'

I thought, 'Where was I?'

He said, 'It was the centre who made the break and you should have caught him over there.'

Ponty made me think about little things as a player that I'd never thought of. He said, 'When you pass me the ball off a lineout [because I used to play and feed off the top], I don't want it over here, I want it here – because I can pass it like that, whereas if you get it to me there, I've got to go like that.'

For the modern players, that's all part of their tuition now. They get so much guidance and the worry I have with New Zealand at the moment is that they're over-coaching players a little. Sonny Bill Williams is a great experiment because he does things 'off the bat', without coaching. You don't coach those things, they just happen with him.

I spoke at a function with Frank Bunce once and he was asked, 'What's wrong with New Zealand coaches? How do you rate them?'

He replied, 'We're all cloned. All the coaches get a manual.'

He wasn't joking. A young coach coming through here at Te Kuiti, he'll get a manual from the NZRU and Graham Henry speaks to all the franchises. The individuality been taken away and that is a bit of a worry because in our days everyone was so different. We are tending to clone our players, clone our coaches.

Meads emphasises the importance of constant innovation, doing something different to gain the winning edge:

A lot of winning teams have done things differently, like Hawke's Bay in the 1960s. I can remember a chap called Barry Bracewell, he was coaching Counties and they did some very innovative things. They had a 14-man scrum – sounds silly, and once everyone got to know it, everyone could stop it. We're not getting coaches experimenting today with moves. In our day we had a move called 'Canterbury'. It was: go out to the first five-eighths, the fullback comes through on the blindside. What a great move. The first time we did it, we scored a try, but then after that no one scored a try!

Innovation has been removed from our coaches. We're getting too built around theory. The coaches that do try different things probably don't get too far, and don't get any further recognition unless they win. Our top teams are all fairly even. There's no place for this experimental coaching, for want of a word, in New Zealand rugby.

A lot of our team talks were built around me, because I wouldn't take offence. You had it built around you by the coaches to beat the opposition. I can remember one tour where McPhail had read somewhere that Scotland's Mike Campbell-Lamerton was the best lock in the world – this is before we got there in 1963. We were playing London Counties, who had been a good side: they'd beaten the 1953 All Blacks. They weren't a great side against us, but we were and the whole thing was built around, 'I want to look you in the eye after the game and tell you that he's not the best lock in the world.'

Nowadays everyone contributes, the All Blacks are playing well and they've got a good team system. They're going to miss Piri Weepu, however, because he was a cocky little fellow who would do something a little bit different – and that little bit different will open up a game for you.

Captaincy

I don't think I was ever meant to be a leader of the All Blacks. I came in with Whineray and he was a born leader. He was a natural. It was easy for him, not just on the field, but off the field, too. He was a good orator; he was a good and a clever guy, a very brilliant man, whereas I only became captain because of my seniority. I'd been there so long and they just made me captain because probably they didn't think anyone else could've been.

Their greatest achievement was making Lochore captain, because there were about four of us in the running to be captain of that 1966 team. 'Bunny' Tremain thought he might be captain, and would certainly have been in the running. He and I were great mates. I never thought I would be captain, though. I was of more value to the team not being captain, because the captain is often restricted in what they can do and my portfolio was to be able to say to the captain, 'Well, don't play me in the lineout. I'm having a bit of trouble here.' I'd be telling Whineray, 'I've marked a player only once, don't throw any to me.'

Collective leadership

Graham Henry talks about it a lot now, with his players. Brian Lochore proved such a great leader. I remember when BJ got appointed, Ken Gray was the other one that they thought could be the captain. Ken was probably too quiet, a deeper fellow. Tremain, when we first assembled, made a speech about how we'd all get in behind Lochore and I thought it was one of the greatest things I'd heard. I thought, 'Bunny, he'll do me.' Tremain had said, 'Pinetree and I'll get in, and Ken Gray will get in behind you. A lot of people thought we were going to be captain, but we're on your side.'

Leadership is within the team. I had a role as a fixer, if there was trouble going on – not a dirty role, but as the one able to talk to the opposition and tell them, 'I wouldn't do that again, if I were you.' When they make you captain, that's largely taken away from you. I enjoyed captaining King Country because they were country boys. They were followers. In the All Blacks, you've got to be more astute and you've got to be able to give directions and guidance, and I wasn't that sort.

BJ just grew into captaincy. Whineray admitted that in his first two or three years he wasn't a great captain, but by the time he got to 1965, after having come through 1963, he was a great captain – he often spoke about that. After the 2007 World Cup, which skipper Richie McCaw got a lot of the blame for, Whineray said, 'It's one of the disappointments that they never came and asked me to speak to the captain. I could have given him so much advice just on the mistakes I made, how I learned and what I went through to be there.'

Richie is now a very good captain, but he's grown into it. It doesn't just happen.

CHANGE TO PROFESSIONALISM

I wasn't manager when they were professional, they were only semi-professional then. But there was talk of money and there was literature left in the bus – 'How to make your money go further' and other money-matters pamphlets. I thought, 'Gosh, in our day it'd be a comic or a wild-west cowboy story.'

Professionalism is handled pretty well by New Zealand. I really think the NZRU has done it right by the players, contracting them. We're more settled as a team because of our professional approach, whereas it must be hard for players in the United Kingdom – they're employed by a club and get contracted from the club to play international rugby. They get huge amounts to play international rugby, above what they get from their club, but they've now got two organisations with whom they've got to be speaking, determining how well they're paid. Then they might play in a test match, play terribly well and want more from their club or province. Those negotiations must carry on a lot longer than anything a New Zealand negotiator or agent would have to do. So from that point of view, we handle professionalism pretty well.

The social side and friendships after the game finished have changed, however.

They don't have the friendships that we used to have. I don't think the modern player finds that friendship in rugby. They try and tell you they do, but I've been to test matches as an old fella. Two or three years ago, when we were over in Ireland, we went to the after-match function. The All Blacks sat here and the Irish team sat way over there and if you wanted a signature or something, you had to get up and go way across the other side. They never sat together, whereas in New Zealand it was a tradition: you were meant to go and sit with the guy you played against and have a few beers together, laugh, joke, and tell stories about what happened during the game, in a nice way. You became friends and you had drinks together.

The French are the greatest 'social' players. Even though I couldn't speak French, we had some fabulous dinners with them. Overall, we just don't have social games like we used to have. Five New Zealanders went back to South Africa for their 75th anniversary, Tremain and all us lot. Rugby wasn't as important as the social aspect. We were a World XV playing against South Africa. Then they mixed them up and they had the World forwards with the South African backs – so it didn't really matter who won. I also went back for the English centenary. They don't have those sorts of things now – it's all tied up in this professional thing: it's got to be test matches and money spent. I just don't think it's quite the same.

Physical conditioning

How does Meads view technological changes in areas like nutrition, physical conditioning and turf management?

I have the odd suspicion and doubt. Nutrition is one thing that keeps changing by the generation. I still think they need just a basic diet. No two players are the same. If I like meat, I should be allowed to eat meat, as long as I'm playing well. The moment you're not playing well, then you've got to listen to someone. Dietitians at one stage were stopping the All Blacks from eating meat on Wednesdays. To me, that was criminal because, I suppose, I'm a farmer. I used to eat it on Saturdays.

The conditioning of the players is different to what it was in our days. We were put together different physically. Not as heavy – nowhere near as heavy as they are nowadays, where they're all two or three inches taller. Ours was mainly just farming or physical work. They call it aerobic fitness now. They go to the gym rather than go for a run, whereas we'd just go out for a run.

Chris Laidlaw was always different. He was just a natural, never that fit, but just did what he had to do. He was a clever enough tactician to be able to get away with it. The average forward had three or four runs in a week. He'd go for a run on the road and then club football started. He'd do those trainings twice a week, and have another couple of runs probably, and that was his lot. Then rep rugby came along, so he found he was training three or four nights a week on a footy field. And that was running. We didn't go down there and go to a gym; we never had conditioning. They test them now – is your right arm stronger or your left arm weak, etc.

Grounds

There have been significant changes to the playing surfaces. Nowadays the pitches around the world are that good, they're like bowling greens. They have a problem in Cardiff with shading from the roof, but 90 per cent of the time the pitches are great. In our day we had some terrible, muddy pitches at Carisbrook, because it wasn't ever protected. They played on them every week: the curtain-raisers, two or three games on Saturday and so some of the grounds were in atrocious condition by the time we played a test match on them. We weren't worried, though; it was just part of rugby.

By way of contrast, I went with Laurie Mains to France [in 1995, when Mains was coach] where we weren't permitted to train on one of the main grounds because they were getting it ready for a test match against Italy. I said, 'We can train over there, on those soccer fields.'

Laurie kept saying, 'This is the All Blacks. We're meant to be the best team in the word. We shouldn't be training on soccer fields.'

'Laurie, we used to train on cow paddocks. What's the difference? There's a line down there. You've got a touch line. You can work out if the first fellow stands five yards back and just work it from there.'

'It should be fully marked out.'

That incident has often made me think, 'Rugby has changed.' The expectations of rugby players now, and at that level, are so very different to what they used to be – and, probably, rightly so. I was the rough country manager. Laurie found some holes somewhere and said, 'If they break their ankle . . .'

Did players in Meads' era adapt to changes in the game?

We went through a phase in the 1960s changing from the big, slow forward to a more mobile type of player. Back in the 1940s and 1950s they used to talk about dribbling. If you talk to a modern player, he wouldn't know what you're talking about if you were talking about dribbling a ball.

The game has changed completely: it's now a game with ball in hand, whereas it wasn't always that. Lineouts were just so different. You kicked it out and the opposition threw it in, but the opposition never dominated lineouts on their side. The lineouts were a lottery; you just went for everything that was going.

POLITICAL INFLUENCE
South Africa

You thought about it, but it never affected me and I was never, ever not going to go, because it was my one life's ambition. My old man used to talk about the Springboks and Danie Craven – the Brownlie brothers (Maurice, Cyril and Laurence) were the greatest loose forwards we'd ever had, so that was the tremendous contest. Tradition told you that you wanted to play rugby in South Africa, so not doing that because of politics never entered my mind. I never held it against people that did not go, however.

I did get a little upset with Chris Laidlaw, not to his face, but because he wrote in his book that South Africa wasn't the right place to tour. Well, why did he go? He went there because he wanted to be an All Black.

When it got more critical in New Zealand, in about 1967, and we didn't tour South Africa, we went to the United Kingdom instead. Then it became 'no Maoris, no tour' and we in New Zealand all accepted that. When South Africa accepted [the inclusion of Maori and Pasifika players] for 1970 that was a huge concession on their part and they never got any credit. It was still a white, racist country over there that was running the country, but they accepted the Maori from New Zealand.

We had three players of Maori ancestry – Blair Furlong, Sid Going and Henare 'Buff' Milner – and one player of Samoan ancestry in Bryan 'Beegee' Williams.

Williams was such a star that just him being there did more to create peace. He was an unbelievable winger and he never played like that again in his life compared to the heights he reached playing over there, when he was just out of this world. It did much for us as All Blacks and for New Zealand as a country. We were loved by the black people of South Africa, they used to cheer for us rather than South Africa. So it was, in a critical way, good to witness being an All Black in South Africa under the white regime. You were treated by the rugby people as great, but you were also treated that way by the blacks, who just loved the All Blacks.

SOCIETY AND CULTURE
Alcohol
Well, once again every player is different. There are some players we've played with that should never have drank. They can't handle liquor. If you're going to drink and get angry or get vicious, you shouldn't drink. It's quite sad: I've seen one or two players that became All Blacks and drank and shouldn't have, and therefore didn't stay All Blacks because they couldn't handle it. In our day, most players drank and had a few beers after the game in the dressing room. You don't see that nowadays. They'll be having bananas and sandwiches and a cup of tea whereas that was unheard of to us.

So the culture and image has changed, but I just worry that they get told now, when they can have a drink – they don't have any drinks for two or three weeks. Both in my day and now we've had, in New Zealand, binge drinking, but one key difference is that after every game we had a few drinks – invariably with your opposition because for all the games we played on tour, there was always a dinner afterwards. That's not the case nowadays. While players of later generations came to hate dinners, I used to actually like them and thought they were a good way to meet up with the opposition. It might be the halfback you played against, you probably kicked him in the arse during the game, but you could talk about it afterwards over a beer and become great mates.

I always think of some players, like a little fellow called Chico Hopkins [who toured with the 1971 Lions as understudy to halfback Gareth Edwards]. A lot of people rated him better than Edwards. He was a cheeky player. King Country/Wanganui played them in Wanganui. At the after-match function they had to be presented with 30

ties from Wanganui, and I was silly enough to go and say to the captain,
'I'm so sorry we haven't got any King Country ties, but I guarantee to
get you some.'

Well, I wished I'd never said it. Chico Hopkins kept reminding me
every test. Another two tests and he'd still be saying, 'Where's my tie? I
haven't got a King Country tie yet.'

The King Country union wouldn't give me any, so I had to go and buy
30-odd ties . . . and they charged me for them.

Maori influence

There was never any conflict on our part with Maori players. Every team
was full of them and indeed we played some teams in New Zealand that
were all Maori. The Huia team was Maori; there was always a hiss and a
roar and they were a very good side, at times. There used to be a fair old
battle on the field, a lot of comments on the sidelines and it was all go
with a beer afterwards. So I don't think there was ever racial disharmony
through rugby, not that I know of.

A New Zealand XV played against New Zealand Maori. New Zealand
Maori (or Maori All Blacks as they are sometimes called) used to have
the odd game and toured to Australia in 1958 before coming back and
playing that New Zealand XV. It wasn't ever called the All Blacks, just
the New Zealand XV playing the New Zealand Maori XV. It was a good
game, and we won. People say if you played those games now it would
be racist, but that's not how we saw it – not in New Zealand. It's never
worried me because there's a big Maori population here in Te Kuiti.
When we went to school, we were the only white kids on the bus. I learnt
how to handle myself and live with Maori and became great friends with
a lot of them.

Attitudes to women

The modern-day player, and I'm only observing here, seems to have a
much flasher woman than we used to have. Women were outcasts of
rugby in the early years, the 1950s and 1960s, and even at club rugby
down here, women didn't go to after-match functions. I know with my
wife Verna I was lucky. She had her parents in town and she'd go there,
and I'd perhaps give her a ring and say, 'It's time to pick me up' – and
down she'd come with the kids to pick me up from rugby.

There is a place for women's rugby. I don't know when it first came out, but I wasn't in favour of it. I didn't think it was a game for women, but we've got to accept it and when you see them play, they're playing with a lot of skill and expertise now. There's also a place in rugby for women administrators, but we men tend to think we're the only ones that can administer rugby. I always think of 'old Cath' (Cath McLean) over on the East Coast who was there for what seemed like hundreds of years. Without her, they'd have been completely gone.

As strange as it may seem, the players' wives all became great friends and they'd meet, say, for the Auckland test. We'd go to the dinner that night while the wives would go out to a function, or a play or something would be on in Auckland and they'd go to that and have a marvellous time. They'd think it was a pretty good life. Later on, Andy Haden had a lot to do with getting women involved in rugby at after-match functions. We'll see a bigger role of women being administrators in the game and that mightn't be a bad thing.

Schoolboy and provincial rugby

There's some brilliant rugby at First XV level, but schools are also putting too much emphasis on rugby and First XVs and you see brawls and goodness knows what, which should never happen. The big schools are going overseas and recruiting players. There's a good chance you'll get a good education these days by being a good rugby player at the age of about 11, 12 or 13. Around here, we lose two or three from King Country every year – they get taken by Hamilton Boys' High School or Cambridge Boys'.

Once upon a time we never had divisional rugby: you just played within your region. We used to play Auckland, North Auckland, Waikato, Bay of Plenty, Taranaki and into South Wanganui, and that would be our lot. The first year we only played four games, that's all the union would play; then they got to six and then to eight. We were playing the top teams, but invariably we'd have a win. Now, with divisional rugby and professionalism, all the good players go to the big unions and they are hand-picked as youngsters. The schools are helping it by putting so much emphasis on winning their First XV competitions.

It's good stuff, it really is, but it means for country districts like this, they're going to miss out, because we never get them back. We've got nothing to keep them here. In King Country we haven't got an education centre, a varsity or polytechnic. So they all go away and never come home again, if they're a good rugby player. In the New Zealand Under-20 side in the last three or four years, we've had about five King Country players. You'd like to think you could play Auckland, but they would give King Country at the moment a 120-point start and still probably beat them. That's the sad part. Once upon a time, they'd have been fair crapping themselves to come down and play King Country in Te Kuiti or Taumarunui or wherever it may have been.

THE FUTURE

Tradition is going to carry us a long, long way. People used to talk about us in the 1960s, still saying we'd been let down by the 1937 All Blacks and the Springboks thrashed us in 1949. We've got all this history. I can remember the great Tom Pearce, who was on the council those days, before the 1956 Springbok tour and he came out with statements – he was a great orator – but he said, 'If we don't beat South Africa, it will be the ruination of rugby in New Zealand.' Of course we beat them and everything was fine and dandy. We were taught how great the 1924 team was, that they were the benchmark back in those days and it goes on and on. Each new generation that comes through gets fed the same stuff, and to me it is tradition.

The one worry we have in New Zealand is our other winter code and that'll be soccer [association football], because of mums and the kids. We have soccer grounds down here below us and on a Saturday morning you can hardly get out of the roadway, it's blocked off by all the parents with their kids playing soccer. That's the big threat because a lot of people now think rugby's a bit violent, whereas back in the 1950s, 1960s and 1970s we accepted that type of stuff more than they do nowadays. If we saw blood, they never, ever changed a jersey – someone just bandaged or wiped it off and just let him bleed and carry on playing.

The game has changed, and the laws are getting too pedantic. Head-high tackles, as an example: some of them aren't dangerous at all, the way they are done, it's just a little guy next to a big guy and they're running close together. There are not enough margins in the rules for the referee. It must be a lot harder to referee rugby now than it ever was when I played. The ball was the off-side line: we had the technical rule which is still in today, but apart from that you were onside as long as you were behind the ball. You didn't have to be an expert, a scholar to work out the rules and to know when you were right or wrong. Today you've got to be a little bit more astute when you can play the ball as to what you can then do with it.

I think we'll keep our winning way because our youth teams do well. At one stage we were even picking a New Zealand Under-16 team. You've got a New Zealand Secondary Schools team and surely that's enough. Instead of being Under-21s, they've gone to 20s: I don't know the reasoning for that. Anyway, if we keep those two teams and they keep winning (they don't have to win everything every year, but as long as they're up there), we will keep on our winning ways. We're very good at lower levels, so the development of young players is pretty good.

The big thing is keeping the initiative in our coaching system, with young coaches. Back in our days a lot of the good coaches, the JJ Stewarts, they started at schools rugby level. You don't see that now. We need to keep imagination in young coaches at that schoolboy level. One thing we've got to stop doing with these Under-18 teams is having coaches that tell them, 'You're our future All Blacks.' By the time he's 21 and he's not an All Black, he'll go overseas. We've got to just tell them it's a stepping stone: some of you will be and 90 per cent of you won't be, but we don't know which ones are the 10 per cent. It's not the best players, it's the ones who will stick at it the most. They'll keep coming through and then our future will always be good.

CHAPTER FOUR
BRIAN 'BJ' LOCHORE

There are few All Blacks more respected for their mana and personable ability to lead than Sir Brian Lochore. He was born on 3 September 1940 in Masterton, his career beginning when, in 1959, he debuted in senior club rugby for Masterton and for representative rugby team Wairarapa-Bush.

After playing six tests, including all four of the 1965 South Africa home series, coach Fred Allen selected Lochore as All Blacks captain to play against the Lions in 1966 – 18 of his 25 tests in total were as the side's leader. Allen wrote, in his foreword to the book *Lochore*: 'I was fully aware of the controversy that would ensue when I was the principal architect in appointing Brian as captain of the 1966 All Blacks . . . He was chosen ahead of greats such as Meads, Tremain, Graham, Gray, Laidlaw and MacRae . . . History has proved it was the right decision . . . he turned up absolute trumps as an All Blacks captain and then as an All Blacks coach.'[1]

Indeed, Lochore proved to be one of New Zealand's most successful captains with just three losses in South Africa in 1970. He continued as skipper until his retirement that year (although, at the selectors' request, he returned to play one game against the British Lions in 1971 for an injury-hit All Blacks side).

A farmer by profession, his involvement in the game did not end with his playing days. He coached the Masterton club before moving on to coach Wairarapa-Bush in 1980, taking them to First Division status within two seasons. Lochore became an All Blacks selector in 1983 before taking the side to victory at the inaugural Rugby World Cup under his coaching tenure, which spanned 1985 to 1987. Lochore continued to be involved in All Blacks rugby, firstly as campaign manager for the 1995 Rugby World Cup and then as one of the All Blacks selectors from 2003 to 2007. He was knighted and inducted into the International Rugby Hall of Fame in 1999. The Lochore Cup, contested as part of New Zealand's domestic competition, is named in his honour. On 6 February 2007, Lochore was inducted into the Order of New Zealand, the country's highest honour, for services to rugby.

PRIDE IN SELECTION

All Blacks selection for me was quite dramatic. I'd played flanker and lock in the trials, the two positions I occupied in Wairarapa and at club level, and of course as they announced the team under the stand at

Athletic Park they started with fullback, working up to the forwards. They got through the locks and flankers and I wasn't named as any of those so I assumed that I was gone; it would be back home to the farm.

My name turned out to be the 30th called out of the 30 players selected – as the second number 8. That was quite remarkable. Funnily enough, it's the only position in the forwards, apart from hooker, that I'd never played in my life. As time went on it was an inspirational selection, I guess, on their part, but more importantly for me. Number 8 suited me; it was a position I probably should have played all of my life, although it was good having played another position so that you understood the role properly.

It was every young rugby player's dream, and probably that of quite a lot of other guys who don't even play rugby, to be selected for the All Blacks. So it was enormous. In retrospect, more interesting is the fact that I remember saying to my friends that as long as I'm selected, I didn't give a stuff whether I played hooker or any other position. It wasn't very long before I realised how important it was to be a *good* All Black and get games, because on that first tour I didn't get many games initially. In the end I got a lucky break and ended up getting two tests, which was brilliant, but it had been tough going. That was probably the best learning curve for me as a captain, later on – knowing how it felt to be just a team member.

Competition for the All Blacks jersey was always intense and of course tradition has it that it was harder to get out of the test XV than it was to get in. So, although form does play a part, experience in those days was very important at test match level.

RITES AND RITUALS
The haka

We weren't very good at it and didn't really understand the ritual, certainly not as well as they do now. We always had Maori players in the team, but not always a Maori in the playing XV, so I had to lead it on a number of occasions – which, thinking back, I'm very proud to have done.

Later I was instrumental in getting it to be performed also in New Zealand. That happened at the 1987 World Cup. We believed it was the first time an All Blacks team was effectively 'on tour in New Zealand', and saw no reason why we shouldn't perform the haka as basically we felt the same as if we were on tour.

The back seat of the bus

The guys in the back seat had a large part to play in terms of discipline around the sort of things that we did as a team socially – and more than that, in some aspects. The back seat was a very, very strong protocol when we played and has continued to today. When I have worked with the team in recent years, it's been exactly the same as it ever was. I nearly got to the back seat myself in my time, and would've been in it, but I became captain and so I got shunted up the front again! But I was able to be a 'guest' in the back seat on the way home from the games, which I enjoyed.

You learnt to be strong real quick, to be seen and not heard. I think that's why many players over the years have only ever played one or two tests for New Zealand, not necessarily because of purely rugby skills but because they didn't cope with a whole lot of other things. It was tough going. You either sank or swam, and I guess you could say that the strong people come to the surface – or the strong get better and the weak get worse. That's the way it was all the times when I played, pretty much.

Induction

Now they have an induction ceremony when you have your first test. You get a cap. We didn't get caps. You might have got a few 'Congratulations' from some of the guys for your first test match, but that would be all. There's much more interplay and opportunities for players to feel included now than there was then. We always ultimately did feel included, but as I say, it was much tougher going to get there. Sometimes you've got to be thrown to the wolves to actually know how tough you really are.

The 'dirt-trackers'

There were the senior players and those who were just making up the numbers. When I first started playing, we only had 15 test players and the others, none of them were going to get on the field: we didn't have reserves, so that difference was very clear. Today you've got a squad of 22, they're all involved with the game and most of them seem to get on the field at some point. So that also means they've got 22 actively preparing to play now, whereas previously there was only ever 15. Having 22 preparing for the game and only eight dirt-trackers changes the dynamics of the squad completely.

Mental and physical fitness

I think for me, in a test match, I needed two weeks' preparation, ideally. Then I could mentally sort out what I had to do and prepare physically. You never got that on tour, of course, but when you were home you needed those two weeks to prepare mentally. It's a little bit like going to war. You know if you just throw it in, you make bad decisions. You wouldn't be prepared for the things you needed to be prepared for. I liked to think I was a pretty good trainer and did a lot of running – no gym of course, but a lot of running. I found I used to slacken off a little bit, a bit like a boxer doing a lot of work before the bout, then just sort of winding down a little bit so you've got all this stored energy. Today's player would call it 'tapering'.

I used to play a bit of squash the week before a test match because you can get sick of grubby training every day, strapping the rugby boots on the whole time. Just to sharpen the old mind up was great. I felt the preparation was very important for me. On tour it was quite different. We always had a Tuesday game – and a lot of us often played on the Tuesday. In 1967, I only had one game off in the whole 15 games, playing every Tuesday before a test match. That is very tough because you're a little tired after a Tuesday game, and maybe a little sore, and you've got to get your old head around and ready to play within two or three days.

You're now looking at a different shape of All Black. A crude description is that we were marathon-trained. We were much leaner than today's All Blacks. All our forwards were lean, even props – Ken Gray was a lean guy. There are few players today who still maintain the old running-the-roads and running-the-hills and all that running. I think it's a mistake. I think the game of rugby is still a running game and you have to be aerobically fit. If I played today, in the playing weight that I played at in the 1960s, I'd now be the lightest All Black forward; that's how much things have changed.

Being lean in our muscle mass, our legs weren't as big. We didn't have big thunder thighs like they have now. I have always had the feeling that that's why there are so many more injuries today. When you have lean muscles and longer sinews, you don't get the muscle tears and things that they get today. I'm sure we had better elasticity. It all starts as young kids – you're climbing trees and up on jungle gyms and doing things that young kids don't do today.

Most of our forwards were farmers so they were physically active all the time: shearing, crutching, fencing, feeding out hay. Now there are no farmers, so they have to go to the gym. I use the example of hooker Andrew Hore. He was the strongest forward in the team because he was farm-bred. In 'townies', everything's symmetrical. When they get on a flat floor and lift, everything's perfect. Again, I believe that's why they have pulled muscles. What do you do when you're haymaking? You're throwing stuff around on different angles.

VALUES AND BELIEFS
Pride in winning
Value and belief in winning was very important. You gain it just from being a competitive player, then a provincial player, and of course only the best of the best (the most competitive) are going to go through to the All Blacks. We were lucky when I was playing in that we had such an incredibly good record. If you did anything that was going to stop that team from winning, whether it was on or off the field, you'd be told, and rightly so.

Winning was everything and sometimes we put a bit of the pressure on ourselves come test match time. Winning the Tuesday game was important to us – so we'd make sure we had a strong enough team to win that one, when we probably should have rested some of the players and just played them on the Saturday. They don't have those midweek games now that we had, that got in the way.

Memorable wins
The best rugby match I ever played in was against France in 1967, in Paris. We kind of underestimated them. We'd had a pretty smart run through England, all of the British Isles in fact, then we went to France and a couple of warm-up games we had prior to the test were so much harder than we'd encountered to that point. The French team at that time was a very good team, and it was a game that went from end to end. I have never been as tired as I was at the end of that game. I have such a clear memory – they scored a try right on full-time because we were absolutely spent. They were able to go from one end to the other, no trouble. However, we won reasonably comfortably in the end, 21–15. We certainly weren't in danger of losing, at that point.

We all went back into the dressing room and were just slumped with our hands on our heads, trying to recover. The dirt-trackers came down from the stand and came in whooping, made a lot of noise – and then they looked at us and all went quiet. They couldn't believe that, instead of us celebrating, we were absolutely drained, worn out. Yet it was the most brilliant feeling that I've ever had in my life, because I'd given everything. We'd all given everything on the field, we'd won, and we were at total peace with ourselves. That made me realise why you play test match rugby.

Memorable losses

Probably the most frustrating loss for me – and there have been a few in my different capacities – was the fourth test in South Africa, 1970. It was a test in which we had played well enough to win, and there were quite a lot of opportunities to score and take that win. But several times, when we had four or five All Blacks bearing down on a loose ball, a fly kick or something similar destroyed our chances. It was a very frustrating loss and we weren't destined to win that series.

After my playing days were over, the other one would be when I was the campaign manager in 1995, having lost that World Cup final in South Africa. They should never have lost that final. If you'd asked me, before the game, what the score was going to be, I would have said 30 to South Africa, nil to New Zealand, because of widespread illness in the All Blacks team. They didn't play that well, they were sick, playing at altitude, yet they battled away and were 9–all at full-time [South Africa won 15–12 in extra time]. It was just amazing to come through it to that degree, but of course there was disappointment for me there because I was involved in the management.

LEADERSHIP
Coaching

We had good two-way leadership between captain and coach in the All Blacks in my era. Confidence is absolutely vital as a captain. You must have confidence in what the coach is telling you, and you must be confident that you can carry it out. He's got to respect you and you've got to respect him. If you have a captain and coach that are not on the same wavelength, it just won't work. You'll find the strategy that the coach gives you will not be obeyed by the captain because he doesn't believe in it – he's the one that ultimately makes things happen on the field.

Most of my time was with Fred Allen and I was lucky in that he gave me enormous comfort and support always. I think the greatest thing he ever said to me was, 'BJ, what happens, what you do on the field, I will support.' Now that doesn't mean to say that he agreed with it, of course, but in public he supported me. We used to talk about it afterwards and he might say, 'Well, maybe we should have done this a little bit earlier, or done that, or whatever.' 'Yeah, fine, that's great, thanks.'

There were times when we would sit down, just the two of us – or maybe we'd bring in three or four other guys – and get the strategy right. I believe in that, because the more people you have on your side, the better it is going to get through to all the players. But firstly it is so important to have the captain and coach on the same wavelength.

Captaincy

I don't know why I was selected as captain. My ambition was to be an All Black, and then I wanted to be a good All Black. I never, ever had an ambition to be the All Blacks captain, and never had an ambition to be a coach. Everything in my life after I became an All Black has not been something I've actually aimed at. So it was an enormous surprise to me to be captain over Tremain, Meads, Gray, Laidlaw – I thought they were probably the four that were being touted as possible All Blacks captains when Wilson Whineray retired. I had to really work hard initially, but the best part of that was the support I got from those other guys that I have just mentioned. They all individually came to me and said that they would totally support what I was doing. In the end, I grew into it.

I'd like to think I was an inclusive captain. I liked to use other people's skills and experience as well as my own, and by doing that I probably got stronger as I went along, as a captain. I'd like to think that I had the ability to communicate well with players and, because I'd gone through a real rough patch myself initially, I understood how some of the younger and less experienced players were feeling when they were in the All Blacks environment. I made a big point of helping them if I could, at least telling them what they had to do. Nobody had ever told me what I had to do to be an All Black.

It was with humble pie that I ever held the role. I was lucky enough to be there in a time when we had a Rolls-Royce team. I didn't have any enormous challenges. We had seven provincial captains in our team,

so they were all already thinking about the game. I'd played a lot of
tennis, where you have to make quick decisions, and ran a farm, where
I had to make decisions. I never had too many problems in seeing what
needed to be done, then it was down to communicating that to the other
players. The off-field part was the most difficult bit that I had to deal
with. On-field was no problem.

Whenever we played, we had to try and read the game as we were
going along. I found that really interesting. I'd had a lot of practice
playing and captaining Wairarapa for a number of years, where I didn't
have good players in every position and so couldn't be quite as tactical as
I could with an All Blacks team. I think one of the interesting things is
the psychology, the psychological battles that you have out on the field.
Some guys you can kick in the backside, really give a hard time to and
they respond. If you do that to another guy, he'd just sort of disappear –
you'd lost him. That was something that I took from captaincy and put
into my coaching. I tried to learn what made each player tick so that I
wasn't going to screw up. I could give one guy a 'burst' and another guy
I'd sort of put my arm around and encourage him.

Collective leadership

Lochore has observed that senior players consistently play an important role
in inducting players into the team and, increasingly, have mentored younger
players.

It's so important, undervalued in my view, and I think they are getting
to grips with it much better now. They actively try and allow the senior
players to take on more of a mentoring role. Off the field, probably at
training, they do it as well.

I often tell this story as it was so vital for me. In 1963 I wasn't getting
much rugby, playing just one in every four or five games and that's not
enough to be match fit. Late one night, having had a few drinks, I was in
a room with DJ Graham. It was the first time I had enough courage to
say to him, 'What the hell am I doing wrong?'

He said, 'Nope, you're fine.'

'Why am I only getting a game every four or five matches then?'

He said, 'Nah, you've done nothing wrong. I only played two games
in the first eight when I was in South Africa in 1960, and yet I ended up
playing two test matches.'

I couldn't believe that anyone else had even gone through the same sort of disappointment that I'd gone through. We didn't have mentors in those days – you just had to do your own mentoring. I went out of that room thinking, 'Oh, gosh, isn't that interesting? It's great that somebody else has actually gone through the same thing.'

Well, you wouldn't believe it. A week later I was playing my first test match – and I had only had four hours to prepare, I might add. DJ and I are great mates, not because of our attitude to rugby, but because of what we each achieved in the game.

POLITICAL INFLUENCE
South Africa

I'm pleased to be able to say that I was part of the first multi-racial All Blacks side that toured South Africa. I totally believe in it. It was really after I finished playing that things became much more difficult. My coaching period was terrible – I went through hell.

The All Blacks team Lochore selected to tour South Africa in 1985 never toured because of the legal injunction that led to the rebel 'Cavaliers', coached by Lochore's good friend Colin Meads, touring South Africa in 1986.

SOCIETY AND CULTURE
Alcohol

When I was playing, we drank a lot of beer after a game. You had a good night then the next day you dried out. You sort of crashed then you'd slowly wind yourself back to the point where you were really full bore for the next game, and night after the game. That has changed dramatically. There are now a lot of players who don't drink at all, whereas there were very few who didn't drink in our era. There are others who drink occasionally, and when they do, they go right over the top and it's not only beer that they drink.

The big thing that has changed is the advent of night games. We always played in the afternoon: by midnight we were starting to get a bit grizzly and tired and went off to bed. In the last few years, the team often hasn't got back to the hotel until 11.30 p.m. at the earliest and the players are not ready for bed. They've slept all day and probably the previous night as well, and are now wide awake with the game still buzzing in their heads. They don't feel like going to bed until four or five in the morning and that's where the key difference is in my view.

In my time, we used to make our own fun, provide our own fun, and we were always there together as a team. It didn't matter whether you were playing club rugby, provincial rugby or international rugby, we enjoyed each other's company as a team and made our own fun, whether it was at somebody's house on a Saturday night or down at the local club or whatever. The change happened quite quickly, between the time I finished playing and the time I started coaching. The players started to go out and 'buy' their fun. They wanted to go out to nightclubs and basically dispersed.

When I came in as a coach with the All Blacks, I said, 'Look, I know that you want to buy your fun but, hey, we're a team. We need to enjoy our victories with the mums and dads and wives and girlfriends.' I remember I made that compulsory after one test in Auckland, and I was looked at as if I was a dinosaur. Anyway, it happened and we all had a pretty good night, I thought. Nothing outstanding – we certainly had better nights when I was a player. They came to me the next day and said, 'Oh, that was great, BJ!'

After an All Blacks test recently, I came back with the team and about two players sat in the team room and enjoyed one another's company, the rest headed to a nightclub to buy their own fun. But when I had left the All Blacks, two-thirds of them were still staying in the hotel and enjoying one another's company – so it is changing. They have gone into that era where they just disappear and do their thing and that's fine. You can enjoy that, but why work with a guy all week, why train all week with a guy and not socialise with them afterwards? It just doesn't make sense to me.

Attitudes to women

I've never been a fan of having women excluded from the game. I think they're absolutely vital to the game of rugby. Our wives got badly treated when I played – they were lucky if they were on a temporary seat somewhere on the goal-line, sitting out in the rain when all the people who went to a game probably once a year were seated up in the main stand. I started playing in an era when women didn't go into the after-matches. During my playing years, they slowly became able to go to after-match functions to the point now where I think they're absolutely vital. I think it's essential to have the womenfolk around when possible.

I don't think they should be on tour with the players, however. I don't have any problems with players spending their spare time with their wife or girlfriend – in 1987 with the World Cup, I talked the NZRFU into bringing the 'girls' to as many games as possible. They came to about four games and, when we were in camp in Wellington, Auckland or Christchurch, the local boys stayed at their own homes. We said it was probably a good idea that you come back to the team hotel on the night before the game, or stay in the night before the game, just in case there's an emergency, but all the other days they went home and lived a normal life. I think that's absolutely vital.

Multiculturalism

There was only one set of rules and everyone adhered to them. I didn't care which ethnicity you were – 'These are the rules in the All Blacks, and this is what you've got to do.' That's pretty much the same today. They are more conscious, and need to be more conscious, clearly, of the backgrounds of the many players today, but when I played we only had Maori and Pakeha. We all knew one another well and were aware of the patterns of the history of rugby.

Now there are other ethnicities that are, in general, much newer to New Zealand. They haven't been here for 150 years, so there is an adaptation period that you've got to be conscious of. But there was never a conscious 'race issue'. We never saw any of the other players, whether they were a little bit browner than we were, as different. We judged them on their personality, as a person, and on their playing ability as a player, nothing else.

I think we're more conscious of the background and make-up of the players now, which is good. One of the beaut nights we had when I was with the All Blacks recently was when we got one representative of each of the different ethnic groups in the team to talk about how they were brought up, the family strengths and their values, so that we understood what made them tick, what made Maori tick, what made Pakeha tick. That was very interesting. Tongan is different to Samoan, and they are both different to Fijian. I thought it was a very good thing to do and I think it brought the team a lot closer.

ECONOMIC INFLUENCE

None of us were getting paid. Your achievement was driven by wanting to be a good rugby player, nothing to do with being better paid. The motivation is quite different, now: it's about playing well to make more money. The only manager you had in my day was your wife at home or the guy you worked for. Now players have their own personal managers who look after the money, negotiate deals and provide them with investments, and all that. I think it is the biggest problem that we face today.

We were all working, and because of that, how many decisions would we make in a day? Just being a simple farmer meant you'd make 100 easily. In other professions it may have been more or fewer, but at least you're all making decisions every day. You would need to ask yourself things like, 'When am I going to find time to train?' We were self-motivated, self-driven, organising ourselves. Today players are not making those decisions; all the decision-making has been taken away from them and placed in the hands of others, whose job is then to motivate them.

They wake up in the morning and look at a bit of paper that is their team-issue daily schedule. 'What are we going to do today? Oh, yeah, I've got training, then lunch at this time, the gym at three, a bit of promotion for something later, then dinner is at seven.' Their whole day is worked out for them – they don't have to switch on or make any decisions at all. The only decision they have to make in the morning is what socks they're going to put on.

The biggest problem the coaches face is the absence of that decision-making – and the coaches themselves perpetuate it. Players get 'padded up' by all the support around them. They go to the gym and somebody's even there for them counting how many times they've lifted things. They've been told what to do all week. What happens on Saturday night or whenever you have the game? Suddenly they have to make decisions out on the paddock. You can't. Okay, the water boys running out all the time can tell them a certain amount of things, but that never compensates for making snap decisions on the field in such a fast-moving game.

Players still value the All Blacks jersey as strongly as they did in my era. They get a lot more games and I think that is the difference. It took me eight years to play 50- or 60-odd games for the All Blacks: well, nowadays they could do that in four years, so that's changed. They still want to be All Blacks, so the jersey hasn't been devalued.

THE FUTURE

Rightly or wrongly, I think the All Blacks brand has an enormous value
overseas. I'd like to think that will continue, but it's up against some
pretty good other brands as well. From the New Zealand point of view,
I don't think you could ever underestimate how valuable that All Blacks
brand is. We will never compete [financially] with other countries in the
world of professionalism; we just have to be smarter. Now, how long that
smartness can last, I'm not sure.

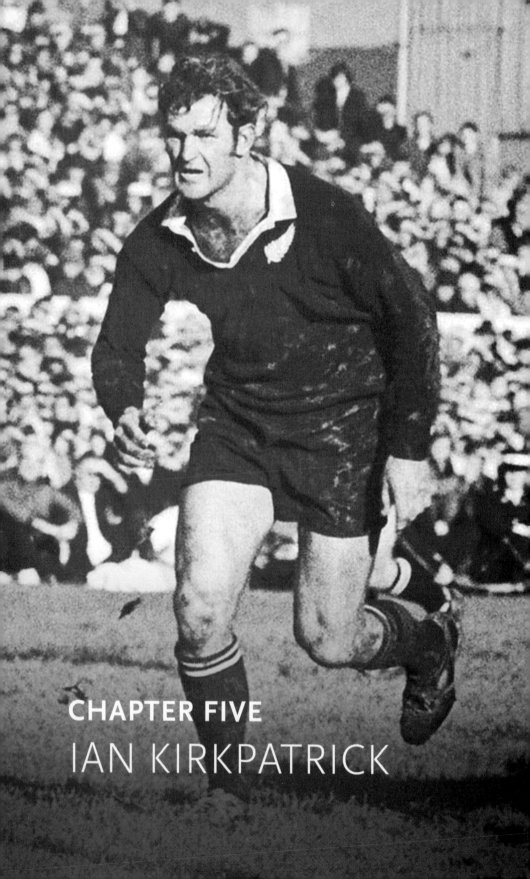

CHAPTER FIVE

IAN KIRKPATRICK

Ian Kirkpatrick was born on 24 May 1946 in Gisborne and first selected for the All Blacks to tour North America and Europe in 1967. As a dynamic loose forward he made an immediate impact, presenting a particularly fearsome sight to opponents while running with the ball. In the first test against Australia in 1968, he created history by becoming the first All Black to appear as a replacement for an injured player (previously, injured players were not allowed to be replaced at international level), coming on for Brian Lochore. He marked the occasion in fine style, scoring three tries.

Kirkpatrick was captain of the All Blacks in 1972 and 1973, earning respect for the way he conducted himself as the leader of an inexperienced team, notably on the 1972/73 tour to Britain and France when they had to cope with the shock of prop Keith Murdoch being sent home and the accompanying barrage of unfavourable publicity. At 20 he had begun his first-class career in 1966, playing for Poverty Bay. One year later he was in the Canterbury team and, later that season, made his international debut for the All Blacks against France, in Paris. Over the next 10 years, Kirkpatrick would appear for the All Blacks in 39 test matches (nine as captain), scoring 16 test tries – which would remain a national record until winger Stu Wilson surpassed it in 1983.

In total he made 114 appearances for the All Blacks, his last in the fourth test against the 1977 Lions, which the All Blacks won 10–9. Sadly, after such a distinguished career, he learned he had been left out of the All Blacks team to tour France whilst he was travelling on the bus with his teammates from Poverty Bay. Domestically he scored 115 tries in his 289 first-class games, becoming one of few forwards to reach their try-scoring century. He was also the only man to have captained both islands: the South in 1969 in his last season with Canterbury, then the North in 1972 and 1973, when he had returned home to Poverty Bay. He also appeared in 33 Ranfurly Shield matches for Canterbury and, with his brother David, represented New Zealand at polo. A farmer at Ngatapa, near Gisborne, in 2003 he was inducted into the International Rugby Hall of Fame.

PRIDE IN SELECTION

I went down to Canterbury from Poverty Bay in early 1967 at about the end of January, early February, and had a job on a farm. For me it was more an experience of getting away from home and working, rather than wanting to play for Canterbury. Having got down there, in those days National Service was in vogue. There were three ballots a month and you were unlucky, or lucky, whichever way you saw it. I was balloted the year before and thought that they would give me the opportunity to maybe defer it, because I knew the university guys had had that. Maybe I missed something, because I had to go to Burnham in April – so I spent two months working, then had to go into the army. Rugby-wise it wasn't that well organised. I had trouble getting to play. I was playing for my club, Rangiora, but couldn't really play for them very much in the winter because I wasn't allowed out much. So I looked to get out of the army, and somewhere during all this the little rugby that I did manage to play included a 'Town' versus 'Country' game, which was quite a big game in Canterbury in those days, a trial for the Canterbury team. I made the side. I remember getting picked up in Burnham by the Canterbury team bus as it was heading around to play mid Canterbury, which was always a traditional early-season fixture down there. I felt as embarrassed as hell about being in my army uniform and all the gear.

That's how I got my chance to be looked at for further honours, progressing from the Canterbury team to the All Blacks trials and eventually to Wellington for the final trial before the team was to go to the United Kingdom in 1967. In those days we had North Island trials and South Island trials. I played in the South Island trials in Christchurch, then went to Wellington and played in the 'main trial'. You had a pretty good chance unless you played your way out of it. When I first heard I was in the All Blacks it was in that shemozzle under the Athletic Park stand where there was every man and his dog and you could hardly move. The team was read out and I heard my name.

It all happened pretty quickly for me. I was in shock and didn't have any great build-up or momentum of consistently playing well. Compared to a lot of guys, I felt really honoured and lucky to be there, to be honest. It was a dream come true, not that I had had too many dreams about it – but it was unreal. I remember feeling completely knackered, sitting in the loo there for a while trying to come right. I was shattered physically and emotionally overcome. One of those old learned gentlemen from the NZRFU gave me a 'barrel' because we were supposed to have been somewhere and I was a bit late getting out of the loo. It was old Maurie Ingpen. It was a pretty emotional time for me. If you had any rugby ambition, that was the ultimate.

RITES AND RITUALS
The haka
We did it in the United Kingdom, but in those days it wasn't like it is now. I can't say we did a lot of practice. It wasn't held in the regard that it is now. We certainly didn't do it in South Africa.

The back seat of the bus
It was there in the Canterbury team, so it was obviously going to be there in the All Blacks. It didn't take too much to work out who was going to be in the back seat. Kel Tremain was going to be in the back seat. He was a Magpie – from Hawke's Bay. It was a seniority thing.

I don't know how far back it went, but the back seat was a great part of the team's history. I didn't really have to be told too much about All Blacks history. I knew about every team since the war, through an interest in the history of the game, and what it meant.

It was a culture that set things in place, that straight away created a good environment, and a respected environment. The back-seat tradition put you in your place. If you were a young guy, you kept quiet, did as you were told and spoke when you were asked to speak.

Induction
Induction? The fact that you had made the All Blacks was the ultimate and you wanted to be there as long as you could, and play as well as you could as an All Black. You really didn't have to have too much explained to you; I didn't think so anyway. That was all there, and it was always what I hoped it would be. It's obviously changed now, but there was no great induction of sorts. I didn't really feel that there should have been, to be honest.

The 'dirt-trackers'
When I went away as BJ's understudy at number 8, I knew I wasn't going to play too many games. I didn't really care where I was going to play, either, to be honest. Injuries came about and you had to go and play in a different position; I went out there and I was going to give it everything I had. I had to train as hard as I'd ever trained because, if you weren't playing that much but all of a sudden were called on, you

had to be there. The ambition was always there. The incentive was there to be ready when you were needed and that was exactly what happened to me.

Midway through our 1967 United Kingdom tour, we went to France – we had had an Ireland test on the schedule, but couldn't go to Ireland because of a foot-and-mouth outbreak so it was cancelled while we were over there. So we now had four games in France. We were playing against 'selection' teams and some hard men, but it was great rugby, on better grounds than in Britain. We had three of these games on the Wednesday/Saturday scenario for two huge weeks and I played in the second game, which happened to be France B. Then we played the third against another French selection on the Tuesday before the test in Paris, and I played in that one and got picked in the test team. I had put Tremain out [Tremain hadn't been displaced by anyone since 1962]. He wasn't really 'a hundred' – he was 90 per cent fit, so I was lucky to have been hanging around when he was not quite right. All of a sudden I'd gone from not having too many games in the United Kingdom, to then playing three in row, and now being picked for the test team. It was a bit of an emotional shock, but it was what you were there for as a dirt-tracker – you take your chances.

I had played for Poverty Bay and then, having gone down to Canterbury, I was playing with guys who were in the All Blacks like Fergie McCormick, so there was a bit of that culture instilled down there. The All Blacks proved another step up from that, but similar protocols, similar disciplines. It was what I thought it would be.

VALUES AND BELIEFS
Pride in winning
Without anything ever being said, if you wore the All Blacks jersey, you didn't lose – that was it. If we lost, it wasn't a good time, I tell you. It was quite difficult with the guys down. If you lost, boy, you had to pay. There had to be some reviews done. Losing wasn't part of it.

Memorable wins
My first test was one that I remember. We were up against it, those 'Froggies' were good then and we were having problems in the lead-up. They weren't easy games. We went to Paris and they played a similar

game to us, an open-type game, and it was great. We won 21–15. The fact was they were a good team, and had some good players.

The other one was in Cardiff [against Wales on the 1972/73 tour]. We didn't want to lose any game on tour, let alone a test match. A Grand Slam was what we wanted to achieve, but you took it game by game. The whole thing was stuffed up by an off-the-field incident a few days after that, but that win in Cardiff – we ended up winning 19–16 – was a pretty good performance by a young side in those days. The average age was only 23 or 24 in that 1972/73 team, so it was pretty inexperienced. Take into account that British rugby at that time, the 1970–74 period, was the best it's ever been. Wales were the top dogs then, so that was a good win and it was the most notable win.

Memorable losses

Any loss stands out, but the real low point, as far as I was concerned, was a game against England in 1973 at Eden Park, when we had come back from that British tour and were supposed to have hosted the Springboks. Early in the season, in about May, or it might have been April, the Springbok tour had been cancelled. So the NZRFU decided to have this stupid internal tour that consisted of four matches and included playing the New Zealand Juniors in Dunedin. A team was picked – but we lost to the Juniors!

I don't say this lightly but when we came back from the United Kingdom and the Springboks weren't coming, that whole incentive had been lost. We came back, after four and a half months, wanting something to really rejuvenate us, yet this internal tour was the most ridiculous thing you could ever think of having. You had 25 in the squad then, and they were 25 guys who didn't want to play for the All Blacks or really didn't want to play rugby at all to be honest, because they'd been 'rugbied out' and here they were touring . . . their own country. It was ridiculous. Then we lost in Wellington. We went to Rotorua and played New Zealand Maori in the rain. We won that and then we beat the guys we'd lost to in Wellington [The President's XV] at Eden Park – and then England came.

They played Waikato, Canterbury and Taranaki and lost all three of these warm-up matches. Then they played us at Eden Park and beat us 16–10! That was the end of the end, I tell you. That was the lowest part of my test career, that test against England.

LEADERSHIP
Coaching
The big change that I noticed was with Fred Allen. When I first got in that All Blacks team, Charlie Saxton (the manager) and Fred wanted to play this Kiwis type of running game, which suited me. He was never beaten in 14 tests as a coach. It was never the same after Fred left in 1968.

We went to Australia that year and carried on from where we had all finished off in 1967 – although we had finished off in 1967 pretty lucky, to be honest, against the 'Baabaas' [Barbarians] at Twickenham. We scraped out of that one, but really it had been a great tour – it was the type of rugby we played, so attractive and enjoyable. Then we went back to being not quite so open as far as wanting to run the ball goes – and scrummaging changed in 1971, when the Lions came. They taught us a thing or two about scrummaging, which changed the forwards' psyche. We had been content with winning our own ball, while they brought that culture of wanting to put pressure on our put-in. So that changed us, but overall there weren't too many alterations. Certainly not the degree of change we've seen in the last 10 to 15 years.

Having had Fred first, he was a benchmark and everything from then on was judged by his standards. Fred was a hard taskmaster. He was pretty disciplined on hard training. There was no mucking around, no fooling. The actual training methods never changed much, but one thing, in 1976, didn't really work.

JJ Stewart thought that we should be training at the same hour that we played, so he'd delay training till two in the afternoon so you had to hang around. Some of us used to go for early-morning runs to make the day a bit shorter – because JJ wasn't like Fred Allen as far as hard training went. I don't know if that change was a good idea, because we always liked training at about 10 in the morning, putting in the hard yards and then that was it. Having to wait all morning, you couldn't do the odd thing you wanted to.

Captaincy
I never really wanted to be a captain. I don't know why that was – I'd been there a while and had captained at school. However, I took it as being part of being an All Black that, if you were there long enough, showed responsibility and had a reasonable guide on things, maybe one day they would pick you. The media were writing it up anyway, after BJ

then Pinetree went, that I was going to be next.

So I took it as something that simply came along. Like anything, I was giving 100 per cent, and if it wasn't good enough, too bad. My attitude towards it was really shaped by those who had gone before me. They had done the standard-setting, and I took what I liked about other captains. BJ had been a good captain. Pretty simple in some of his philosophies, but he was the main one I had from 1967 until 1970, when we toured Africa. Then it was Pinetree in 1971. They were the only two whom I played under and they had principles that were as good as you get. There were plenty of great things about BJ, but nothing fancy, nothing out of the ordinary; his were good, basic, straightforward leadership principles.

I felt you had to try and strike a balance where you didn't favour one player over another. On a tour of the United Kingdom, or any longer tour, you had 30 players who were all different, but you tried to treat them all the same. You would try to spend a little bit of time talking to, say, the younger guys if things weren't going good for them and they weren't playing much. You didn't want to get too heavy with them, but you'd explain we all went through that scenario on tour and if you didn't play, you gave it more so that when you were called upon, you were 'there'. These were some of the little things that weren't ingrained in stone. It wasn't something we *had* to do; it was something you *felt* you had to do.

As captain, there was always plenty of dialogue with the coach, and there would always be discussions with the vice-captain, in those days, about what we were going to do, so that when we prepared for a test match, we were all on the same page. The discussions were reasonably simplistic, particularly when we came in together the night before the match, the 'captain's night'. Generally we had only a few days before each test, or if we had a midweek game on a Tuesday, we'd only have Wednesday and Thursday to specifically prepare for the match as a test team. We couldn't get too complicated, not like they do now. No video analysis or any of that stuff, patterns of play and systems that they've got now. It's chalk and cheese when you compare the eras. Unbelievable.

Collective leadership

Today players have leadership groups and all these leadership-facilitating type of things. We had nothing like that at all. The closest we ever got was talking about leadership – and whether leadership is the right word, I'm not sure. I'd call it more 'accountability' as far as individuals go, really. There was a selection panel when you were on tour: the captain, vice-captain, manager and coach. Outside of that, there was no leadership group or senior management. Leadership was anybody who fronted up. If you were a leading player in the team, if you were a provincial captain (and a lot of All Blacks teams did have captains from the provinces), if you were a senior player, it was expected that you would help lead the charge. There was no dialogue as a group about that, however, as whatever needed to be said was up to the captain.

'Willie' Whineray had started 'captain's night' before the 1963/64 tour of the United Kingdom. The night before the game, depending on who was the captain (on tour, captains can change between test and midweek games), the captain would take the team talk. The coach wasn't there, which was the best thing we ever did, I reckon. Fred Allen didn't like it much, I don't think. There was no change from what the coach wanted; it was just a matter of emphasising it all, getting the guys to be focused – not that they needed much focusing before we played on some of those grounds. It was the only time when it was just us, when the captain 'led'. It was excellent.

POLITICAL INFLUENCE
South Africa

Going to Africa was one of the big ones. If you were part of a tour there, there was always going to be pressure from some quarters and it was not always that good. However, if that's what you wanted to do, if that was your ambition, well, you've had to do it [Kirkpatrick managed the 'Cavaliers' tour of South Africa; Andy Dalton was the captain]. If there were a few hassles on the way, like the Olympic boycott of Montreal, well, 'too bad'.

That was the general feeling amongst the team. There may have been the odd individual exception. Old 'Cutaway' (Chris Laidlaw) was the only one I can remember feeling differently on any of the tours. Mind you, 'Cutaway' was a bit hard to follow. He came all the way back from attending Oxford in the United Kingdom to play in those trials before the 1970 tour. I felt he was trying to tell everyone how intelligent he was, as he would have known what the situation was in South Africa. Then, once he got there, got in the All Blacks, he was dodging the whole thing. 'Is that the way to go or what?' I would have thought he wouldn't have wanted to go in the first place – that's what Ken Gray did, at least. Ken said he didn't want to go and that was fine, no one held that against him. 'Cutaway' could have done the same thing. We knew it was going to be political. There was always going to be an element of that there, although it never got the coverage that they get now.

ECONOMIC INFLUENCE

Amateurism was particularly enduring. It was camouflaged by the fact that we wanted to be All Blacks and, for some guys, being an All Black was assumed to be difficult financially. Going on a three-and-a-half-month tour of South Africa or four and a half months in the United Kingdom was hard, but because you wanted to be an All Black, you would have done anything. Some were married guys and I hate to think what would have happened back home in some of the cases. It would have been extremely difficult – it was difficult enough for the unmarried individuals to go away for up to four months. We all worked, all in different walks of life, and some never got paid while they were away. They had to rely on their clubs. When you go away for that long, you need to spend a certain amount. You can't go away and stay in your room and not have a night out somewhere or spend any money, so it was extremely difficult.

We had team funds that covered that a bit. We'd sell [the players' complimentary allocations of] tickets and, boy, the hierarchy hated it! They didn't want to know about it, but they knew it was going on. Some of the guys got caught selling tickets outside one of the bigger grounds in the United Kingdom by one of the hierarchy. That caused a bit of a kerfuffle, but we were saying, 'Get real, man. This is the real world. This is what we survive on.'

The guys selling the tickets were pretty well camouflaged, but the facts were known by some of the individual hierarchy. It was always talked about. We should have got a bit more money than we were getting – we were given an allowance that was supposed to keep us in pocket from the time we left the airport. The best it got up to when I was playing was about $1.50 a day on tour [$1.50 in 1975 was equivalent to about $14 in 2013]. It wasn't a huge issue, but all our counterparts were getting big amounts. We thought, 'Oh well, that's rugby. Maybe one day we'll change it and so fair enough.'

These [current] guys earn what they are paid. The NZRU uses the players to the maximum, like having a test in Hong Kong when they want more revenue to help fund the game. It is difficult to fund everything now, as New Zealand rugby is finding out, but the amounts the top players are getting are fair enough. We've done that professional part reasonably well with the Super Rugby contracts. Some say they might be getting paid too much, but what is too much? Where's the benchmark? Our top echelon of All Blacks, from the core down to, say, the top 12 in the test team, is getting in excess of $400,000 each a year. I think fair enough: it's not easy. It's a great lifestyle if you're young, but you're only there while you're fit. If you get a broken leg, you might be history, so it's a bit of insurance for down the track somewhere. It can end in a blink as soon as they don't want you. Rodney So'oialo, for instance: back in 2009, was signed on until the end of 2011, then all of a sudden the selectors couldn't play him. When he signed, the selectors wanted him till 2011 – they saw him as part of their 2011 World Cup campaign, and then they didn't. But that's the way it is.

What's happened has had to happen here. The game was always going to run into difficulties further down the track.

SOCIETY AND CULTURE
Alcohol

Drinking is a big issue now, it gets more exposure. As soon as a professional player gets hammered, if it becomes public people make a big thing of it. In our day there was only beer anyway, but it was an unwritten law that if you weren't playing, you could go out and do what you wanted to do during the week – if you were playing, you put those things away and concentrated on the game. There were no problems.

All the same, there was always talk about discipline around alcohol as far as our general behaviour was concerned when we were touring. We were conscious of being under the spotlight, but again it was nothing like today. If we were in Africa or the United Kingdom and you put a foot out of step, they thumped you – the media would nail you for it, but nothing like they do now. We all knew the rules and, by and large, there may have been the odd time when there was a bit of a kerfuffle, but there was nothing much, nothing much at all to write home about.

Attitudes to women

It was shocking really. Women were treated like second-grade citizens by our hierarchy. As far as doing things for them after matches, there was nothing at all. Old Andy Haden changed all that in the mid to late 1970s, but before that, if you had a partner or wife, they weren't treated that well.

Multiculturalism

We all came through with Maori boys at school or club level and they were part of the team. The fact that they were Maori didn't mean anything to the rest of us. We were all part of the team. There certainly weren't any cultural issues or anything. In Auckland, they complain about the 'spot a white guy playing rugby' aspect now, but if you look at Auckland's demographics and who makes up the rugby population, that's what it is. Polynesians like playing rugby or league because they like that physical thing. The fact that the game has gone very physical, with more collisions and a bigger style of back, has played right into their hands. They always mature earlier than a person of European descent does, and so they dominate the game early. It is a problem because 'Mrs Mum' doesn't want her little boy getting hammered at school by these big, physical Polynesian boys, so then we don't have Grant Foxes or Dan Carters coming through.

TECHNOLOGICAL INFLUENCE

It's huge. Some will criticise what they do now, but it's pretty scientific. I wish we had had even a quarter of it – in some way, it would have been so much better. Our training methods were our own, read out of a book. We had a little bit of guidance towards the end about pre-season training, but by then we weren't really going to change.

Now, whole training programmes are built around the individual, their position, what they do in a game. They spend a lot of the pre-season in the gym, but only spend a certain amount there once they start playing. It's about physical conditioning, keeping up. When I was with the Hurricanes [in a mentoring role], players would ask me, 'What did you play in, weight wise?'

I said, 'Oh about 105 to 107 kg, depending on how fit I was.'

Well, if you were playing now, I would have been 115. You put on 10 kg through all the conditioning. These guys are all well-proportioned and when they put on muscle mass, boy. At our peak we wouldn't have wanted to go out and play against these guys, we wouldn't have lasted five minutes. Physically, we'd be all right if we played our game, but we wouldn't have competed well in the highly physical game that it is now. My big criticism of the game now is that there's too much physicality in it. It has become too much like league. That's one of the negatives to have come out of the game's professionalism: the coaches spend hours and hours trying to get an edge, but they haven't really changed the rules to suit the new breed of athlete.

However, when the game went professional in 1996, I reckon that was the best rugby that I've seen. I'd like to have played like that too, and people enjoyed going to see it – there weren't too many people who didn't want to watch a Friday- or Saturday-night game in the original Super 12 years. But as we've gone further into professionalism and the coaches have started analysing oppositions, it has become very defensive. That's where rule changes were needed. They never took those lines of defence back behind the last foot or anything like that, so now you've got the scenario where you can come right up to the mark (in fact, they check now). So depending on the attitude of the attacking team from where they stand – whether they want to run it or kick it, you've got two lines of eyeball-to-eyeball contact stuff: one pass, contact, contact, contact. You've got the breakdown, you've got contact the whole time. As we went into the 2000s, it became very boring. The game never evolved. When they did change any rules, they did so for all the wrong reasons and got the wrong results. It really wasn't until recently that it came right. The All Blacks decided they were going to go for it: move it fast and play a real fast game, which required a higher rate of fitness levels. You can hold that for a while and then you get 'analysed' out of it, because your opponents will find a way of combating it.

The Hurricanes, Blues and maybe Chiefs in New Zealand utilised the services of an Aussie-based consultation outfit called 'Leading Teams'. It was all about 'facilitating', getting guys to try and think outside the square. Some thought it was all right, others didn't. It worked for some players and not others. It was trying to get guys to be more open, getting the guys to criticise other guys in a peer review system for the good of the team and the way they were playing. At the end, it cost them between $50,000 and $60,000 a year. They ran out of money and couldn't carry on, but it was good for some of the coaches. It gave them a new perspective about how to go about getting guys to think outside the square.

PART II

WINNING THE WORLD CUP

Shamateurism, as the term implies, was a deceit. The authorities turned a blind eye to under the table payments in the hope of buying off the players with the proceeds from their clandestine transactions . . . They could stall the push for professionalism while still, on the face of it, preserving amateurism . . . Furtive and demeaning though it was, shamateurism worked after a fashion because there was something in it for both sides.
– *Paul Thomas in* A Whole New Ball Game[1]

SEMI-PROFESSIONALISM OR 'SHAMATEURISM' CIRCA 1970–1990

As shamateurism took hold, the All Blacks' results wavered with two losses to South Africa (in 1970 and 1976) and, in 1971, a lost series against the British Lions – the first time that had ever happened. The 1970s were a time of shifting ideologies. Questions abounded about amateurism versus shamateurism, and the encroachment into New Zealand's sporting contacts by government – who had signed up to the Gleneagles Agreement, a Commonwealth commitment discouraging sporting contact with South Africa – before backing away from rugby matters by leaving future tour decisions in the hands of the NZRFU.

Those leading the union at the time, Ces Blazey in particular, thought their job was to administer rugby, not politics. Meanwhile, the players were not only questioning their time commitments and the demands being placed upon them for physical conditioning, but were also dissatisfied with the leadership and direction of rugby. Underpinning some of the latter was the need for the IRB and NZRFU to resolve matters such as whether players could receive royalty payments for books or payment for sponsored advertising without breaching their amateur status, at the same time fending off criticism that centred around their small-mindedness and lack of moral courage.[2] A few years on, Andy Haden would depict it as a lack of foresight and innovation as the NZRFU tried to maintain the status quo.[3] The union, apart from its shortcomings, faced an array of changing external factors for which they were not equipped to cope.

Chris Laidlaw's criticism of rugby's amateur status in his 1973 autobiography *Mud in Your Eye* was made when he had just ceased playing as an All Black and when the writing of books was considered by the game's administrators to be 'professional payment'. Laidlaw's criticisms gave an indication of an All Black player's typical perception of amateurism and the game's officials and administration at that time. He described the NZRFU council as a body 'which bears resemblance to the Vatican College of Cardinals whose pronouncements are equally doctrinal'.

The internal turmoil created an environment in which coaches were appointed who exhibited big differences in calibre, experience, and strategic and tactical capabilities. Not all coaching was visionary and skilled, and the door was opened for senior player input and contribution. Much of the responsibility fell on the captain and senior players. Graham Mourie had a strong rapport with All Blacks coach Jack Gleeson in 1977/78, but in other instances the captain and senior players effectively ran the team. If matters needed changing during the course of a game, they were the ones with the maturity, confidence and combined intelligence to change tactics.

CHAPTER SIX
ANDY HADEN

orn in Wanganui on 26 September 1950, Andy Haden made his All Blacks debut as a 21-year-old in New York in 1972. He would have to bide his time for his test debut – that came against the British Lions in 1977, but he would go on to make 41 appearances and score two test tries. His last test appearance was in 1985, against Argentina.

Infamously, in the dying moments of a 1978 match against Wales, at Cardiff Arms Park – the score 12–10 in Wales's favour – Haden suddenly fell to the ground, as if pushed. The referee awarded a penalty, which Brian McKechnie kicked to win the game for New Zealand. Although the referee subsequently stated that the penalty was awarded for an infringement against Frank Oliver, rather than anything to do with Haden's 'dive', Haden didn't deny it was a preplanned move. He was an infrequent captain, but was unquestionably one of the longest-serving 'back of the bus' leaders, particularly in the period between 1977 and 1985 when he re-established himself in the All Blacks. An imposing, central figure just shy of two metres tall, Haden was gregarious both on the field and off, earning a reputation as the unofficial 'minister of lurks and perks'. He was also one of the first All Blacks to play rugby overseas, playing two seasons in France and two in Italy. As a result, he became an unofficial liaison officer and interpreter during the All Blacks tours to France in 1977 and 1981.

Haden was damning in his criticism of the rugby administration of this period.[1] He was one of the first New Zealand rugby players to write books in a manner which challenged amateur regulations, criticising how rugby was led and managed. In a full chapter on rugby administration in his book *Boots 'n All!*, Haden regarded the NZRFU as a remote, obdurate, intransigent body with a status quo mentality.[2] His comments covered the various structures and processes of both the NZRFU and the IRB at that time, and he was also critical of their lack of democracy, transparency and innovation. It is a reflection of the stringent attitudes towards amateurism that Haden was subsequently placed 'on trial' by the NZRFU in 1984 for the views expressed in the book, and threatened with expulsion from the game.[3] His defence in the NZRU's 'trial' was successful, he was allowed to continue playing and remains in demand as a commentator on the game.

PRIDE IN SELECTION

I was called to Wellington to the All Black trials and the ceremonial reading of the team afterwards. The gong sounded, Jack Sullivan came in with the selectors and read out the team they had chosen, as was done in the day. The trials were for the 1972 side to go to Britain, a traditional All Blacks announcement.

I suppose I had a very typical background for a rugby player. My father was keen on rugby. Farming people from Wanganui, we went to Wellington whenever there was a test match, and we watched every King Country/Wanganui combined match when they played a touring side. We went and saw international matches whenever we could get to them and listened at night on the radio to the 1960 All Blacks in South Africa and the 1963 All Blacks in the United Kingdom and all of those great tours. I used to picture myself being a part of an All Blacks team, even though at the time I thought I had no chance of ever doing that. The Meads brothers were born into a small farming community – not far from where we lived – so that was my connection to the team they played in. I used to go with the rural delivery guy and drive past the farm that they'd left probably 10 years before. I knew the topography of the terrain and where they would have trained, and we had the same on our farm and I thought, 'I could do that, too' – run in my hobnail boots across the hills; as good as any gym programme, might I add.

RITES AND RITUALS
The haka

I had no connection to the haka whatsoever and, in fact, it was a wee bit like the Bledisloe Cup: a non-event at the time. The All Blacks never used to do it at home and we didn't practise it. As anyone can see from those old pictures, it wasn't done very well. I would have loved to have been in a more organised haka and to have done it better, spent more time on it, known more about it. I even led the haka. I think it was in Argentina in 1976 but I really knew little about it. I'd grown up with a lot of Maori, but as I say I had no connection to the haka at all. I didn't think the haka or the Bledisloe Cup meant very much in those days. Haka tend to break out in all sorts of situations these days so it's no longer that special. If you come third or turn up late to the Olympic Village, you get a haka, which cheapens it. I'd like to see the specialness of it return, the symbolic status. The haka can be a fantastic part of the uniqueness of

New Zealand rugby, but it has to be kept special and done with the sort of feeling that All Black teams these days give to it.

The back seat of the bus

That was an important part of the internal disciplines of the team. I grew up in the post-war era during the 1950s and 1960s, and heard a lot about that old era. I was probably thought to be a little bit maverick and 'new generational' in the 1970s and 1980s. The All Black touring teams I played for during that time were very influenced by the 'back seat'. It removed the captain, coach and management from the day-to-day discipline of the team and it preserved traditions. I thought that was very important and it did maintain a very efficient and highly respected part of All Blacks rugby – I believe that is still the case today. Protocols were important.

I was in the back seat for perhaps 10 years. We didn't have people going to the game or to training with their headphones on listening to rap music. You need to be able to talk to the guy that's sitting next you about things like the weather, changes that may be happening, or things that just come into your head about the game that you're preparing for. You can't do that if the bloke you want to talk to is bopping up and down with his rap music on. That's something that the back seat of the bus in my day would have dealt with.

Induction

You provided your own induction to a large degree – by how you played. I replaced 'Pinetree'. I was asked by the media at the time if this was something significant. I said, 'Oh, he said that it's all very well being an All Black, but you might wish you weren't one unless you're a good one.'

I had made that up, thinking that that's what he would probably have said if I had spoken to him. It became one of the things that the press have attributed to 'Pinetree' ever since, so I hope he didn't mind. Call it 'passing on the baton', if you like, in that I wanted to tell him that I respected what he'd done, what had gone before me, and that I wanted to try and live up to the example he had provided. The years from 1972 to 1975 were disappointing for me because when I got in there I didn't find the type of environment I was expecting. It wasn't structured or disciplined; it was quite fragmented. Afterwards I came to think that leadership is the single most important part of All Blacks sides. Our leadership, not just on the field, but right across the board, was too haphazard for us to be a great All Blacks side in those years.

We were poorly prepared for the 1972–73 tour to the UK – four and a half months and 32 matches. We lacked ideas. There was virtually no positional input; no one could help with things like feet position of front-rowers or jumping techniques of second-rowers or anything like that. In today's game there are a raft of experts who are handling these sorts of things. I don't think they need them all.

In terms of the leadership and the way that the team was operating, it became obvious that if you had a good, strong leader who was clever enough, then the rest fell into place. We have always had such great depth in New Zealand rugby and the eras when everyone became contributors were the most successful. In the most unlikely set of circumstances would come the most imaginative ideas, when everyone contributed. Have a look at the short lineouts we pulled against the French in Paris in 1977, after we'd been totally smashed by them in Toulouse a week before [beaten 13–18]. One week later, they were begging the referee to stop the game and start again after 20 minutes, because this was not a game that they wanted to be part of. Too much running. Too fast. At that point we knew we'd won, it didn't matter what happened after that. We ended up winning that test 15–3, which in those days was a massive turnaround.

The 'dirt-trackers'

I was one of the dirt-trackers during the 1972–73 tour. We had the impression that selection was a closed shop, not that the test team played terribly well.

Geography plays a larger role in All Black selection these days and few from country districts make the team. The main centres are where the professional teams are based – that's where you have to go.

I had worked out a strategy of how to win a place in the All Blacks team and deal with the circumstances of the day, when I moved from Manawatu to Auckland in 1971. There were a lot of Auckland clubs I could have joined. Waitemata chased very hard to get me to come play in the west. I thought I should maybe play for University, having played for Massey the previous year. Ponsonby was a team I'd never heard of and had no intention of going to. Then I thought, 'Well, [All Blacks lock] Peter 'Pole' Whiting plays for Ponsonby and if I play for another club that plays against Ponsonby, he probably won't turn up on match day and that'll be it, I'll have to wait another year to get a crack at him.'

So my strategy was to have him in my sights every Tuesday night and Thursday night at training. And then on game day on Saturday, minute by minute, right through the match and the whole season, I'd wear him down.

So I ended up in Ponsonby because that's where Peter Pole was – not because I knew the club or anything else. You don't know much about Auckland clubs if you come from the backblocks of Wanganui. I took him on because I thought that was the way to get into the Auckland side – if I could nail the top dog, I was halfway into the All Blacks and a part of that was learning from somebody who was as skilled as Peter was. If you've got the next level there right beside you all the time, and you constantly try to be at his level or try to beat him, then the job is half done.

VALUES AND BELIEFS
Pride in winning

It was the fear of losing more than the importance of winning that drove me, and the fear of losing was a lot to do with understanding just who it was that you played the game for. Coaches often say it's the colour of the jersey or the name of the team that you're playing for. A club coach, a provincial coach, an All Blacks coach – would all bang on the same drum: die for the blue-and-white jersey, or the black jersey. They all had the same message: eventually, after dying enough times, the penny will drop. It's not the name of the team or the colour of the jersey, but the people around you that you play for. Good All Blacks sides work that out. They are playing for a very tight group that they are part of, and playing for each other. JJ Stewart wrote me a great letter telling me why I wasn't going to be in the 1974 All Blacks team to tour Australia. He talked about the 'ethos' of All Blacks rugby, how important the central core of the team was and how that central core had to be kept intact and the rest of the team selections rotated a few around it. Losing someone out of the central core was like a death in the family.

JJ wrote about ethos: 'It's a word that's not as big as Weet-Bix or wheelbarrow,' he said, 'but it means more . . . ethos is the value around which you build a team and its beliefs.' It's about the people that you go into battle with, the central core. If you're one of that central core, the others are counting on you for your contribution, the same as you're counting on them. I read that Carl Hayman didn't want to be rotated in or out of that central core. I can understand that. It's the most special part of All Blacks rugby. It may have been diluted with rotation policies and the number of games the All Blacks play in a season these days.

The ethos is what defines the central core. Whilst, from time to time, a player will drop out due to injury or very occasionally a loss of form, the central core remains pretty much intact, evolving slowly.

They don't give you a manual and say, 'Read this, this is what you have to do when you get in the All Blacks.' A lot of it is about time at the coalface and building experience. And it's often the case that All Blacks have a great first year, and not such a good second year, and return to form a little while later. If you turn over players by rotation, you lose the central core very quickly. The central core of All Blacks coaches and players learn about ethos as they go through the experience of being a part of the most successful sports team in history.

Memorable losses

The memorable wins aren't as easy to remember as the memorable losses. The losses are the ones that stay with you the most – especially if they were 'avoidable losses'; times when we know we didn't prepare properly. For example, we all got measured up for our blazers the day before the second test against France in 1979 at Eden Park. We'd just beaten them in the first test, and some of us were mentally already on the plane on our end-of-year tour. France won a famous match, 24–19 on Bastille Day.

They beat us with 14 wings and a fullback. That's what it felt like. We may have done New Zealand rugby a disservice because we weren't prepared and had played poorly. We could have avoided that. So the opposition turned up and we didn't. We gave them the confidence that they could run the ball at us and win. They did it at Twickenham [in 1993], and again in Cardiff [2007], and they've done it in other places around the world, and on our own grounds on tour, because now they believe they can.

LEADERSHIP
Captains and positional skills

I made some comments about Todd Blackadder being added to the All Blacks as a lock. I thought he was a great workhorse-type player as a blindside loose forward, or number 8, a Trojan of a man, but I was highly critical of him being an All Blacks lock because I didn't think he brought the skills necessary for the position. The locking position, in my mind, required the ability to catch the ball above your head, whether that be at kick-off or at lineout time or with a loose ball bobbling in all sorts of circumstances – controlling what I called at the time 'the aerial game'. The media, particularly Phil Gifford, clambered all over me and said I was a heretic for making such comments about Blackadder. He is a fine bloke and his captaincy was unquestioned as far as I was concerned, but I was critical of the skills that he brought to the lock position.

We went through a time when we had several wingers who couldn't catch the ball above their heads. We saw it in league with Manu Vatuvei, who you would think would have come to the position with a specific skill set that his high salary demanded.

I equally have no complaint about the heart and commitment of a bloke like Brad Thorn, but he brings league skills to the second-row position. He often finds it difficult to catch the ball above his head. It doesn't matter much unless you are marking someone like Victor Matfield, who has that skill. You're waiting for the ball at shoulder height but it never arrives because they've snapped it up out of the air. If we didn't have that skill set and the opposition did, we were at a disadvantage. It is a skill that takes a lot of practice, as professionals know!

Early in his career, Sean Fitzpatrick didn't throw the ball into lineouts well – it's well documented that I sent him away from a lineout practice session and got another hooker who did; I wanted to make sure that Sean got the message.

You can't build a winning culture in a team with technical and skill deficiencies. If you've got someone who can't pull off a tackle, and you know he's in a position where there's a lot of tackling required, you have to upskill in that area. The ethos demands that each player does as much as they can. Sometimes it is possible to compensate for deficiencies by concentrating on other areas.

In 1978, for example, we stuck to our tactics and wore oppositions down, winning in the last quarter in a number of games. We delivered a grand slam, but really we weren't very much better than most of the oppositions we played so tactics played an extraordinarily important role in our success.

The lineout 'dive' was a desperation thing: I knew I had to take a hit for the team. There were things that had to be done because the team's success was much more important than mine. The desperation to win for your teammates was more important than any other factor.

We encouraged each other to be absolutely searching in what we could bring to the team.

We didn't want the captain in the back seat of the bus. I was offered the All Black tour captaincy on one occasion but didn't want to give up my back seat of the bus position. I was quite happy to contribute from the back seat. If the captain wasn't playing midweek, as happened eight times in my career, I was happy to captain. To me the captain was the bloke who sat in the middle of the photo, led the team out of the dressing shed and then, in many cases, stood back and got out of the road.

Leadership has got to be much broader than the captain, because one person can't run the All Blacks, and one person can't set on-field standards.

Collective leadership

Bryan Williams and I, in our wisdom, once mentioned to Jack Gleeson that we had played against Dave Loveridge, a halfback and club player in Auckland. We'd seen him over a couple of seasons and knew, or thought we did, what sort of player he was. We hadn't followed him very closely when he went off to Taranaki, but we knew him from being a top club player around Auckland. We said to Gleeson that we thought, however, that there must be better halfbacks in the country. We thought if we lost [incumbent All Blacks halfback] Mark Donaldson, we would be at a big disadvantage if we were touring and recommended that they look harder elsewhere.

During the course of our subsequent tour, which happened to be to the United Kingdom in 1978, we called Loveridge down to the back of the bus and apologised. We told him what had happened and said, 'Well done, and you've played outstandingly.' Well, Loveridge went on to a great All Blacks career and just kept getting better. The better company he got, the higher the level, the more he went up. So you can be terribly wrong, based on what you'd seen in a club player who was never going to get into the Auckland side. He might have been up against Lin Colling or Bruce Gemmell, or one or two like that, and we knew at the time that his club form didn't challenge them.

CHANGE TO PROFESSIONALISM

I was in the vanguard of the transition. However, the minute it went professional, even though I was in the sort of [agency and promotions] business that could profit from that, I dropped out and I have avoided involvement with current players since. I did that for deliberate reasons. I hoped that the players of the new, modern professional era would retain some of the standards that were set before. That was certainly the basis for being able to be better than the rest of the world – we have the luxury of a depth of talent that comes out of our rugby nursery.

The professional era may well offer an opportunity to spend a lot of time training, building a great physique, sprinting very quickly between two points, but I remember discussing with [All Blacks coach] Eric Watson the reasons why, if you wanted the two fastest endurance runners, you wouldn't pick a John Walker or Dick Quax or Rod Dixon, and put them on the side of the scrum. The answer is simply they don't have the rugby nous required. They have the fitness and the stamina but that's not enough. Athletes playing the game today can develop their fitness in the gymnasiums of the world, but great physiques and great strength is not what's going to win matches.

I remember a classic story from 1977, when we toured France. It was an end-of-year tour, quite a new squad. We went to the first training run and there were a lot of expat Kiwis following the tour, all hanging over the fence and watching. At the second run the next day, there were not so many, but the army of campervans and VW Kombis was still growing, more people following along with the tour. Then the following day we had fewer people still at training, but more people were coming to the hotel and after-match functions and things like that. There was one bloke who was leaning over the fence at the same spot at every ground we went to. After maybe about 10 or a dozen training runs, when the spectator numbers had dropped off quite considerably, I noticed the same bloke in the same place, and went up to him and said, 'I've seen you here at each training run. Would you like to come and have a beer after lunch with us?' He said, 'I'd like to do that.' He turned up at the hotel and he had a drink with us and a bit of a lunch. 'So what's your interest in us?' I asked.

He said, 'This doesn't look that hard to me. I could do a lot of this. I want to have a crack at it. I'm just watching to see what I can learn.'

I said, 'Well, good on you and I wish you luck. Where do you come from?'

'I play in Levin.'

I suggested it might be a good idea to get into a First Division province.

He said, 'Oh, yes. I'm moving to Manawatu.'

Well, Mark 'Cowboy' Shaw turned up at the trials within a year or so, and he quickly became a core member of the All Blacks pack. That was a guy with a plan.

Rule changes

From my point of view, the most significant rule change was no longer having to jump at lineout time. I'm surprised that halfbacks, who can catch the ball very well, aren't out there as lineout jumpers. My guess is that the locks can lift the halfbacks higher than the props can lift the locks.

Tinkering, I call it. I remember being in a game in 1980, at Cardiff Arms Park, when Stu Wilson slid towards the goal-line on his back, then flipped a pass to Hika Reid, who ran round and scored behind the post. I was way back on halfway with a similar view to the law-makers in the grandstand, and thought, 'I bet that's outlawed very shortly.' It looked too ridiculously easy, but that's what the rules allowed at the time. Sure enough, at the very next meeting of the IRB Rules Committee it was outlawed because it looked too easy.

Rule changes were reactionary. The Northern Hemisphere teams couldn't ruck as well as we could. The ruck was eliminated from the game. We just add page after page to the law book, making it into something that players and referees can't understand or adjudicate, and spectators in the grandstand or at home on the couch are bewildered by. Nobody seems to get fired for coming up with more and more nonsense to splice into the rule book.

Mental and physical fitness

We had a distinct advantage in the Southern Hemisphere because New Zealand, Australia and South Africa were countries built by physical, pioneering immigrants. The beefy, meaty Poms were fodder and the gymnasium products of the Northern Hemisphere, but no match for the rugged colonials. The physical conditioning wasn't terribly scientific, as 'Pinetree' with his fencepost over his shoulder was just as effective as some guy with a 300-kg bench press.

Of all the changes that have come into rugby, from diet to the surfaces we play on, the equipment we're using, the preparation techniques, all the training techniques, the one great area that is least explored is why the team that beats everyone this year beats no one the next year. Yet they're the same team, and they're playing against virtually the same opposition.

The mental part of the preparation has always been where there's a gap. I'll give you an example. The NPC started in 1976 and Bay of Plenty won. They might have lost one game in the whole of the NPC season. The following year, the same Bay of Plenty side won only two games with the same team. So, from 1976 to 1977 they went from beating everybody to losing to everyone, yet the opposition remained similar. Assuming they have done similar things at training, played a similar style of game, and the opposition have not been drastically different, that has to be something to do with mental preparation because, in the course of a year, all of those others can't have assembled a whole lot of different training equipment or techniques, or all have had new coaches, or all have had new tactics, or all have done something different that the Bay of Plenty side didn't do. It must be mental. Mathematically, it can only be mental.

I'm sure it's simply a combination of leadership together with how they go about preparing mentally for matches. That's where we used to 'beat ourselves' a lot, as an All Blacks side. We would be slightly underprepared and know damn well that the opposition, be it Munster or suchlike, were more up for it than we were. If we played them another 25 times, we might have beaten them in 24: it was one of those things that, if you didn't have your mental preparation right, your skills weren't always going to get you over the line. The area of the rugby game with the least development has been mental preparation. The trick is to combine the ability that your brains trust has to research the opposition, and choose tactics and practise them and get the team to deliver on the day.

POLITICAL INFLUENCE

When you are involved in a team as dominant as the All Blacks, in the context of the national importance of one sporting team, there is always going to be a political influence – probably more so in days gone by than today. The parliamentarians' rugby team is a symbol of how much rugby means to New Zealanders. With that degree of importance comes an equivalent weight of responsibility. You learn quickly to get it right or your days in the black jersey are numbered!

South Africa

The '81 tour was eventful! I didn't care that there were often people protesting on my driveway when I drove out because I had a job to do. I knew what my job was. Anything else that was going on, whether it be demonstrations on the way to the game or in the streets or overhead, was irrelevant. It didn't matter whether there was an injunction stopping the team going to Africa. We were focused on one thing; we were going to represent that team wherever, against the best opposition in the world. It was unbreakable. If you talk to the ones who were in that central core (and it's easy to guess who they were, because they were the ones most often selected), then you knew that that's how they all felt about the responsibility of representing their country to the best of their ability.

I regret that [social conflict around the 1981 Springbok Tour] happened. It was sad that it had to happen that way. It was what it was – and it would have been lovely had it been avoided.

SOCIETY AND CULTURE

Again, these influences were somewhat incidental to our primary objective and the reasons we had been selected. Rugby did get out of step with society probably because it became stubborn and overtly insular. The last thing that was going to change was probably those central core pieces of teams. It is the same with rugby committees; they will hunker down and resist change because they think it's going to disturb what has been successful in the past, when being able to adopt other things is more likely to be successful in the future.

I read about players leaving the All Blacks team now to go home because their wife is having a baby. 'I've got to go home because my wife's going to have a baby in two weeks' time' is not something I'm familiar with. This was just not something that would happen in my day, if it did there was no place for you in the central core.

Maori and Pasifika influence

The Polynesian influence was dramatic in Ponsonby, which was the Polynesian area of Auckland until the 1980s. Inevitably, in our club side there was a Polynesian predominance. I had also had a relationship with Maori people from school and from work on the farm in Wanganui. I had no problem at all dealing with that. The Polynesian aspect was different because this was where the Polynesian community was based.

Ponsonby battled to win the Auckland Championship. We had had a period of around 25 years without ever having won it, despite having a club team full of great All Blacks – we had the majority of the Auckland side and the majority of the All Blacks from Auckland. When I joined in 1971, we had already had some 20 years of not being able to win the championship, and that continued for the next five years. I joined at the same time as Lin Colling and Terry Morrison, adding another couple of All Blacks to the numbers, and still we couldn't win. Eventually the penny dropped and we found a way to deal with Polynesians and they worked out how to deal with us. The answer was to make exceptions for no one. Demand the same standards, the same training regime, demand the same disciplines and off-field disciplines. Make no exceptions and build a team on solid principles and stick to them.

Finally, in 1976, after four or five years of having the best team on paper but underwhelming results, we won – and then won again in 1977 and in 1979. And over the last six years straight, Ponsonby has been winning the Auckland competition. The Polynesian players are now setting the standard. It's not just a quirk of fate that we couldn't win a championship between about 1950 and 1976, then all of a sudden dominated for the next 25 years.

I would take Ron Rangi back home after training because I was mates with Ron – not because he didn't have a car or had brown skin. It was just that I enjoyed his company and those sort of things were more to do with rugby in that generation than anything that was ethnically oriented. I had no experience of anything that set them to be different from us. In fact, I thought they were quite lucky. They were advantaged to a degree because they seemed to have more skills. They had a better grip and they could catch the ball better than we could. They seemed to be able to swerve or side-step when we couldn't do that very well.

In my First XV days in Wanganui, we would travel to play the Maori college in Feilding, Hato Paora. We had a good team, but we could never beat them there because they were so motivated. They had about 10 rugby teams and a school roll of probably 150. The entire school turned out and if they weren't playing they were on the sideline with their haka and sticks banging on the ground. We experienced just how much influence the surroundings can have on a rugby match, how distractions can affect your concentration, and how that can disturb your ability to deliver your role in the team. Our whole team was affected by what went on on the sideline. We could play them at home and beat them by 50 points because the haka guys didn't come on the bus to their away games. But they usually won at home.

It was that mental part of the game that I became quite interested in. As an aside, many years later I went to play domestically in France where most clubs lost their away games, but took reprisals when their same opponents came visiting. We were having 60-point losses away and 60-point wins at home – and there wasn't 120 points of difference between the teams. I knew whether we were going to win or lose by how much wine they used to put in with the water at lunchtime. If they were putting a lot of wine in, we weren't going to win. Coaches have always grappled with the different temperaments as much as with the ethnic make-up of their teams.

CHAPTER SEVEN
ANDY DALTON

Andy Dalton was born in Dunedin on 16 November 1951, the son of All Black Ray Dalton. He earned his first All Blacks cap during the 1977 tour of France and, little more than a year later, found himself achieving one of the great, unfulfilled goals of those who had worn the jersey before him, playing all four tests on the first successful Grand Slam tour of Great Britain and Ireland.

By 1981 Dalton had become the regular All Blacks hooker – captaining the side for the first time when Graham Mourie declared himself unavailable for that year's series against South Africa. He has often been called one of New Zealand's greatest captains, players of his era praising his team leadership, particularly during the 1981 Springboks series. How many All Blacks have had to captain a team being flour-bombed by a plane, as happened in the third test at Eden Park in 1981? His own view of the protest movement at the time was, 'You have to ask yourself what is the motivation of a fraction of our population who would go to any lengths to get their own way . . . if the downfall of South Africa is their objective, then it is only communism which can gain from that.'[1]

Dalton became the full-time captain upon Mourie's 1982 retirement, notably leading the All Blacks to a 4–0 clean sweep against the Lions during their 1983 tour. He was also chosen as captain for the aborted 1985 tour of South Africa, but captained the unofficial Cavaliers tour in 1986 until he suffered a broken jaw in the second match. He was also named captain of the side that eventually won the inaugural 1987 Rugby World Cup, but suffered an injury in a practice session that ruled him out of the entire tournament, leaving the honour of lifting the Webb Ellis Cup to David Kirk. Despite being injured, it is acknowledged that Dalton was a leading influence off the field and statistically he is one of the more successful All Blacks captains in history, victorious in 15 of the 17 tests he captained.

A Bombay farmer, after his retirement from rugby immediately after the 1987 World Cup, Dalton continued his career in agriculture and later became a corporate manager. He coached Counties from 1989 to 1991, and was president of the NZRFU from 1999 to 2000. In 2006 he became CEO of the Auckland Rugby Football Union.

PRIDE IN SELECTION

We had a trial down in Dunedin in 1977, just after the Lions tour – I
played against John Black in that game. It must have been a few days
later that I was playing in a Counties game against Poverty Bay. Ian
Kirkpatrick was playing for them. That's when the end-of-year tour
team to go to France was named. Being a D, I was fairly early on in
the announcements, and 'Blackie' was there as well. That was a very
exciting moment for me, and the fact that Ian Kirkpatrick hadn't made
it that same day was lost, certainly to me immediately, and to most
of the people in the Counties crowd. It was half an hour after the
announcement that the buzz went round that Kirky had missed out. In
hindsight, that was a lesson for me at the time; you're never safe in this
job. It was a real blow too, because he could have contributed so much
to what was an extremely inexperienced team that went over to France,
where we took on some pretty tough customers.

That was massive. As long as I can remember, right from when I
first knew about the All Blacks, I used to listen to them on my little
transistor in my room at two or three in the morning in South Africa.
My father Ray was an All Black of course, not that he ever spoke of
that, but I was aware of it. From the age of seven or eight it was just
an unspoken, but very strong, desire of mine to head into the All
Blacks. Given the fact that I didn't play regular senior rugby until
I was about 21, maybe 22, it was a dream. Had I spoken about it, it
would have been laughed at, but if you stick around as long as I did,
you never know what might happen. I was 25 when I was named
in the All Blacks – quite late. It was the most important thing that
I had ever wanted to achieve as I was growing up, and I got there
despite getting a lot of disappointments along the way, including
not getting into the Lincoln Senior team for three of the four years
I was at Lincoln.

RITES AND RITUALS
The haka

I shudder when I look back and watch us do it, because we weren't
anywhere near as good as these guys are today. It was impressed upon
us early on that it was very much a part of the All Blacks mystique,
more so even then, I suspect. Bryan Williams, who was in that team,
made it very clear to us that it was a requirement to do it as best as we

possibly could. We spent some time practising, although clearly, when I look back on some of the footage, not as much we should have – it was pretty rough. Still it was very much part of the culture and it was impressed upon us by the senior players that we had to do this properly.

The back seat of the bus

I wasn't so much aware of it until I got on the bus to go out to the airport and got a call from Bryan Williams to come down to the back of the bus. I was right up the front then, one of the new boys, and in the back were Brad Johnstone, Dougie Bruce, Bruce Robertson and Bryan Williams. He asked the question, 'What does being in the All Blacks mean to you?' and I told him what I thought. Then he said, 'What are you going to do to contribute to this team?' It was a very, very sobering and quite daunting prospect for a not-so-young, but inexperienced, player to go and see these guys for whom I had (and still have) a huge amount of respect. They did that with all the new boys and they went through the same routine. There was no question as to who was in charge, and what their expectations of you were in making this team. It wasn't that you'd made it; you had a lot of work to do.

Induction

In terms of an induction, it was more a case of what we were told to do and how we were going to behave. There had been incidents of poor behaviour on recent tours away, and there was some discussion about that. Bryan and Bruce in particular drove that need for discipline, as well as the necessity to set extremely high standards. It was set out very early on in the piece that those were the expectations.

The 'dirt-trackers'

In those days we were playing midweek games so everybody was actively involved. I never saw that distinction given the role I was in. I can only think of one player who didn't really fit in and that was [Southland player Ash] McGregor who got pretty well left out. He didn't really get game time on that 1978 tour, and he must have found it very difficult. Whenever I was in the reserves, we made an effort to play really hard so that those who were playing the main game could see we weren't just slacking and going through the motions. It was important to make sure that everyone was part of the team.

VALUES AND BELIEFS
Pride in winning

Every time we were together, I felt a massive responsibility, to the players in the team first, but also to those players who had represented New Zealand previously, to represent them well and equally. The country was riding on your back expecting a positive win and I was very, very aware of this. That was always the strength of the All Blacks. They had this wonderful heritage and I played on that a lot, on many occasions. For instance in 1984 when we were in Australia one test down and we had a team that was inexperienced. The Wallabies were a lot better than us, but we won the second test and the third. The guys had pulled in together.

During the Springboks series in 1981, there was massive pressure on the team. For all the drama the country went through, had that series been lost I just can't bear to think what that might have meant to us – but we won it. Winning was always the expectation. I can remember being absolutely shattered when the result didn't go our way. It was a massive expectation and I welcomed that.

Memorable wins

That second test against France in 1977, which was my first test. I was lucky to get that one, to be honest, but the manner in which we won, changing the game tactically, was memorable. We out-thought and out-ran the French and that was a very exciting moment. The game against Scotland, the last of the Grand Slam games in 1978, was exciting [this was the first time an All Blacks side had achieved a Grand Slam]. The third test against the Aussies in the 1984 series I was talking about above, too, and the fourth test against the Lions when we won the series. It was such a complete performance from the team that day, a great feeling. The 1981 series against the Springboks would be hard to beat. The pressure of all the off-field events, with what the country was going through, meant it was more relief than elation. While we were very excited to win the games, to me it was an expectation.

Memorable losses

I could tell you more about the games we lost than I could about the ones we won. That's again a significant negative memory in my life, of times when we had an expectation from the supporters of being unbeatable, and we were beaten.

LEADERSHIP
Coaching

They'll get upset by me saying it, but there was no question senior players ran the show. We had Jack Gleeson, a very astute coach, and Ron Don as his manager, but there was just no question at all that the players were in charge. That's not colouring them in a negative way. Ron was in charge of the chequebook, Jack was in charge of the on-field, but in terms of setting standards, behaviour and expectations, no question it was the senior players.

Captaincy

When Graham [Mourie] made himself unavailable, it was a case of who was best to step into that role. At that point I'd been in the All Blacks for essentially four years. I had seen captains come and go and Peter Burke [then All Blacks coach] thought that I could do the job. I guess he saw in me the fact that I could lead these guys. It wasn't difficult, given that there were good leaders within that squad and they were generally very supportive. I was more a 'follow-me person' than one to do a lot of talking – and we had plenty of talkers.

I was always, for whatever reason, captain of the teams that I was in. Even at Counties, I got thrown in there in the first year and I didn't do a very good job of it at all. I had to 'learn my way through' and relied heavily on senior players and that organisation to help me. Right through my times as a captain, I drew on those senior players a lot. People still do it in business nowadays. I was fortunate to have very good people around me who made me look good.

Coming into that Springbok Tour series, I was following Graham Mourie who had done a good job. I remember Andy Haden and Murray Mexted coming to me before my first opportunity to speak with the team and telling me that this was going to be the most important speech I would ever make. That was on one side, and on the other, Mark Shaw came up to me and he said, 'You'll do me, pal. Congratulations, I'm right behind you.' So I was pretty annoyed with 'Mex' [Mexted] and Andy Haden insisting that I needed to be told that, whereas 'Cowboy' gave me full support. They were All Blacks for a long time, and it was the support from those guys that helped me tremendously. It was quite a daunting prospect, given that it was a very strong South African side and the circumstances under which we were put with the off-field events: a pretty challenging time.

Collective leadership

The collective leadership of the senior players is critical – without it you would end up with a shambles. It's absolutely critical to have the values of the team, the behavioural standards, the expectations spelt out very early in the piece and, the minute somebody wavers away from that, to have them jumped on immediately. If you have guys in senior leadership who are not performing at that level, you've got major problems.

Their importance was never more clear than between that first and second test in 1977, after we got hammered in the forwards, muscled and bullied by this massive French pack. Gary Knight got his eye ripped open; they just played with us. To sort out the pack, to keep the ball in play, to not have lineouts, to keep the ball away from their backs, to break up the attack – that was quite a learning curve for me. I felt very fortunate that I had had Barry Bracewell (Counties) who was tactically a very astute coach. He was the first real 'tactical coach' I had had, followed by Hiwi Tauroa and then Jack Gleeson. A combination of Jack, Andy Haden, Bruce Robertson and Graham Mourie set the tactics and strategies in this All Blacks team, and the team bought into it. That was the biggest change from the first to the second test that I ever saw, and identified tactically how important it was to go in with a new approach to the game. It's not always the best team on paper that will win. We proved that in that second test, when they were still a much better team than we were.

CHANGE TO PROFESSIONALISM

The only difference is dollars, in terms of the attitude of the players. When I was playing, there was absolutely no question at all in terms of our attitude and values; everybody was as professional as the players of today. The difference is they get paid for what they do and we didn't, and possibly it changes some people's attitude to the game, given where the best dollar is. I guess you can't blame them for that. There is more exposure for them these days with some of the media outlets chasing them, but in terms of their responsibilities, no, I don't believe that has changed at all.

The game is a better game now. Players are faster, fitter and the technology is much better. The ball they are playing with is not a pig's bladder full of water on a wet day. The fields are vastly improved from some of the early ones we put up with, which elevates the skill level and the spectacle. The first time I went into the gym was in 1987 for the World Cup. We'd played around with weights a bit, but we ran the roads and I would get out on the farm and throw a few sheep around, crutching them or something. That was probably the reason I lasted as long as I did and maintained myself at the level – I was fitter than most of the other players whom I played against. I worked harder than them, but in terms of strength and speed, the technology has just moved in leaps and bounds ahead of where we were. Video analysis has added a new dimension to the game nowadays, possibly to the extent that there's too much of it. Again, it's improved the game, particularly in terms of defence patterns; it's a positive influence.

Our trip to Italy, which was part of the first tour I went on, was a long haul. Getting to France was 36 or 39 hours as I recall, but nowadays you'd do it in about 22 to 23 and be sitting up the front. We were cattle class, which was okay for a little shortie like me, but for the Hadens, the Laurie Knights and the Gary Seears of this world it must have been very uncomfortable. So travel improvements have made it easier, and it's now a totally global game.

POLITICAL INFLUENCE
South Africa
People respected Graham Mourie for his background. He was a personal friend of mine. He explained why he wasn't going to play against South Africa and that was fine, we respected that – there was never any issue when Graham came back into the team that I recall. I remember the media getting hold of some story about Peter Burke possibly making

Dalton or Mourie captain, and I rang Peter and said, 'Look, Graham was the captain beforehand, so don't think you're going to upset me by reinstating him.' It got him off what he thought might have been a bit of a tricky position and Graham came back as captain, which I was more than happy with.

Clearly the South African issue was the major one that we had to work through. Where I came from (and still do) is that as long as the person and the team are playing by the rules of the game, I'll play against them. The minute you start hand-picking who you're going to play against, you leave yourself widely exposed as a sportsperson.

I acknowledge things have changed in South Africa (some for the better, not all). Right now, given the history with South Africa, should we be playing against Fiji and some of those other countries, and should we have gone to Romania? The government intervention – I struggle with it because it's not from a sporting perspective, but maybe I'm naive.

ECONOMIC INFLUENCE

It's a challenge for New Zealand. The marketing determines the payment of players so it's critical for all involved in the game that we can still make it an attractive game to the sponsors and to the fans. The fans will drive the sponsors, so we need to make sure that we are producing a shining spectacle and the players need to buy into that. We are extremely young in terms of professional sport – there's still a lot of learning to go through. The market will continue to determine where payments come from.

Players and coaches going overseas is part of the game now. We should embrace that. I'm very strong on the fact that the NZRU should not select players from overseas. The minute you do that, the floodgates will open. I had a look at the Football World Cup recently, where the lack of unity in those teams has just destroyed the best players and the best teams on paper in the world – because they've lacked leadership, and they've lacked the unity that you get from teams when they are not driven by selfishness. The players are there for all the wrong reasons, I suspect. I implore the NZRU to carry on with their current policy of not selecting from overseas, because, as I say, as soon as we do that we'll be in trouble.

SOCIETY AND CULTURE
Alcohol
The alcohol, I guess, has always been there and in moderation is fine.
It does sometimes have to be managed. In terms of the binge drinking
we are seeing now, it appears that it is a societal issue and one that is of
real concern.

Attitudes to women
In terms of feminism, I see that 45 per cent of our crowd now at our
Super 15 games are female and it's fantastic to have them part of the
scene. Trecha Haden and my ex-wife were the first to walk into an after-
match, in Wellington. When they came in, they created a hell of a storm,
but from that night on they were invited and so they should have been.
It was just crazy, the separatism that existed in that era. Women are very
much part of the game now and we need to embrace that.

Polynesian influence
We would be in trouble without Polynesian players so I certainly
welcome them. There are different challenges that come with it. They
are so much bigger and stronger, and they develop a lot more quickly
than the little white boy – and unfortunately that limits their own skill
development because they can hold onto the ball, tuck it under their
arm and just run it through people. It gets found out as they move on
and suddenly come against someone as big as they are. We are really
pushing hard to develop those skills, but at the same time making sure
that the late developer (and I was a classic example of it a century ago!)
is getting an opportunity and not getting knocked out of the game. We're
changing our whole current talent identification system, bringing in
Under-14, Under-16 and Under-18 age groups to widen the spectrum, get
more players involved, give them the skill development to ensure we get
those late developers coming through the system.

In Auckland historically we have had one Under-14 team for the
whole of Auckland, yet we have 1750 players in that age group. Only
picking 25 means you're killing 1725 players: 'Thanks boys, go and get
your snowboard because you're not going to be a future All Black.' In
Under-16s it has been the same thing. We've got one silo of 25 players
that we're bringing through. So, as I say, we're changing all that now.

We're breaking our city into four regions and we'll have 100 Under-14s from east, west, south and north coming together for skill development, showing the light to all these people that they do have a future in this game, and keeping an eye on that number of players coming through. Doing the same with the Under-16s, Under-18s, we're investing in putting coaching into those regions to make sure that we do give them encouragement.

I never saw any ethnicity in a negative sense in all the All Blacks teams that I was involved with, and it's the same now with the Blues in Auckland. It is a supreme environment and what happens out there on that field is Auckland's, it has nothing to do with being Polynesian or religion or anything else: what you do out there is all about Auckland or the Blues, and that was true of all the teams that I was involved with. Everybody played together and got on well. Ethnicity was never an issue.

CHAPTER EIGHT
WAYNE 'BUCK' SHELFORD

Wayne Thomas Shelford was such a popular All Blacks leader – unbeaten during his captaincy – that even today's generation of New Zealand rugby fans refer to him simply as 'Buck'. He was born in Rotorua on 13 December 1957, first playing for the All Blacks in 1985 as a dominant number 8. Joining the unauthorised Cavaliers tour of South Africa the following year (as one of 28 of the 30 players who had been originally selected for the cancelled All Blacks tour), Shelford made his official test debut in 1986, in Toulouse against France. He was a notable victim of the infamous 'Battle of Nantes' in the second test, however. Roughly 20 minutes into the match, Buck was caught at the bottom of a ruck when a French boot ripped his scrotum, leaving one testicle hanging free. He also lost four teeth. Remarkably, after some hasty stitches, he returned to the field before a blow to his head left him concussed, at which point he was finally substituted and watched the remainder of the game from the grandstand, witnessing the All Blacks lose 3–16.

At the first Rugby World Cup in 1987, Shelford played in five of the six All Blacks games and was a core member of the team that won the final against France 29–9. In the semi-final match against Wales, Welsh lock Huw Richards punched his All Blacks opposite number Gary Whetton. Shelford reacted in defence of his teammate, landing a punch that knocked Richards to the ground, but escaped punishment while Richards became the first player to be sent off in a Rugby World Cup. Shelford took over as All Blacks captain after that tournament during the 1987 tour of Japan. His captaincy continued until 1990 and, during that time, the All Blacks did not lose a game (including one draw, against Australia in 1988). Upon becoming captain, it was Shelford who insisted the team finally perform the 'Ka Mate' haka properly.

In 1990 the All Blacks selectors controversially dropped Shelford, the unbeaten skipper, the man with the mana, after a test series against Scotland. The general public was plainly unhappy with this decision, especially when the All Blacks lost the third test of their next series against Australia, ending a 17-test winning streak (and a 49-game streak overall). Fans started appearing at games with signs saying, 'Bring Back Buck' – but Shelford never regained his place in the All Blacks side. He had scored 22 tries and had played 48 games for the All Blacks, including 22 tests, captaining 31 times, 14 of those occasions being in tests. He retired from rugby in 1991 and later coached in Britain and at NPC level with North Harbour.

PRIDE IN SELECTION

I heard it on the radio, like we did in those days. It was lovely to hear it with your family – brothers and sisters, your mum and dad. Then all of a sudden the phone starts ringing from the extended family. For the next few days (it could be a week), you're running around trying to organise your life because you'd made it into the All Blacks.

It's quite humbling, but it's something that we all feel so proud of, hearing that name being called out. Sometimes you wonder whether you deserve it or not, because there are other players around the country who were just as good as you were, but you're the one who got the nod.

I used to wear the jersey with total respect. It's a prized possession and I never called myself an All Black till I actually put that jersey on and ran out into my first game. Back in 1985 I was picked for the South African tour, but that was cancelled. They were looking at arranging something else at the end of the year, and that turned out to be Argentina. I still didn't believe I was an All Black until I put that jersey on. It is a small, special club. You're representing a lot of honour, there's respect for that jersey, pride in the jersey from all our rangatira who have worn it before. We're basically the guardians of the jersey and you've got to give it your best shot to uphold those values.

I was only there for five and a bit years, and those five years were very successful. It was a proud moment in my sporting career, because I never thought I'd be an All Black. I didn't have, even up to the age of about 20, high aspirations of ever making the All Blacks, solely because I played a brand of rugby that was, I suppose, a bit rough. I didn't curtail my style to the normal things that happened on the rugby field. At the same time, I was right into my mates in the military and we were tripping overseas all the time [Shelford joined the navy at 17 and served as a PT instructor until 1986]. I was missing the odd half-season here and there. I was all over the place, but I remember an older guy coming up to my dad and saying, 'Your boy's going to be an All Black when he grows up.'

We listened on the radio all the time to the rugby coming through at three in the morning, and half the time when we were little fellas we always fell asleep, never got to the end of the game. It's just very humbling to actually be a part of that unique club and in the era that I made it, the turnover of All Blacks per test match wasn't too great. There weren't too many people that went through the All Blacks in those days compared to the modern era, and you didn't come off the field to give the other guy an even break. I played my first game when I was 27, so I wasn't going to give a sucker an even chance. Making it at that age, there were a lot of top players around that same stage. Dale Atkins was a huge performer of the Canterbury era and he could have been an All Black as well. Then you had Mike Brewer and Zinzan Brooke coming through, and John Mitchell with Waikato; there were about six or seven and I just thought I was very honoured to wear that jersey. I was representing them, as Kiwis, and knew that I had to be the best I could be all the time I wore that jersey.

RITES AND RITUALS
The haka
Hika Reid came up to me [during the tour of Argentina in 1985] and said, 'Buck, the boys want to do the haka.'

'What are you asking me for?'

'The boys want to do it.'

'Well, unless there's 100 per cent support from the management and 100 per cent support from your team members, don't even go there.'

We had grown up together and he had been brought up in kapa haka. I hadn't, but when I was in the navy I was into kapa haka. I learnt that there was always total respect for kapa haka, total respect for the tikanga of it.

We made sure that the players bought into that, and they had to do it correctly otherwise we would be embarrassing ourselves, shaming our tupuna on the Maori side – and we didn't want to do that. We said that we're going to train to do it, we're going to do it well. They're going to learn what it's about – and that was the start of it. We just got better and better at it after that and in the end the players enjoyed doing it, because they understood it. There was, at that time, a Maori renaissance, especially in using our Te Reo, so everyone bought into it and it's been here ever since.

The education process was very simple. Let's do it properly and let's do it well so we're actually looking after the Maori component, not embarrassing the Maori people, and we're doing it correctly, the way they would want it to be done. It's just grown from there and what we've got today is fantastic. Many of our national teams in other sports have picked up on it now, they're using it as well, and it really shows you that Maori has grown within our society over the last 30 years.

The back seat of the bus

When I made the All Blacks, the back seat – Andy Haden, Dave
Loveridge and guys of that mould – were seen as respected old-timers.
I thought the back seat was fantastic. The players, if they wanted to air
any dirty washing, could go and talk to the 'back seat' because there was
deep respect for these players – that is, when players wanted to talk to
somebody or sort out problems without having to go through coaches or
management. Or the senior players could drag you to the back seat and
say, 'Pull your head in, otherwise we're going to sort it out.'

As time moved on, and when I started captaining the team, we lost a
little bit of respect for the back seat from some of our younger players, and
likewise the players might have lost respect from the people in the back
seat. The back seat was, when I first made it, a good thing. I never sat in
the back seat at all, whether I was playing for Auckland or North Harbour.
I just watched what they did and sometimes I didn't agree with some of
the things they did in my era. We talked about that with senior players,
and then we moved on and sorted it out: 'What's on tour, stays on tour.'

That small little club is about the way you handle yourself on tour,
on and off the field. You're actually an ambassador for this country and
you have to do it 100 per cent well. If you don't do it well, you can be an
embarrassment to the country and to the team. No matter how big you
are, the little negatives can get back to the country and end up in our
newspapers, and in today's environment it's got even worse with cell
phones and cameras and all that sort of thing.

Now, rather than having one or two captains, they've got five or six
leaders – leadership groups have taken over from the back seat. The
senior players maybe still sit up the back of the bus, but they don't have
the back-seat mentality.

The 'dirt-trackers'

I was a dirt-tracker when I first became an All Black and then I became a
regular test player once I got the captaincy – but because you're the team
captain doesn't necessarily mean you're going to be a regular test player.
You play one bad game and you can be pushed out. Being a dirt-tracker,
you learnt a lot. I was one for a couple of years. I didn't play many Saturday
games, I played the 'midweekers'. I played the odd Saturday game – that was
in 1985 on that last tour of the year – but in 1986 when the Cavaliers went
to South Africa as a pseudo New Zealand team, I actually led the midweek

team and that was a great honour for me. Here were all these great All Blacks that had played for years and I learnt so much off those guys – Jock Hobbs, Andy Dalton, 'Cowboy' Shaw – just by being a dirt-tracker.

These young guys today get promoted very quickly to the number one team, and they're raw. For many of the young ones on that tour in 1986, we learnt from our peers and from the rugby players over there how brutally hard it can be in South Africa. We never won that 'test' series; we didn't win every game on tour, so the lessons we learnt fast. I believe that was a huge catalyst to winning the very next year at the World Cup, because all those guys came back tougher, harder in the head, mentally. We lost to France just before that World Cup, so that gave us an edge, but I believe all the younger All Blacks of 1985 and 1986 had grown an arm and a leg come 1987. It was huge.

VALUES AND BELIEFS
Pride in winning
Winning was very important. Winning becomes a habit, because success is fantastic, but when you take those plaudits you've also got to learn how to lose, lose well and graciously, and learn from your losses.

We've gone through an era in our education system that has created a lot of mediocrity. You see kids coming to rugby now and they're just not the hard-nosed kids that you used to see when I was young. Fifty per cent of New Zealand teams lose every week. You've got to learn how to lose. We don't know how to lose graciously sometimes. You learn more from losses than you do from the wins. Teach people to give their all, but walk off that field and be proud of their performance – that's all a coach can ever ask of them.

Memorable wins and losses
Winning the World Cup was fantastic, winning the Bledisloe was fantastic, but the greatest satisfaction I got out of my football was always the games where you came from behind, where we had to dig deeper to find that extra. Against Australia, the second test in 1988, we pulled our way back into it. We could have stolen it; but we drew 19–all. I honestly believe that the tougher the game was, the more we had to dig inside ourselves to find something extra – and they are the games that you always remember. Some games you never forget.

We learnt so much from losing to France in 1986 and in that same year we lost the series to South Africa (with the Cavaliers). We learnt a lot about ourselves as people and as team members in those particular teams. We didn't want that to ever happen again, so we had to look at ways of being better than anybody else. We found that in the World Cup, a recipe for the next three years. It was just a pleasure to play for that team. In hindsight, by the time we got halfway through the second half of most of the games, we'd won, because we'd put so much pressure on ourselves in that formative year of 1987 that we took the game to another level. Everyone was chasing it. The All Blacks are doing that right now to the rest of the world.

LEADERSHIP
Coaching

Coaches do a lot off the field, but it's when you're in battle that it really counts and the coach is not there, it's the captain. Your greatest learning is actually on the rugby field. You learn more on the field in the heat of battle than at training. That's when your captain comes in. If he's calling good shots on the field, you're going to have more chance of winning and guiding the team to that win.

We had Andy Leslie, Laurie Mains and Peter Thorburn. You took something from every one of them. I was probably with Pete the longest as a coach and I was his captain. We were fast approaching professionalism at the time; it was 1985 and it was seven years later, when I finished with North Harbour, that the game turned pro. Pete did things that didn't include me, like naming the team, which is fair enough – that was his call, but on the field I was the captain, I carried out the wishes of the game plan. We disagreed, to a degree, sometimes on the way things happened, but that's just the way it was. We didn't see eye to eye all the time and that's good because you're challenging each other.

A lot of the communication that I worked within was military. It was very one-sided from the top down, with Pete or whoever I had as coaches.

Captaincy

Coming through club football with the players that I'd played with over those years, the reason you become pretty good is because you've been schooled really well by your senior peers within your team. By the time I got into playing for the All Blacks, I'd played a lot of football: Maori rugby, Services rugby (both some of the toughest rugby I've ever played). I played league when I was a youngster as well and the learning that you get from all those years just mounts up and gives you all this knowledge, which is probably why I became such a good rugby player.

With the knowledge base that I had in my head about how to play the game, I seemed to be ahead of everybody else. You're organising them to get to places. Their fitness levels aren't like yours, so you're cracking the whip: 'Come on, work harder.' That's probably natural leadership, even though I wasn't captaining at times.

You got picked because they believed that you had the leadership qualities to take over that team at that particular time. For any All Black who gets named captain of the team, it's a big responsibility and it's not something that you're groomed for. It's something that's bestowed upon you and you can turn it down if you want to, but it's a great honour. I felt very privileged to become an All Blacks captain, because you had so many other very good All Blacks in the side at the same time.

The leadership the military had instilled in me was one in which everyone was in a pecking order and you all had somebody to look up to at a certain level. You went from a junior to a private to a corporal to a sergeant to a warrant officer (WO2), then a WO1 or a sub-lieutenant – you all had a boss or leader in front of you. That was no different to the All Blacks. Within the All Blacks management you had the coach, assistant coaches, manager, assistant manager, captain, and then he had lieutenants around him. Everyone had a part to play. It was a pretty strong side.

In the amateur days we probably lost our way, at times. There was never any set format for management within a team. Compare that to now where, if you joined a company, they'd probably have a template of how they want things run. When you go into the military, there's a template of what a leader does, what a sergeant does, what a petty officer does and that's your job description. So you move from one job description to another. Within the All Blacks, you were learning on the hoof half the time and there wasn't any job description as such for captain. 'Vice-captain, you support the captain.' The captain supports the coaches, supports the managers and everybody gets in behind.

Collective leadership

In All Blacks rugby it was different. Senior players got together and talked about tactics with 'Grizz' [Alex Wyllie] and 'Harty' [John Hart]. All those guys during that time always talked about tactics, and in the end we came up with a specific brand of rugby. The higher you go, the more you communicate with the senior players about playing the brand of football. You're actually empowering players to make decisions or embrace a brand of rugby. If it is not successful, who gets burnt, the player or the coach? In the world of gridiron or basketball, if you're losing it's the coach who gets burnt, not the player. We're still adjusting to that and learning. Many of our professional coaches are realising that we have to have a bit of buy-in. As long as our captain and two or three of our senior players agree to what we're trying to do, as long as you can paint the picture for them of how we're going to run the season, you can have that buy-in.

Challenges to leadership

A lot of the players wanted to play a different brand of rugby, but I was still of a mindset that 'Grizz' was the coach. I was the captain who carried out the orders. When other players in the team wanted to do something else, that's when I struggled. I got outnumbered. There weren't too many North Harbour players in the All Blacks in those days, it was predominantly Auckland. I said, 'Okay, we'll do that, but be prepared to wear it if it doesn't come off.' That was probably my toughest period, the last years. In the year before I got dropped, a few egos started to fly and they thought that 'Bob's your uncle, we can do it, no matter who's here'. I left the team when we hadn't lost a game and only two or three games later they started losing.

CHANGE TO PROFESSIONALISM

The transition from amateur to professional rugby hasn't been easy. It's created huge holes within our club system, because we don't get to see the top guys play at club level any more unless the coach decides to send somebody back to club football to get some game time. The players that make the top tier are leaving school at 18 and 19. They're Super 15 players then and really haven't done any hard graft in the system. Talented, but they haven't really honed all their skills, and they still haven't got out of the schoolboy mentality, haven't worked in a coal mine or built houses or worked around the farm for two or three years. Much of our professional-era rugby is trying to fast-track our youth to knowledge and maturity, and that's something you can't do overnight – it takes years.

For example, [Isaia] Toeava from Auckland – he was a talented young Samoan boy. He had his injury problems, was shy, introverted and they got him in early [he made his All Blacks debut against Scotland in 2005, aged 19]. He's a much better rugby player now than he was five years ago, but why couldn't we have harnessed him and done that without bringing him in too early? Sometimes you can destroy a kid's career by bringing them in too early, when they're not ready for it mentally or physically. You can't transplant experience into young men's heads.

I left home when I was 17 and made the All Blacks when I was 27, a full 10 years later, after 10 years in the workforce. What was in my head as a 27-year-old becoming an All Black was different to an 18- or 19-year-old becoming an All Black when he's just come out of school. Many of our young kids want success early, but they've done no work for it, living off sheer talent. They don't realise that once you make it into these teams, you have to work hard to stay there. They haven't had a work ethic, so they think it's going to be really easy, but they find out they've got to grind. The transition between the amateur world and the professional world is still hard. Some of the young ones who make it find it very difficult. They can fall back to an amateur very quickly by getting dropped out of the top team, or because of injuries, and then they can't make it back. Then they turn around and say, 'I'm still only 22, I'm off to make money overseas.'

Club football misses out as well as it's a loss to New Zealand: 'We knew he was talented. Why did we put him in so early?'

We are losing a lot of players [overseas], but I'd like to see them come back and be a part of developing the next tier. Bring back a guy who's been involved in All Blacks rugby, who dropped out at the age of 24 or 25, went overseas until about 28 or 29 and comes back and plays club rugby and maybe rep rugby for the next two or three years – like Tana [Umaga] has come back and done. He's got so much to offer rugby.

POLITICAL INFLUENCE
South Africa

To take away the dream of a young player of playing rugby in South Africa is pretty tough. The reason I went [on the Cavaliers tour] was selfish. What was I going to get out of it? Probably being dropped from the All Blacks or being reprimanded. Whatever happened, I was willing to take that chance. In my era the greatest thing was to be able to play against the Springboks, and this was my chance. I missed it in 1981 and they didn't play another Springboks team until 1992, so that was the selfish part for me. I wasn't worried about the politics of it all. I didn't really worry too much about my family – because I had walked out of my job as well – but I knew things would be all right.

Within the military, after I came back, there was a bit of politics there regarding the government getting involved in me coming back into the military, which was quite sad. We got stood down from playing a couple of tests when we came back, and when I applied for my job again, they wouldn't give it to me. The military gave me a limp reason, but it was actually a political directive from government. So I didn't go back into the navy, but went to join the army. They wanted to use me as a recruiter. I went out on the morning I was going for an interview with them, basically to sign the forms to go into the army, and I got a phone call. I'd just left the house and the phone rang. My wife said, 'Come back, there's a phone call.' It was the guy who was going to do the interview and he said, 'We've just had a directive from the government not to employ you.'

That was sad, so we just moved on. At the end of the day you've just got to move on.

SOCIETY AND CULTURE
Alcohol

You still had a good night out and got hammered (to put it bluntly), and that was seen as fine as long as you didn't create trouble. On the 1989 tour we had a bit of trouble with people in the bar and a fight ensued. I wasn't there at that time. It was later in the morning, a big fight. That's the sort of thing you don't really want on a tour. There are lots of other things that had gone on during previous tours that have been quite devastating, not just for New Zealand rugby, but the franchise that the players come from. There are high expectations of everybody out there to perform on the field, but also off the field, making sure that the values you have in the team are also there. In my family, we're very values-based and it's about looking after each other. If your mother would not be proud of what you are doing, why would you do it?

Present day society, for example binge drinking, requires an education process. Our forebears had the six o'clock closing, was that a social change? Everyone finished work at five and by the time six came around, they'd have put 20 jugs away. Then all of a sudden it went to ten o'clock, and now it's all hours of the day or night, depending on your licence.

I don't know how we created this binge-drinking culture. Is 10 p.m. a good time to come home? I think that it is, but our young kids are not going out just until 10 or 11 at night, that's why they want the bars open till three or four in the morning.

I remember going over to England back in the 1980s and the pubs there shut between certain hours. They opened at lunch, then they shut for two or three hours. Social change has evolved in all the countries we visited.

Attitude to women

It's great that women are playing rugby. It's fantastic. For certain things I am old school, but for some things I don't mind change. You've got to be adaptable and flexible in business. You've got to move, otherwise you get left behind. It's the same in sport. We now live in an environment where there is so much sport, and the thing is we're losing so many sportspeople from rugby because of all these other sports. So it's great that women are playing sport and the game of rugby.

Maori influence

Back then you would go to play against East Coast Bays or the 'Ponsonby Ponies' – Bryan [Williams] was probably the only Polynesian in that team, and wherever you went, there was always banter where Maori were called 'darkies' and 'Blackie'. I'm not that dark, but we didn't take it seriously in those days, it was just a bit of jibe – that's what I perceived it to be. We gave back as much as we got.

The thing is, now people take it really personally. We've got to be very careful about what we say. We're becoming a little bit too precious at times. Within New Zealand, there would be no full-blooded Maori. They will always have some foreign blood in them. Our European culture is predominantly English, Scottish, Welsh and Irish and now we also have to deal with all the other cultures that have come in. We've just got to get it together and I can see that, but a lot of people can't.

[Dame] Whina Cooper was one advocate for Maori, very pro-Maori, and she said, 'It doesn't matter about what's going to happen because by the time that I'm gone and your children have gone, we're going to be such an inter-mixed race here that everyone is going to have Maori in them anyway' – or be some sort of Polynesian Indian.

Everyone talks about the Maori issue with Pakeha, and we've got all this Waitangi stuff, which is fantastic. They're vying for rights that they lost many, many years ago and lands they lost many years ago. There are a lot of people complaining about New Zealand and complaining about Maori when they're not even from New Zealand. If you don't like it, you've immigrated here, why don't you go home? The issue is that Maori have got nowhere to go. We were here before the European came, we are basically the tangata whenua of this country.

Polynesian influence

It's had a huge impact on rugby. There's nothing wrong with it, we just have to manage it because the Polynesian boys are huge, they're big brutes. That's only going to enhance our rugby and our league. In another generation or two, you're going to get the Kiwi South Africans coming through too. There's something like 30,000 in North Shore. We just have to manage our rugby so it's organised correctly. We're pretty precious when we say, 'Oh, we can't have little Johnny playing with these big Island boys.' We have to teach them how to be tough too; we're breeding that out of our kids.

There's a little bit of a problem at grassroots because our Polynesian boys are much bigger than our Maori and European boys. The education process of coaching has got to evolve. We've got to be better coaches at the lower level – and if league can teach their kids to tackle, why is it that the rugby kids can't tackle our Polynesians? There are a lot of Europeans playing league as well, and they're playing it from youngsters up, but they're learning to tackle whereas we got rid of tackling because our young Johnny's 'not up to it'. If he's not up to it, why isn't he up to it?

Mum has a big impact on the loss of kids from rugby. I did a programme for eight- to 12-year-olds, a skills-based programme over four or five days. I had all their coaches and I said, 'You teach your kids to tackle and you won't have to worry about the big Island boys, they'll be able to tackle anyone.'

Tackling, defence patterns, catching, and passing a ball in contact situations: if you teach them those four basic skills, any kid can play rugby, but tackling is a big thing. If you take that out of the system for two or three years in the five- to nine-year-olds age bracket, who's going to teach them to tackle? If you teach them well as youngsters, they'll come through from the lower grades. It's a 'no-brainer'.

At lower club level, there are a lot of people putting in their time for nothing and that's fantastic. Clubs have to be more proactive in teaching our youngsters better skills. A big thing that has gone away from many of our primary schools is that skill level at playtime. Should we take it off the schools, so that clubs take over full-time, running all the age groups? You don't know what's happening from school to school, how good or how poor the coaching may be. If you've got poor coaches, you can lose rugby players. You've got to have enthusiastic coaches who can communicate, can have fun, and are good enough to teach the skills of the game.

All my coaches, coming through, were very good coaches, teaching catching, passing and tackling. I had a coach at primary named Ron Woolgar. We had a fantastic team and I was playing league at the same time. You tackle more in league, so you have to learn to tackle. I was a better tackler after I'd had five seasons of league: it improved my rugby a lot. I stopped playing league when I was 17 when I moved to Auckland and made a senior team. There was no practising of tackling at all there, whereas in league it's practised all the time. You only get good at things if you practise them. That art of tackling has been taken out, and I brought it back in – our boys are tackling all the time. We're making them tackle because that's what happens in the game all the time. They reckon there are 150 to 160 tackle components, tackle areas in a game, so we should be moving towards it again.

TECHNOLOGICAL INFLUENCE

The advances in technology for grounds has been fantastic. It's great to play on good fields all the time: you're playing on the surface instead of playing in it. Man, there was some mud around – even I played in a lot of mud, but over the last 15 years, with the era of professionalism, all of the unions around New Zealand have upgraded their fields: club fields, union fields and test fields. There's nothing better than playing a brand of rugby you want to play on a field that permits it, compared to sloshy mud. You can still play in the rain and play running rugby, but you used to get a lot of mud. That's a thing of the past, but if you go over to places like England, you still see it at the lower-end clubs.

Video analysis is part and parcel of professionalism, but it means we try and clone players. Many of our players lose their individuality because of the coaching. We've got this 'guru scrum coach' who goes around New Zealand to every province, to every franchise, to a lot of the clubs, and so their techniques are exactly the same. Where's the individuality? We're taking a lot of the individuality out of scrummaging. Could you imagine everyone trying to be cloned as Tiger Woods? It's impossible.

THE FUTURE

We can still win all the time. The calibre that is constantly coming through is just fantastic: real athletes. They're learning to become athletes earlier now because there's a pathway in rugby and that, too, is fantastic. I wish they'd spend more time working on the other side of things, the academic side, because many of our kids don't have that background and once their career is over, they struggle a little. The professional era has much to offer, but it's hurt a lot of people as well, regarding preparation for jobs outside rugby.

We're playing a brand of football that other people are struggling to keep up with. At one stage, it was all about defensive systems – everyone went really defensive and the next thing is, 'How do you win rugby by becoming defensive?' All you're doing is stopping the opposition from scoring a try, but you're not scoring anything yourself. England – all they're doing is scoring penalties. They won a World Cup by being defensive and kicking penalties from halfway, but then they lost their next 17 games in a row. So they're a championship team for that particular tournament, but they lost 17 games in the next two years. Is that a championship team?

I tend to allow players to play the way they enjoy it. I say, 'I want you to think back to when you were kids, when you were running around the yard with your brothers and sisters, in the neighbourhood: How did you run? How did you feel? What did you do? Well, let's see that out there today. Stop kicking the ball away and play rugby.'

It doesn't matter what size you are: play rugby, and when you pass the ball, make sure it's accurate, don't lose the ball in a tackle. You'll go from being an average side to a very good side because you've empowered players to play rugby the way they did when they were youngsters. They all wanted to be a Carlos Spencer or Frano Botica. They wanted to play rugby so they were allowed to play it, whereas as soon as you pull the reins in on guys like that they're not good players. They become stereotyped and don't want to be there. We do tend to coach a lot of the flair out. I'd rather lose playing real 'football' than playing boring football where you're kicking it away and becoming a defensive team.

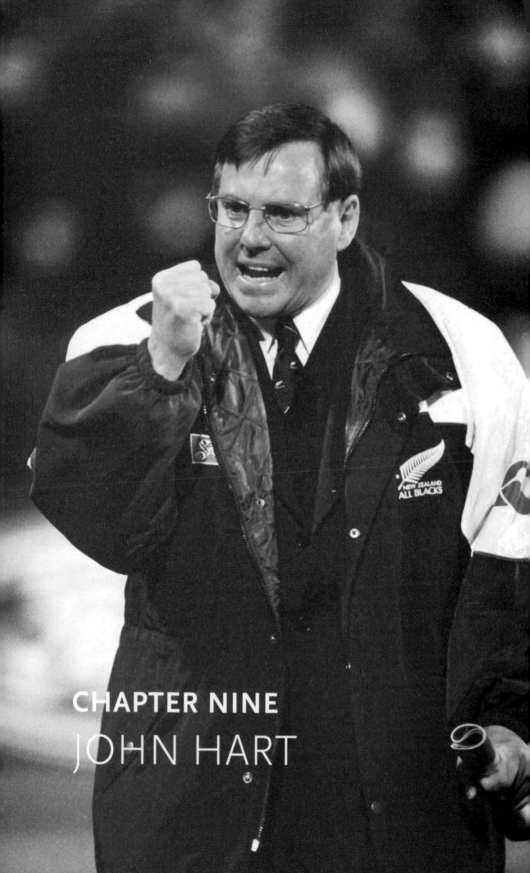

CHAPTER NINE
JOHN HART

Born in 1946, John Hart became a professional rugby coach after making his mark in the corporate world. He had risen to become Group Employee Relations Director for Fletcher Challenge, which was one of New Zealand's largest companies, and began his first-class coaching career with Auckland in 1982, taking the side to the NPC title in 1982, 1984 and 1985. Auckland also won the Ranfurly Shield from Canterbury in 1985 and successfully defended it 61 times, which remains a record in Shield history.

Together with Alex Wyllie, Hart was an assistant coach under BJ Lochore when the All Blacks won the first Rugby World Cup in 1987. Lochore then retired from coaching and Hart took the All Blacks to Japan on an unofficial tour at the end of 1987, but it would be Alex Wyllie who would be installed as the All Blacks' permanent head coach from 1988 until 1991.

Hart returned to the selection panel, however, after the tour to Australia in 1988, and was eventually appointed co-coach alongside Wyllie for the 1991 Rugby World Cup. In hindsight, Hart regarded this decision as a mistake. Following the loss to Australia in the semi-finals, Wyllie resigned, while Hart again sought to become sole head coach – this time beaten to the post by Laurie Mains.

The tenacious Aucklander was finally appointed head coach in December 1995, after Mains had resigned as part of the Rugby World Cup fallout of that year. During his tenure, the All Blacks achieved their first series win in South Africa, in 1996, and won the Tri-Nations three times, in 1996, 1997 and 1999. Hart would resign after the All Blacks unexpectedly lost 31–43 to France in the semi-final of the 1999 Rugby World Cup, by which time he had a record as head coach of 41 games, 31 wins, one draw and nine losses.

In 2005 Hart was appointed to the board of Cullen Sports, owners of the New Zealand Warriors league club, and later served as its executive director of football. He has also served on the boards of a number of other companies and in 2011 took up a position in golf as the New Zealand PGA Pro-Am organising committee chairman.

PRIDE IN SELECTION

I was so immensely proud. I had been a selector for a while, and had been unsuccessful in my applications on three occasions beforehand, so I was a bit relieved as well. I've always been very passionate about rugby and the importance of the All Blacks to New Zealand, so to be involved with them, not having been an All Black myself, was an honour. I had been only an average player myself, but that didn't stop my understanding of their importance.

More significantly, the timing coincided with rugby's introduction to the professional era, so all of a sudden there was a whole shift in expectations and requirements. In some ways, I might have been lucky I didn't get the job earlier. I was better suited to professionalism because of my background in business and HR with Fletcher Challenge. I could understand the transition from amateurism to professionalism and how it had to be managed. I saw that as a great challenge and opportunity.

The biggest challenge was always to honour the jersey, and to honour the jersey meant you had to play well all the time – it wasn't acceptable to have poor performances. You always had to have excellence at the forefront of what you were doing. We had a lot of success initially and in 1996 we played 10 tests in 13 weeks in three countries. Nowadays, these guys rest every week, play a test match, have two weeks off.

Coaching Auckland in the 1980s had helped Hart prepare for the All Blacks role.

I had been lucky enough to be involved with a really good Auckland side. When I left [Auckland], we had 14 in the 1987 World Cup team! I saw the growth of those players, their selection into the All Blacks and what the All Blacks meant to them. That was really beneficial to me, to understand how important it was.

RITES AND RITUALS
The haka

I had a feeling that maybe it was overdone, but I never imprinted on that – I was very supportive. I thought it was a player's choice, not a coach's choice, so while I would have restricted it maybe to test matches rather than every time we played, that was only a personal view and, in retrospect, I think I was wrong. I used to get really uptight that the players didn't sing the national anthem because I thought it was a moment of expression in which we should all be involved. I did try to change that, subtly, but you can't make people sing. The response from a lot of them was that the haka was where they really expressed themselves and the national anthem was where they 'absorbed'. I could understand that, too, later.

The back seat of the bus

There was one ritual to which I was really opposed in the professional era and that was the back-seat concept, because when I had been with the All Blacks as a selector or a co-coach in 1991, I saw some things which weren't good in terms of guys getting smashed up. I thought, 'There's no place for that.' In the professional era I canned that. I didn't can the back seat and the overall principle, because I could understand that: that was part of the great tradition of guys earning the back seat. But the business of 'attacking the back seat' for the right to sit there and some of the things that went on, I did can those. I'm pleased I did, because they're the sorts of things that in the professional era, if people had seen that and everything became public . . . you could get away with these things in the amateur era.

At the 1991 World Cup there were a couple of guys smashed up one night as a result of a back-seat altercation. Well, the media let it go, but today there would be no chance of that; they wouldn't let anything like that go. In the professional environment we had to understand that rituals and tradition were important, and we've got to ensure the tradition is kept, but not some of the outdated rituals. I thought we had too many. Where do they fit in the new game, where you are now public property, you are being paid money, and people think they own you because of that? The public has always thought they owned the All Blacks, but now they thought they owned them even more, because these guys were getting excessive money – going from the dole to $200,000 a year overnight.

It was a whole different ball game with the media. I could see all that changing, so we had to alter the way we did things. One of the things I worked on really hard in terms of our media philosophy was to bring in someone specifically as my media person. I brought in a woman [former TVNZ sports reporter Jane Dent], which was unique at the time, a first. She's the best selection I ever made as an All Blacks coach. I often say that because she was just brilliant at helping us manage the media and the players through a very difficult transition.

The back seat was fundamental to the whole tradition of the game. They supported the captain, and they were an internal discipline mechanism. That was fine and I never impacted on the back seat. I impacted on the way some of the things might have been done. The players understood that eventually. There'd be a few who rebelled, stood up against it early on, but it wouldn't be a good look getting off the bus with your shirt ripped open, you couldn't do it any longer.

VALUES AND BELIEFS
Clash of values

We had a training camp for the 1999 World Cup in Palmerston North. I had a management meeting with the NZRFU while we were there and Bill Wallace and David Moffett, just as an example, said to us, 'We want five All Blacks to go to Auckland tomorrow.'

'What for?' I said – because it hadn't been on our schedule. 'Oh, well, Air New Zealand are launching a plane for the World Cup.'

'Well, tell me more,' I said.

'Well, we've got this photo of the All Blacks front row on the plane that's going to be taking you to London.'

I've never done my stack like I did then. I said, 'All Blacks talk about humility, about values, and what you're doing is totally contrary to all the values that this team has – and you expect me now to go in and tell my team that five of them have got to go to Auckland?'

I was really upset at the total lack of understanding from the commercial arm of the organisation. To be fair, it was driven by [NZRFU board member and later Saatchi & Saatchi executive] Kevin Roberts. He said it was a great idea in terms of publicity, but to me it hit at the heart of what we were not. We never, ever promoted ourselves as being better. I was always the underdog coach. I never wanted to say, 'We'll do this or we'll do that.' I'd do it internally, but I'd never do it publicly, so the concept really hurt me. The players reacted quite badly when we went in and told them. Now, I was in a terrible position because my employer was saying I had to do it (I didn't want to do it) while the players saw me as being the architect of it, when it wasn't anything to do with me. We had to send these guys up but they refused to have their photographs taken in front of the plane – it was a catastrophe. It created a bit of a division, not so much between me and my team, but within the team.

Pride in winning

Absolutely fundamental. We haven't lost a test at Eden Park since 1994: that's pretty huge. The winning ethos was so fundamental to the culture and had been ingrained for years, and it just keeps going. The wonderful thing about the All Blacks is the tradition of its history, the belief by players in what happened before. Winning was something that was an absolute focus, but winning in style was as important. That's evolved. Winning at any count was, at one stage, our philosophy. You go back to 1956: nothing's ever really changed in that how you win may be slightly different, how you might have been prepared to win when you could get away with it, but the winning itself hasn't changed.

I really saw it in 1996 with Don Clarke. I'll never forget Don coming to our team hotel: his eyes were streaming when he got there. He wanted to meet Christian Cullen. He was so proud of winning – of the team winning in Africa, because we'd never done it before. Even though I never played for the All Blacks, I often referred in my preparation or motivation to the history, to those we represented, to why we had to go this other step, and often reflected on this great history of the game and the tradition. The 1996 season was more or less the pinnacle. It was good talking to 'Fitzy' [Sean Fitzpatrick], because 'Fitzy' understood that. He would say to me, 'There are some guys here, like Christian Cullen, who have no understanding of Africa or the history of South Africa' – in the sense that they were too young. 'Fitzy' had been brought up with it through his father [Brian Fitzpatrick had played 22 games for the All Blacks] and sat and listened to the old games with his dad. Generally, there was, in our management team, a huge understanding of the traditions and their importance.

Memorable wins

In the context of what it did for the game, it was South Africa in 1996. We were contacted by so many past All Blacks who had been denied that opportunity to win against them, often not because they weren't good enough, but because of other issues – sometimes because of our own fallibilities, at times those of referees. From a history point of view, that was the most important. There were others. In 1996, we beat Australia in Wellington in the worst conditions. We beat them 43–6 and we played sublime rugby. I used to look for perfection. I used to talk to the guys about how we have the ability to get close to playing the perfect game, but we never will because that game's in heaven. That game was one that will always stand in my mind, because it was such a special performance.

Memorable losses

I went through a terrible time in 1998, a really hard time. We came out of 1996 with nine wins from 10 tests, in 1997 we didn't get beaten – we won every test and drew one, so we really felt it in 1998 when we got beaten five times in eight tests. We lost a lot of the leaders: 'Fitzy', Zinzan Brooke, Frank Bunce and Michael Jones, and we struggled, we all struggled. It was awful, but in three of the tests, if we'd had modern-day [refereeing] technology, we would have won those – there were bad decisions made there and it was that close; it wasn't a thumping.

One that will always hurt me is the 1999 Rugby World Cup semi-final loss. You don't have a right to win, but we were in a position to win it at half-time. I've still got my notes for my team talk at half-time, what I said we had to do. For some reason, some players decided we were just going to go out and play the same as we had been doing, and thought we would kill them because we were already 10 up. We needed to pin the French to the corners and not give them a chance, lock them out, lock the game up. I have a huge regret about losing that game, because had we gone through, we would have won the World Cup that year. We would have had the better of Australia in the final, so that was a huge disappointment. I felt let down, but I also felt that I'd let the country down too, because there was this great expectation.

The aftermath of that was pretty frightening for me and took me away from my normal life for two years because of the personal onslaught of some of the media. It was just some sections of the media, though: I got over 500 letters, emails or faxes, back in those days, and only two were negative. I had support for all that I'd done, but there was just one game that hung – so that was tough, a loss that I always feel.

It got taken away from me too quickly. When you're losing, all of a sudden you've got a lot of people who want to put the knife in. That's

what I found sad about the media: the guys liked you or they didn't.
There's a few, when you're going well – fine, but they were waiting
for you to fail too. It was the tall poppy syndrome that disappoints me
about New Zealand. We don't understand how good we are, how *great*
we are in this game of rugby, how traditionally we are the greatest
team in the world. We've won, historically, about 75 per cent of our
games, which is huge in the international sporting arena – yet we
lose a couple of tests and all of a sudden the world's come to an end.
That was my disappointment in terms of what happened after that
one game.

I had an 87 per cent winning record with the All Blacks and
Auckland, but I'd get no credit because I failed in that one game. The
media were at me because I was prepared to voice an opinion and lead.
Of course, sometimes that was taken as arrogance. I found that sad. You
should always feel good about your own individuality.

LEADERSHIP
Coaching

I was a disciplinarian who set standards that I felt were important for
an organisation. I'd seen it in Fletchers – if you don't have standards
and leaders don't lead by them, and if you don't walk the talk, you're
in trouble. I always thought [coaching Auckland] that we would have
certain, simple standards which we wouldn't compromise: they were
time-keeping, dress and fair play. I instilled that pretty much into the
All Blacks too. Some of it was easy because it was there already, but
things like time-keeping became very important. No one's late for a
meeting, we're early, because why should we all wait around? I started
to discipline them.

The discipline factor was important. It cost me, in the end – my
standards of on-field discipline where I made some pretty strong
statements and made some selection statements about players
who didn't bring credit to the game by their actions on the field. I
still think I was right. You don't get away with anything now in the
professional game, whereas in those days no one yet had video –
players could get away with a lot of things. I might have instilled,
in the end, an attitude where players thought, or may have thought,
they couldn't take their game further. I don't actually think that, but
it became an excuse for some players. As a leader, if you're going to

compromise on standards, you compromise on culture – and if you compromise on culture, you'll see what you've lost. Most of them understood it. I was lucky to have the calibre of people like Fitzpatrick who were of an older age, but very professional. They were the leaders, they led by themselves.

Professionalism caused dramatic off-the-field changes, and on-the-field too, because all of a sudden there was money and technology to understand the opposition and what they did going from here to there. I struggled with that initially, because my strength in the 1980s as an Auckland coach had been that I did a lot of research on the opposition myself, not with video, but just by watching games and knowing plays.

I always think back to when we beat Canterbury in that great game in 1985 at Lancaster Park, taking the Shield. I can still see us having a training run on the Friday night, a light run before we went down to the game and going through about eight plays that we had to do and eight that we had to stop – and they all worked like a charm. We were ahead of our time, in some ways.

When I then got into the first professional era, I was caught short. I was coming back into coaching – I hadn't coached since taking the New Zealand Colts through to 1990/91, and the worst mistake I made in my life was going to the 1991 World Cup with Alex [Wyllie], because that was never going to work. Alex didn't want it to work. I had a manager, John Sturgeon, who didn't really help to make it work, so we were just on a collision course from the outset. I should not have gone, should have just stood away and said, 'No.' I felt the pressure was so great, however, that I had to go.

I'd come from quite a time off coaching – from 1991 to 1995 I did virtually none, then here I was coaching the All Blacks. I started going and watching the Super 12 teams train: clearly it was a different game. I had to get up to speed again. I had to really start to study the game, study the new technology, the professional approach – even the tackle bags had changed from those I used to have, and they had ruck machines, which I'd never seen. We had scrum machines, obviously, but this was far more sophisticated, all the technical aids, the tackling. It was a dramatic culture shock and I had to work pretty hard on getting up to speed with that.

I didn't see too much difficulty with rule changes. New Zealand rugby always did lead in that area. If there were changes, we had often caused them, so we adapted quickly. One interesting note during that successful 1996 series in South Africa was that, after the second test, the Africans were bringing players off and replacing them. They had to go through the injury rigmarole as it wasn't allowed, otherwise: I got annoyed and was certain that these guys were cheating. I remember speaking to Morné du Plessis and André Watson – we got together after the test in a meeting halfway between where we were and where they were. I said, 'Look, you can't do that. We're going to go public on it in a big way if it keeps going on because that's not on,' but I also said, 'I endorse the principle.' So we actually introduced, on that tour, substitution, before such a thing came in officially. We led change, in a way. We had both agreed to the principle at that meeting; we would just go through a doctor in the interim. The guy would come off and supposedly see a doctor as we substituted.

One of the great challenges that you have in the game today is sports science. It's the opportunity of it. I see it with the Warriors. Altitude testing – they've got a whole system there now. These guys are doing altitude testing all the time. The way you prepare, the way you wind down after a match with ice baths. It's all been a dramatic change, and it's got to be good because the player's body needs so much more help. The game's got so much more physical than when I used to play. It's a dramatically different game in the contact area, so the body conditioning is really important. We didn't lead that, we grew with it, but we're as good as anyone else. When I came into the All Blacks, Laurie [Mains] had done a really good job in that physical conditioning area, that was really something that he pushed. We just carried that on. We didn't make any steep changes in my time.

Collective leadership

I grew a twofold attack. We used to have pre-season meetings in which I involved four or five of the senior players with the management team in planning for the year, talking about the whole thing, putting it in front of them. From a tactical point of view, I used to let them do a lot. Guys like Zinzan Brooke, he was an unbelievable thinker about the game. Sean was a great captain because he had 'Zinny' providing the tactical nous, but people don't always realise that.

I had guys like Ian Jones and Robin Brooke at lineout time. I couldn't teach them about lineouts, to use another example, so we used to hand a lot of that over to the players. There was a lot of leadership shown

by the players in the tactical appreciation of the game. I went to Africa
with a plan. Everyone said we wouldn't beat them in the tight five
and my whole plan was to take them on in the tight five with Craig
Dowd, Olo Brown, Fitzpatrick, Robin Brooke and Jones. If we were not
good enough to win there, we were not good enough to win in Africa.
Through our team seeing that we had no fear of South Africa up front,
we created the space that allowed Cullen, [Jeff] Wilson and company to
just blow them away. That all went back to the special part of the game,
which didn't change up front.

Wayne Smith came in with me in 1997. Video analysis changed a lot,
that was his strength. It wasn't my strength. I tend to think you can have
analysis paralysis. It has become too much, at times. We were giving
players too much information, clogging their minds. The great thing
about Auckland was we would say, 'We'll play what's in front of us. We'll
do some moves. We'll practise all these things, but if you think there's
something on, I'll never condemn you if you take it on. If you've got a
chance, I'll never criticise you.' That [individuality] has gone a bit. We've
got so much analysis now that we're too regimented. I'm a great believer
in allowing individuals to express themselves and sometimes, at the top
level, that has stopped.

We handled most things – the odd incident, like Norm Hewitt
[drunkenly smashing someone's glass door], we normally handled pretty
well. I was really prepared to back the players, but they also knew it
when they'd stuffed up. Even if they stuffed up, I wouldn't crucify them
publicly. I regret a statement I made publicly in 1998, however, because
it was taken totally the wrong way. We'd been beaten in Australia
and came back to play South Africa in Wellington. I decided to drop
[Andrew] Mehrtens for Spencer and was quizzed about that. I said,
'Andrew made a number of errors in the test and it's time we gave Carlos
a go as well.' Well, that got taken as me blaming him for the loss – which
was not what I intended or said. It became quite an issue. I had to go
down to see Mehrtens and square that away. It was a regret because
generally, publicly, I was careful in what I said.

Coaching or managing?

I wasn't a great technical coach – I never aspired to being a great
technician. I always believed, at that level, your job was to create the
plan, mould a team, then let them express themselves. My strengths

were selection; the ability to understand what we needed; and organisation in terms of preparation and motivation.

If I compared myself to, say, Laurie Mains, I wouldn't rank myself as a technical coach on his level. He knew more about what a prop does than I ever did – but I didn't feel I had to know it all. If you think you know it all, you actually restrict the expression and ability of players to take over and go to another level themselves.

In the professional era a coach who was effectively a manager was what was wanted and needed. Often I get people, even players, saying that the timing was right for me to come in, at that stage. I knew what I needed to do. I knew how to get it done. If there was something I didn't know, I'd go and find out. I brought Graham Mourie in to help me with Auckland for a while because I wanted my loose forwards to do certain things that he could help me with. Andy Haden was a huge help, likewise. I coached Auckland on my own for three years.

Managing was important. The first challenge was the test series in South Africa. I researched the history of what we'd done in Africa, did a lot of talking to a lot of people and decided that, if we were going to win in Africa, we had to do things totally differently to what we'd done before. I went to the NZRFU with a plan, said I wanted to win the test series in Africa, that was my dream for 1996 in the professional era. Now, that resonated obviously, because that was what rugby wanted. I said, 'We won't do it, however, if we try to do it in the traditional way.'

'Well, what are you talking about?' they said.

'Well, there's a few things I want to do. I want to take a 36-man squad.'

No one had ever taken more than 30 men anywhere, so that shocked them because that meant six more players getting paid. I said, 'I want to go over to South Africa in March, three months before we get there, with the team manager and spend a week there.'

'Doing what?' they said.

'Just going to every hotel, every training ground, meeting every person who's going to be a liaison, looking at all the buses, looking at all the facilities. If we're going to win, we're going to have to plan the whole thing.'

The 36-man squad was the big sticking point. They came back and said they couldn't afford it. I said, 'Well, if I pick three or four youngsters in the extra six, and we go and talk to them about coming along, but not getting paid top money – would you accept that?' They promptly did, so young guys like Taine Randell and Anton Oliver came along and, sort of, they were All Blacks. My strength was planning and preparation from understanding of my business background.

CHANGE TO PROFESSIONALISM

When I was appointed in 1995, I'd done a lot of study on professionalism in league's NRL, basketball's NBA and soccer. I could see a huge void between our knowledge of professionalism in New Zealand sport and knowledge internationally. I spent a tremendous amount of my time in the early part of my tenure starting to prepare the players and the management team for a professional era and the expectations that would come with it.

One of the things I did in March 1996 was hold a forum for the top 45 players: ones I saw as potential All Blacks that year. We had a day's seminar on professionalism and what it meant. I brought in an NFL star who was a New Zealander to speak to us. I had people like [TV current affairs host] Paul Holmes speaking. I had business people speaking about sponsorship and expectation, because there was a lack of understanding from the players as to what was now going to be expected of them.

Sponsors in the past had been treated pretty averagely, to be fair, and now they were the lifeblood of the game. For the professional era to survive, the sponsors provided the money. I've still got tapes of that day's forum. I probably tried to cram too much into a day, and some of these guys weren't used to being able to sit and be lectured or talked to, but it was very worthwhile overall. John Mayhew (the All Blacks' team doctor at the time) said to me, 'Someone should one day go through your tapes about what you said would happen in professionalism – you will find that a lot of it has come true.'

There was certainly a lot of change coming, so I spent a lot of time just working on saying we've got to be professional: the game is professional. A lot of people fall out over issues that come with drink, money and all those things. I came from a background in Auckland where we were very professional, although in an amateur environment. A lot of players took a while to adapt, however. Most did – some brilliantly, and I'm talking here more so from a financial management point of view.

One player, he was a backblocks boy with no money, he had been on the dole, then all of a sudden was earning $180,000. He was buying

Leadership is within the team. I had a role
as a fixer, if there was trouble going on –
not a dirty role, but as the one able to talk
to the opposition and tell them, 'I wouldn't
do that again, if I were you.'
—*Colin Meads*

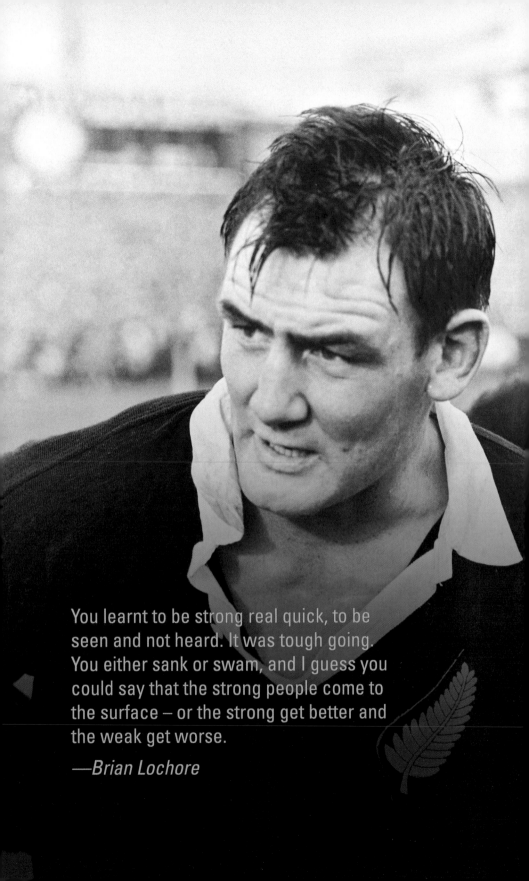

You learnt to be strong real quick, to be
seen and not heard. It was tough going.
You either sank or swam, and I guess you
could say that the strong people come to
the surface – or the strong get better and
the weak get worse.

—*Brian Lochore*

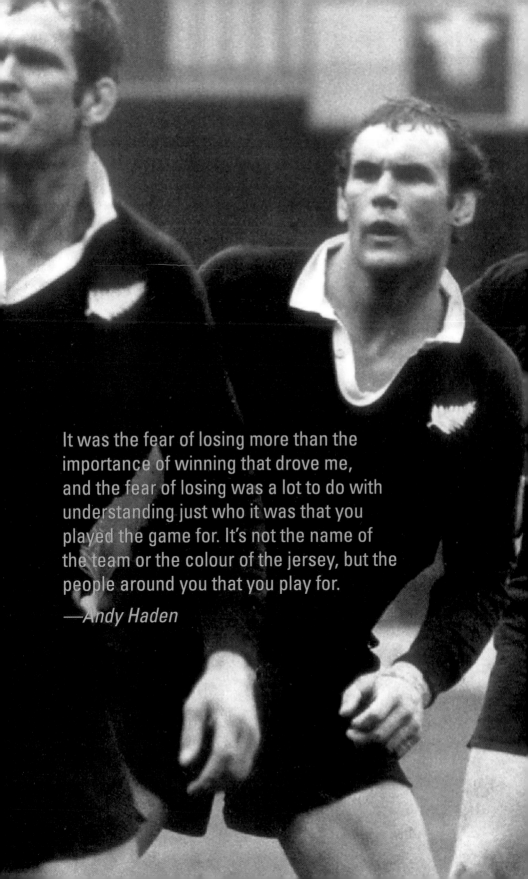

It was the fear of losing more than the importance of winning that drove me, and the fear of losing was a lot to do with understanding just who it was that you played the game for. It's not the name of the team or the colour of the jersey, but the people around you that you play for.

—*Andy Haden*

There was always total respect
for kapa haka, total respect for
the tikanga of it. We made sure
that the players bought into that,
and they had to do it correctly.
We said that we're going to train
to do it, we're going to do it well.
It's just grown from there and
what we've got today is fantastic.

—*Wayne 'Buck' Shelford*

From a tactical point of view, I used to let them do a lot. Guys like Zinzan Brooke, he was an unbelievable thinker about the game. Sean [Fitzpatrick] was a great captain because he had 'Zinny' providing the tactical nous, but people don't always realise that.

—*John Hart*

The areas that we have needed to work on as coaches are developing our ability to grow self-awareness, understanding and problem-solving with these young guys coming through . . . we have had to become questioners. Instead of instructing all the time – technically or tactically.

—*Wayne Smith*

It was a huge pleasure for me to be able to do the All Blacks job. I was very privileged but, in saying that, it fulfilled a lifetime ambition.
—*Graham Henry*

Richie McCaw has appreciated the demands of the professional era on and off the field, and set standards of performance and leadership that challenge others – providing huge footprints for other players to follow.

cars and things. Some of them struggled for a while. Others, Anton Oliver, Fitzpatrick, the Brookes and these guys who had been All Blacks, they handled it pretty well because they were professional in their lives already.

I remember saying to them, 'Look, I don't care what you get.' I never knew how much they got because I took a position that I didn't want to know the contracts as the All Blacks coach. As soon as you know you're impacting on the decision-making if someone doesn't get picked, and then he doesn't get this or that as a consequence; it's best not to want to know. I said to the NZRFU that I'm quite happy to keep away from that. I used to say to the players, 'Look, you've been living on $50,000 a year. That's your challenge now: to live on 50 and save 100, or whatever you're making. You might only have four or five years of this, but you can set yourself up.' Overall it was a huge, steep change, but I'm really pleased we did it.

POLITICAL INFLUENCES
South Africa

I went through the worst time of my life with the Cavaliers in 1986. I was terribly compromised by that, because I was opposed to what they were doing. I wasn't opposed on the grounds of apartheid. It was the fact that these guys were going to go under their own umbrella, which wasn't the All Blacks, which wasn't New Zealand, and yet be perceived to be the All Blacks. I was coaching Auckland at the time, so there was some deceit from some of the players – they weren't saying anything. I got to know about it through guys like [John] Kirwan and [David] Kirk saying they wouldn't go.

I found that all a shocking mess and all of a sudden at provincial level I had to coach a side without all these guys. They'd walked out on their team, walked out on Auckland, but it was the perception that they'd walked out for money that was most damaging. Money was an issue then and it tested my relationship with Andy [Haden]; we were very close and he was in a very difficult position. I understand that, but it would've been better if he'd been right up front and told me what was going on. He says, and he's right, that if he'd done that, I would have stopped it because Wyllie and I were of a mind. We found out late, we talked about it and we were both totally opposed to it.

We were playing Canterbury the day the Cavaliers flew out – that night. I struggled with that. There were a lot of moral judgements going on, it wasn't just apartheid. Apartheid was part of it, but going was seen to be supporting that regime at the time. The reintegration of the players became a bit of a problem, we did it and we got through it, but that was difficult.

The 1981 Springbok Tour was way before my time as coach, before I coached Auckland, and we had nothing of that kind in my era. I remember it though, of course. It was one of the worst things I'd ever seen. I went to that Waikato game, was sitting in the stand watching it all unfold. I thought, 'This is not New Zealand' – but it just showed you what rugby does, how big it is. The All Blacks' stance clearly divided the country. We were robust enough to come through it and that's the great thing about our game: we go through a lot of drama, but we come out.

SOCIETY AND CULTURE
Alcohol

There was always this culture of drinking a lot. I used to struggle a bit with some of the team sessions when young guys were put under pressure to drink a lot of grog, but I was lucky in that I had guys like Michael Jones and a few others who didn't drink, and finally that tempered it. I don't know how it is today. All I say is, today, you can't drink and play the game. We got away with it in the 1980s because you had plenty of time between games. I came from the amateur era, when there was still a lot of drinking. I didn't like it, and I made moves to change and control some of it – how much grog they would have in a team session and certain rules around not putting pressure on individuals to do stupid things. So I changed some, but it was difficult and that was a conflict area for me.

Attitude to women

I led change with Andy [Haden] in the 1980s with the Auckland team, because when I came in women weren't anywhere near the place. I used to think it was important they were, because I worked on the basis that if the partner was happy, the player has more opportunity to express himself. So I was one who encouraged it and, during my time, we did a lot to involve the women. I always struggled, however, when we were on tour in regards to having women around, because that was a bit of a distraction. Now there is a more open attitude and players manage it better. When should they be around the team and when shouldn't they? I certainly endorsed the principle that we needed to involve them much more than we had been doing. I broke the mould, too, by bringing in Jane Dent. That changed attitudes as to how the All Blacks were seen. I see in more recent years that the All Blacks had a female team doctor [Dr Deb Robinson]. I never would have thought that would have happened.

Maori influence

We don't understand Maoridom enough, to be fair. That was a weakness [in rugby] and that's very sad, because it was so much part of our history. I struggled to grapple with the concept of the New Zealand Maori side – it was the principle of picking a side on race or colour, but I totally supported it because it is part of our history. I was lucky to grow up with and play in Otahuhu with players like Waka Nathan and Mackie Herewini. Maori culture wasn't something that we were taught at school at that stage, or understood, so you didn't grow up with it otherwise. A guy like Waka changed it for me and gave me a far better understanding. I went to a few [Maori] games with him, and a marae. The influence of a person like Waka and, to a different extent, Albie Pryor helped educate me. Today, there is far more education and understanding of Maoridom and that's a good thing.

Polynesian influence

The Polynesian factor brings a lot of positives and a lot of negatives. It is now a 'New Zealand factor' and therefore we have to adapt to managing and understanding it better. The weakness is that we don't see Polynesian coaches [Pat Lam and Alama Ieremia are exceptions], we don't see Polynesian administrators, so the governance process has no Polynesian content or understanding to it. We're going to become a heavily populated Polynesian environment. We have to manage and grow it a lot better than we currently are. That means encouraging people to take leadership roles, which is not natural to some Polynesians, even to some Maori.

When I was back in the Fletcher days, we were going through the whole idea of growing leadership. For some young Maori, it wasn't a position that they could take, because of other people around them. We have to understand all that, yet encourage the growth of people into areas of significance. Then there will be more understanding of the Polynesian and Maori factor. That's a challenge. If you look at most [union] boards, particularly in Auckland and Wellington where there's a really huge Polynesian factor, you don't see too many Polynesians.

I see a person like Bryan Williams as being very important. He has done a marvellous job at Ponsonby. It's a really nice appointment to see him being President of the NZRU as a Polynesian, and a successful Polynesian – that's important. Role models in that area are really important. We've got to work a lot harder at it.

I think that if you've got a totally Polynesian team, you've got problems. I'm not saying that from a racial bias. Look at the Warriors. When I came in, Polynesians dominated the club, and there were a few Australians. For us to be successful, we had to integrate, we had to have a far better balance. If you were going to have a dominance of Polynesians, you had to have intelligent Polynesians – and there's plenty of them, Jerome Ropati and people like that in the Warriors who are really intelligent young men. But we've also got a lot of other guys who lack confidence and need leadership, help and understanding. The most important thing to getting Polynesians integrated and playing is actually to understand them – to understand what makes them tick.

We had a young guy who was playing in the back row for us. They wanted to sack him because he'd been late several times and was breaching the protocols in that way. I said, 'Okay, do you think it's a good decision?'

'Well, we're sick and tired of what's happening.'

I asked, 'So how much have you done to find out what his problems are? Before we sack him, I want you to go and understand what's happening at home. Why is he late?'

It turned out he was late because there was only one car at home, there were 20 in his family and he was being told to drive somewhere else, take people here and there – the family was controlling what he did. So I said, 'Well, that means you've got to talk to the family about what he's got to do.'

You've really got to work hard at understanding the culture – don't make excuses for them, because it's not excuses, but understand where there are differences. Polynesian culture is different and many live their culture – they're not all 'integrated'. That's the challenge, to understand the culture well enough to get integrated.

THE FUTURE

Rugby today, I'm really worried about where it is, to be fair. The NZRU has huge credibility issues in terms of leadership of the game. I look at what's happening to viewing numbers. In the Super 14 from 2006 to today, they've halved. Now, that is dramatic. I look at what's happening with attitudes. Sir Graham Henry's a great coach, but he made a terrible decision to stand again after the 2007 World Cup. The apathy that we have in the game still goes back to that 2007 World Cup – not because we lost it, but because of the way we did things leading into it. All the money we were seen to spend on trips and whatever, the conditioning windows and reconditioning, the absolute abuse of the Super 14 and its sponsors. I was dealing with sponsors, I was employed by Ford at the time and saw what they were thinking. They hated it, they lost contact with the game. The decision by the NZRU to reappoint Graham – forget about whether he was the best coach or not – was about what was right for the game. If they had gone with [then Crusaders coach, later Australia coach] Robbie Deans, which they should have, the game would have moved on quickly out of 2007. We would have been stronger and in a far better position.

I still think we're in a position of apathy, even though we win a lot. I talk to business mates of mine with whom I play golf. They don't go to games any more, not even on Saturday nights. I've got a good mate, a really big businessman and lovely guy who loves rugby, and he said, 'Oh, I've lost my appetite for it.' Now, that never happened before.

The NZRU got it wrong and there's a lot to understand there. They were out of touch with grassroots. I tried to tell [NZRU CEO] Steve Tew that three or four years ago and he laughed at me. I said, 'Be careful what the Warriors are doing, because they're going to hurt you.' [For example, sales of Warriors merchandise compared to Super 15 team merchandise are significantly higher, reportedly.]

That is frightening because I don't expect league to take over from rugby. I'm a rugby man, I'll always be passionate. I'll never forget my roots, but I don't see the leadership in this game now standing up and saying, 'We have issues and we're going to have to change. We've got a vision as to the whole way the franchises are working.' They're making some moves now in terms of giving more responsibility to the franchises, but [the NZRU] will never give up control. I said to Tew, 'Look, you don't have to own the game. You have to own the principles. You've got to control the All Blacks and whether players can play for the All Blacks, never compromise: the All Blacks are your brand. You're trying to own everything, and therefore you're suffocating growth.'

Professionalism would be far better, in my view, to permit private ownership of teams, to let people invest in them. To allow public ownership, list these companies, list the franchises, get New Zealanders involved – but to do that you've got to let go. You can't say, 'Well, you've got to have this sponsor and you can't do this and you can't do that.' They just don't grasp that. They must realise they do not have to control every stage of it, and can still 'own' the game. They're making a huge mistake with the current [overkill]. It's sad because it's crying out for leadership, and we haven't got it.

PART III

WINNING THE WORLD CUP TWICE

Rugby in the first flush of professionalism is a little like a lottery winner coming to the painful realisation that being an instant millionaire isn't all it's cracked up to be.
– *Paul Thomas in* A Whole New Ball Game[1]

NEW ZEALAND RUGBY AS A PROFESSIONAL SPORT

Professionalism meant different things to different people. As such, there was a sense of confusion in the minds of many who were directly or indirectly involved in taking the final plunge and committing New Zealand rugby, the country's iconic game, to operating as a professional sport. Some commentators saw things in a different light. Joseph Romanos, for example, saw professionalisation as the betrayal of New Zealand rugby, whereas Paul Thomas likened the collapsing citadel of amateurism to the walls of Jericho. He also decried what he saw as rugby selling its soul. Later, Chris Laidlaw saw the grassroots element of egalitarianism being replaced by a new form of elitism.[1] Jock Hobbs and Brian Lochore, bastions of the amateur game, meanwhile had tried to dissuade New Zealand players from joining the potentially lucrative World Rugby Corporation.

The negatives of professionalisation are often highlighted, especially when romanticising rugby as it existed in the amateur era. Laidlaw wrote that finding a way of keeping the umbilical cord intact between the amateur and the professional 'arms' of rugby was becoming a primary preoccupation of most of the world's rugby unions. It should be explained that, whilst the top echelons of New Zealand rugby (the All Blacks, Super 15 players and some ITM Cup players) are fully professional, club players who make up the bulk of those playing rugby are not. Their support, as volunteers, participants, and All Blacks fans and consumers, is nevertheless critical to the success of rugby in New Zealand. So the amateur ethos, at least at the lower levels of rugby, needs to be preserved.

In New Zealand, the professional game subsidises the amateur game. Not so in Europe, where the big clubs attract sponsorship or patronage on a large scale and have parted company from the 'have-nots' or amateur aspects of the game. Under the current professional regime, the NZRU employs the players at All Blacks and Super Rugby level, appoints the coaches for these teams, approves the Super Rugby franchise directors, sets the international and Super Rugby programme for the season, and retains administrative control over the franchises in a variety of ways. Many provinces, some of which operate along semi-professional lines, are very dissatisfied with these arrangements, so the professionalisation or 'corporatisation' of rugby has not had total acceptance in New Zealand.[2]

Most rugby supporters don't begrudge players earning big money and going overseas to do so, knowing New Zealand lacks the critical mass to be able to compete financially with European rugby nations. However, the number of players in Japan, the United Kingdom and France has now reached almost epidemic proportions – over 1000 New Zealanders play rugby overseas.[3] The reality is that money in rugby has changed the ethos of the sport, as was to be expected. The move may have initially alienated many of the old rugby players and supporters who saw the modern player as egocentric and disloyal to a sport they loved, but the change was inevitable and impacted on the organisational culture of the All Blacks.

CHAPTER TEN
LAURIE MAINS

Laurie Mains, born in Dunedin on 16 February 1946, played 115 times for Otago. He made his All Blacks debut in 1971 against the British and Irish Lions, playing 15 times, yet is best remembered for the impact he had as a coach.

Mains' coaching career started with his beloved Otago, overseeing the side for eight years and winning the NPC First Division title in his final year, 1991. He was appointed All Blacks coach the following season, coaching them in 34 tests until the 1995 Rugby World Cup final, which they dramatically lost to South Africa in extra time.

During his tenure with the All Blacks, Mains was initially confronted with the challenge of rebuilding the team after their semi-final exit at the 1991 World Cup and, from his perspective, an NZRFU council that included members unsupportive of his appointment and requests. He established an excellent rapport with a team dominated by Auckland players and captained by Sean Fitzpatrick, but his position as coach came under intense public scrutiny in 1994, after the All Blacks had lost their home test series against France 0–2. Despite such challenges, he held firm and received some recognition for the high standard of play achieved by the All Blacks at the 1995 World Cup.

His career spanned the amateur and professional eras, rugby formally turning professional during that World Cup. The last of his 15 New Zealand caps as a player had been against Ireland in 1976, although he also toured with the All Blacks team to South Africa that year – he was not selected for any of the test matches, however, despite scoring 132 points in 11 games.

As a coach, his loyalty to his players placed him in a particularly difficult position during the sudden contest between the NZRFU and the interloping World Rugby Corporation to secure the services of the All Blacks for their prospective would-be professional competitions. Because of these experiences, Mains provides some fascinating insights into the beginning of the professional era.

Mains was made a Member of the New Zealand Order of Merit for services to rugby in 1998 and continued, as a professional coach in the new era, with South African team the Golden Cats, and the Otago Highlanders in 2002 and 2003. Although he had played his first-class and international rugby at fullback, Laurie Mains was highly regarded by many of his players as an astute coach of forward play, known as a coach with a solid technical mastery. He is also renowned as a straight shooter: someone who expected high standards of his players, but gave them the chance to meet them.

PRIDE IN SELECTION

I can remember standing with my ear to the radio hearing the great feats of Peter Jones and players of his era. I was a rugby nutter at primary school. I always had a rugby ball, kicking it out on the lawn was another world. I would always dream of one day maybe being an All Black, never, ever expecting that it would happen. When it came about, I had been playing under a very good coach, Eric Watson [a Dunedin sports icon who coached the All Blacks briefly in the late 1970s], who developed my rugby and gave me a whole new perspective on it: standards of discipline, self-analysis and honesty were his key words. I had developed my rugby pretty much to its potential – I wasn't a naturally gifted athlete and had to work very hard for everything I did. When that came about, or the possibility of it, it was almost surreal. It had arrived out of nowhere: suddenly I was realising I could actually be selected for the All Blacks.

It was Charlie Saxton who rang me, at two or three one afternoon, to advise me that I had been selected for the test the following week. As I said, it was sort of surreal. The first thing I did was say to myself, 'Right, get your feet right back on the ground, put your training gear on and go down and have a few kicks and do something down at the club.' Not Carisbrook, where I could have headed – my own club, to get my feet firmly on the ground and realise the enormity of what I had ahead of me.

Selection as All Blacks coach

For me, that was a greater achievement than getting there as a player. Coaching is much tougher than playing. With coaching, you have to learn and know every facet of the game, whereas as a player you don't. I had a very grim determination to be the very best rugby coach that I could be. I like leading people, I like developing people and to this day I still get a great deal of satisfaction out of helping people lift themselves: rugby coaching gave me that vehicle. When I received the phone call to advise me that I'd got the thumbs up, there were two things that came into my mind. One was that I now had the weight and expectation of not just the rugby community, but the whole of New Zealand, on my shoulders. This was so significant that economies relied on it, the general well-being and the mood of the country relied on it. The second thought was that I was now one of those people responsible for setting a standard of hard work and achievement.

When we took over in 1992, we knew that we faced a really difficult programme over the subsequent two or three years, but also that our prime responsibility was to build a team for the next World Cup. We decided to bite the bullet and effectively get rid of all of the players we knew wouldn't carry on more than a year or two, except for one or two whom you needed to glue the team together – we needed glue for culture. There had been significant culture issues in the All Blacks in that 1991 period. The manager at that time, John Sturgeon, who's a very good friend of mine, had alerted me to these, as had some of the players. We kept the mature players whom we knew weren't part of that, or who would very quickly rise above it. That was the starting point as we decided to bite the bullet and rebuild All Blacks rugby.

RITES AND RITUALS
The haka
For me as a player, the haka had simply been a bit of history and a good warm-up before the game. I enjoyed doing it, but it wasn't motivation. Of course, there are two forms: you've got your short-term motivation for an event, with which it helped, and the long-term motivation for excellence or standards – here it didn't play a role. The All Blacks jersey and the history (I mentioned Peter Jones earlier, but there are hundreds of players I could have mentioned) provided that. Colin Meads was probably my favourite player. For me, the haka was the most significant icon or 'ritual': recognising the responsibility to those who had gone before and laid this foundation, or legacy.

The back seat of the bus
Every team has its own forms of induction, which I always believed should be character-building and about teaching the new players the responsibilities they faced, about standards, performance, behaviour and all the rest of it. The back of the bus was always an 'earned' position, one that had to be respected absolutely and never questioned, such was that authority of the All Blacks. The All Blacks expect to command wherever they go – on the field, off the field, in whatever they do. The back seat was just part of that, that we as young players had to learn. I was very happy for the young players, when I coached, to learn the hard way. If you were lucky enough to get invited to the back seat for a 'christening' –

drinks or whatever, you were favoured; you were obviously liked by them, because they didn't have you up there if they didn't like you and if they didn't think you were worth it. So that was a great honour.

Induction

At All Blacks' level there was the Laurie Mains induction and then there was the All Blacks induction. The players got their test tie and the back-seat boys or the players' committee, the leadership groups that we had, would spell out in no uncertain terms the responsibility that these players had just taken on. The Laurie Mains induction was – and there's some pretty good stories around about this – about me finding out how much bottle a player had, him finding out what he was in for and that trainings were going to be harder than a game could ever be, and about what All Blacks had to go through.

It may be an appropriate time to tell a story about this. I remember lock Richard Fromont being selected for the All Blacks. It wasn't a totally convincing selection on our part – I wasn't sure that he should have been selected. However, I was told that he would give everything he had and we were going on a Northern Hemisphere tour. I had an exercise that became rather famous, I suppose, called 'Down and ups'. It is an incredibly hard drill to do and you could either do them in sets of six or sets of 10 – whether you did 60 or 100 of them determined how tough you were. Well, I always like to add an edge, a knife, a needle into it. For instance, if one player wouldn't do them properly or wasn't committed enough or too slow, they would have to do another 10. If he was a tight forward, I would look around and ask where the rest of the tightheads were. Would you leave one of your mates out to do his own thing? So the whole five would have to go. Richard, very mistakenly, thought that meant only the others and that he didn't have to do it, so the cycle just repeated itself. I recall seeing 'Zinny' Brooke out of the corner of my eye, his provincial captain, moving about 20 yards along the line to get along in behind Richard when this pain was occurring. I said to Earle Kirton, 'Go and have a listen, see what's going on here.' 'Zinny' was standing behind him saying, 'Go Dicko! Do not let him break you. Just do not show any weakness or you won't get on the bus.'

So that is the type of induction they had, and I had to be convinced in my own mind that any player – you could select them, but whether he lasted determined on just how much he had inside.

VALUES AND BELIEFS
Pride in winning
On the day and the week leading up to a test match, winning was obviously the goal – but it was also almost everything.

I had said this to the interview panel that interviewed me before I first got the job. 'You realise that this team is going to require a lot of changes, a lot of new players, and that it has to be rebuilt?' I remember Kel Tremain on that panel saying, 'So what you are saying is that you accept, in the rebuild, that you may lose a few more tests than if you just selected every team just for the next test match?'

'That's exactly what I mean.'

The World Cup has created a four-year focus towards which All Blacks rugby coaches have to build. I was probably the first of those who specifically did that, and who sacrificed performances in the quest to find the best players – we did alternate players a bit. I studied what [Wallabies coach] Bob Dwyer had done before he won in 1991. He went through something like 62 players in three years building up to that World Cup in order to find his best test team. I was prepared to do that. We wanted to build a team that had 11 or 12 world-class players in it, and when I look back, that team that we produced by 1995 was a great team.

That was the selection side of it and the other key thing we did was develop some new techniques and skills. I will use one that was a classic. The All Blacks started the 'pick and go' and we developed it to a level in practice whereby the clean-out and the creation of a hole for someone to pick up the ball and go through was a critical part of it. To this day I see that tactic as being very badly implemented, because there is not the same work done before the player picks to go. Yet we had developed it. It was a devastating tool. We used it twice in 1993 at Carisbrook and it was instrumental in creating the opportunity for both tries scored by us in that test. Then, against Scotland, it literally tore them apart. We then parked that, didn't let the All Blacks use it again until the World Cup. There were a number of tactics we devised that we 'saved' for the World Cup. In 1994, we should have put our intended game plan to the side and just concentrated on getting our set plays right. Everybody expected winning to be in our priorities, but there were other considerations. Then when we got to 1995, World Cup year, we unleashed it all. Oppositions really didn't have an answer. The ability we had to create space was phenomenal.

Memorable wins

Our 45–29 semi-final win at the 1995 World Cup over England was one of the great games of rugby and epitomised what we, as a panel, had attempted to do over all that time. We did the same to Scotland [beaten 48–30 in the quarterfinal] and other teams on the way through.

Memorable losses

We lost the second test 7–20 to the Lions at Athletic Park in 1993 and I'll say we lost it abysmally. We just didn't really fire a shot. We didn't perform the way we took the field to play, and there were some peripheral reasons, hotels and things like that. Our players weren't 'professional' enough to deal with the sort of luxury that was being thrown at them and we took the field soft. You lose one week, you win the next, and there are two reasons for that: discipline, and my hardness and ability to identify what caused us to lose. In other words, breaking down our game plan and why we never got it going. Sean Fitzpatrick, who was a great leader, didn't fire in that second Lions test. He told me that he expected to get up in the morning and hear the test team for the next week without his name there. I remember walking past Chris Reay, a BBC reporter, the following week. He was sending a report back to the BBC about how there was no way back for the All Blacks because the Lions were improving so much and we couldn't handle them, and all the rest of it. Well, the following week we beat them 30–13, so there's a loss and a win that stands out for me.

In 1995 in France, we had another one of those miserable losses in Toulouse where the team just didn't fire – a similar loss and again we went through the process. I'm going to throw another story in here to illustrate that process of hardening attitudes again, of refocusing and fixing the problems. I recall prop Craig Dowd making a mistake. Now this tells you about All Blacks standards and the intensity at training runs on test week. Dowd and our centre Frank Bunce both made mistakes. In front of the rest of the team, for effect, I said to them that I didn't feel they were mentally prepared to go into this test match. Would they let me know by dinner that night whether they were fit people to take part in the test? And if not, I would put replacements in. Well, we turned it around at Parc des Princes in Paris and annihilated France 37–12. So they were two memorable losses, each followed by great All Blacks performances.

LEADERSHIP
Coaching

In 1992 I believe I significantly enhanced the culture. Stories I had heard of the 1991 culture were centred around the senior clique and the new boys having a really hard time. That was something for me that was just not acceptable. Peter Thorburn, living in Auckland where many of our players were based, did quite a lot of research on it. I also learnt a lot from John Sturgeon, who had been the manager. We set out to improve the culture and that's one of the reasons 'Fitzy' was made captain. We had really good blokes like Grant Fox and John Kirwan in the leadership group who didn't want any part of cliques or mistreating junior players. Before we went to Australia, I recall sitting in the Poenamo Hotel on Auckland's North Shore – a team hotel I loved because it was very basic, down-to-earth, no frills. It was a great place for the All Blacks to prepare and I had them all in the team room and was laying down the rules of this tour. One was: there will be no cliques in this team – everybody gets treated equally. If I see a clique forming, be it provincial or anything else, I will walk straight into the middle of it, get whoever the ringleader is and he will be on the first plane out. Two Auckland players were sitting together and they were sort of trying to shift aside at that point. It had its impact and became a team spirit thing. 'FPH' (first plane home) is the catchphrase that came out of that, meaning if someone digressed, they were gone. We had a fantastic culture and that team went on to greatness as a very special, close-knit team.

We certainly progressed in tactics and game plans. We introduced to the rugby world a whole new way to play test rugby. In 1995 at the World Cup, that was evidenced to everybody. Critical to it was the development of techniques and individual unit skills to allow the end product to mature. I brought a lot of structure and discipline to the All Blacks. The coaches before me had had discipline, no question about that, and structure, but this was now part of a forward progression.

The other key area was the players themselves. I always had a leadership group that operated on a two-way system. They fed information to me about how the players were feeling, about the way we played the game, or any other issues, and then I would use them to dissipate information to the players and get their support. I would also use them to control discipline and standards and all of those sort of things that senior players are better at doing than coaches. On occasions it was a tactic of mine – and maybe it was something that wasn't all that favourable with players – to swing the leadership group into thinking that way, so that they were introducing whatever needed to be said to the players. The guys could always see where I was coming from, however, and therefore I had their buy-in to do it.

Before we started preparing for the World Cup, the players were saying that they felt – because of all the work we had done over the previous three years – they were ready to start playing a much more expansive game. Then I outlined the way we intended to play. We developed a game plan to beat England, basically. They were huge and strong, so it was going to be all about the pace game. When I suddenly divulged how we were going to do it, the players were over the moon because they felt that they were ready to move on to that much more expansive game.

Communication was simple, straightforward and non-negotiable. I would do that in a team meeting and outline how it was to be done, go out and walk through it. But on many occasions, if we were going to dramatically change anything, I would get the key players in and discuss it with them first. The key players? If it was a scrum issue, obviously they would be the scrum, the tight five. If it was a backs issue, it would be the skipper and some of the backs. It was very much involving that leadership group of players and in picking their brains, to be honest, I learnt as much off players as players ever learnt off me.

Off-field issues

This is where, in my time as a coach, it wasn't easy. For two years I had a manager who, if he thought something wasn't going to be all that popular with the [NZRFU] council, would never even raise the issue with them. All I'd hear is, 'No, council won't wear that.' I only had the opportunity to meet the council once or twice a year and it wasn't really a forum at which I could be communicating our needs. In the last two years, when Colin Meads was manager, the problem evaporated. Colin would go to the council and tell them straight, and I had enough good friends there that he always succeeded in the requests. It came down to the role of the manager, really.

Change to professionalism

It did have an effect, but not until the end of my time with the All Blacks. In 1995, when the NZRFU paid players, for the year's participation, the figure was around $130,000 to $140,000, a significant amount in those days. At no stage was it an issue or a factor with the players. It had nothing to do with their motivation to get in the team. It was an accessory. I only saw the ill effects of professionalism a little further down the track, when players started to worry about their contracts, rather than about being a better rugby player.

It had a considerable effect at the end of that 1995 year when there was the challenge from the World Rugby Corporation, and that had a dramatic impact on me. I first learned about it after the World Cup, on the way home – Sean Fitzpatrick and, I think, Eric Rush spoke to me on the flight about it. I was very nervous and confused. As time went on, I felt this tremendous loyalty to my players, but a greater loyalty to New Zealand rugby, yet couldn't divulge what had been told to me in confidence. I almost became a bit of a whipping boy over it, in that these WRC people then came to New Zealand and I had had meetings with the players over it. I had said to the players, 'If you go down this track without the sanction of the NZRFU, you need to be aware of the damage that could be done to New Zealand rugby.' Many of the players' attitudes were, 'Well, New Zealand will just have to fall in line and become part of it.' I'm not sure that I agreed with that.

The reintroduction of South Africa to New Zealand rugby [in the post-apartheid era] was a really exciting and significant development in my first year as coach. After we toured Australia, we were off to South Africa. We were a new team with a lot of new players. Not only were we going to play the world champions – the same Australian team that won the 1991 World Cup the year before – but we were off to the Republic. Stories abounded that South Africa was full of steroids at that stage, an unknown factor to all of us. One of the areas about which I was concerned was steroid use. [Former NZRFU chairman and IRB board representative] Eddie Tonks and I, early on that year, really drove the introduction of drug testing to rugby. I was not having my players put up against people with that significant unfair advantage, and we successfully drove that to a level where the South African union and the IRB insisted on drug testing. It was significant and, as a result, there were a couple of South African players who happened to sort of 'disappear' from the scene that year.

Right back from when I coached club rugby, I would have a gentleman film my club team playing and would get the videos and go through them. While I could get a very good gist of what was right or wrong in a game by watching it – of individual failings or good play – you're fooling yourself if you think you can see it all, out in the open.

I would have been one of the first to have gone over videotapes and I learned an awful lot at that club level by doing that. I stopped short of confusing the players with it all, but it brought out enough information to enhance our play. That grew in complexity, the science of it increased steadily right through the remainder of my coaching career.

While I was coaching my Dunedin club Southern, I introduced some new coaching techniques. We used to just call it 'skills practice'. We would do a warm-up and then I would spend 10 minutes on basic skills like passing, falling on the ball (trapping the ball), kicking accurately, all the sort of thing that I had never had as a player myself. I did that for the three years that I was the senior coach and we took a significant step forward against most of our opposition in the Dunedin competition. Now, what happened was in one particular drill I would have my players handle the ball, say, 20 times. During the time I was coaching Otago, [sports fitness guru] Jim Blair was involved with the All Blacks, and also with Canterbury in the same period. Blair developed drills where a player could handle the ball 50 times, instead of 20. I very quickly started to observe what was going on there, and introduced that style of skill training, that saturation, into my practices.

With the University of Otago and its School of Physical Education based in Dunedin, I recall going to the head of the Phys. Ed. school and seeking assistance with weight training. They had a biomechanics division, a high-performance division. We got a gentleman by the name of Martin Toomey involved, and he not only trained Otago and set weight-training programmes for us, but also came with me through to the All Blacks. With Toomey we took a very significant step forward. It became scientific training, as opposed to just run-your-guts-out. Many of the drills that I gave to my players, those players who are now top-level coaches are now giving those to their teams. They weren't an extra, they weren't just the coach going mad; they were an integral new part of the overall training programme.

POLITICAL INFLUENCE

In my coaching era there was really just the reintroduction of South Africa to world sport in 1992, and that was great. The prime minister of the day, Jim Bolger, was an avid rugby supporter and, as a result, we were received at Parliament on more than one occasion. He would ring me regularly when I was the All Blacks coach, offering his support and encouragement.

SOCIETY AND CULTURE

I have a very good story about this aspect. In my search to be the best that I could be and to learn things that I didn't know, I went to Australia with Dr John Mayhew to study the Manly league team, which was coached by then-Kangaroos coach Bobby Fulton. I didn't learn much there, to be honest, but from there we went to Brisbane to spend time with Brisbane Broncos coach Wayne Bennett and learned a lot.

One of the questions I asked him was, 'My doctor is saying that if we have two test matches from one Saturday to the next, that the players shouldn't drink anything in between – is that right?' He looked at me and said, 'Yeah, my medics tell me that, too, but the damage it does to the players by not letting them have a beer is a lot greater than the damage done by letting them have a few beers.'

That was a very significant comment to me and gave me a standard, a gauge to work to. I thought, 'Okay, let's assess this. I draw a limit where I cut the alcohol out altogether, or I draw a limit and say they can have three or four light beers each – or whatever.' We know that rugby is such a psychological game that being happy and motivated is key, so I was always reasonably relaxed about the beers. Not four days before a game, but I never stopped players who traditionally, all their rugby careers, had had a beer on a Friday night, and had never stopped that one beer or two beers before dinner. Some players had done that all their adult lives, so who was I to change a successful habit?

Going back to Wayne Bennett, I watched him, this one night at training, spend 45 minutes with his forward pack. [Halfback] 'Alfie' Langer and the likes went from halfway to the goal-line, repeating the same move some five times, then they would turn around and come back again, turn round and go back again. After practice I asked him if this was a punitive thing and he said no. He said, 'On a Tuesday night I will do one of two things. If we have one of our stock moves that is not performed well the previous Saturday, they will practise it until they can do it in their sleep. Or, it might be a move that I know would score us a try, or two tries, against our next opponent . . . saturation.'

'Don't they get bored?'

'Professionals can't afford to get bored. They don't get bored if they can earn more money. They win by doing this, so they don't get bored. It's a great motivator.'

It influenced quite a dramatic change in the way I coached. I started specialising more in 'saturation' of the key things we needed to be good at.

The thing that was always a very strong part of my rugby culture was 'The Team'. Coming into the All Blacks, getting rid of the cliques: by 1992 we had a settled team to go and tour Australia and the only thing that mattered was The Team. There was no mistreatment of any of the junior players or any other player in it. If there was a problem because a player wasn't pulling his weight, a member of the back seat would come and talk to me about it and I would deal with it. It was for the benefit of the All Blacks group and we maintained that. They were also very strong – the players, the leadership group or the back seat – on dress standards, and they were very strong on behaviour within the culture.

I can tell you a little story here about behavioural standards, this cultural thing in the All Blacks. Hooker Norm Hewitt had a drink problem and was a bit of a larrikin. Whenever we went on tour, Norm wasn't allowed to drink and he stuck by that. The other players would mind him. On the last day of a tour, after the final game he would ask me if he could have a few beers, and I would say, 'Right, you go away and come back and tell me who your minder is. You go and find two players who agree to be your minders who will stay with you all night, whom you will follow around and when they tell you to go to bed, you go. As soon as you bring those two names back to me, I will give you the go-ahead.'

Which he did, and there was never a problem. They looked after him. The All Blacks always knew that if they were out socially and someone had had a couple too many – which happened from time to time – they just stopped and made sure there were no problems. I don't recall any issues, but while we were under the spotlight, it was not as bad as it is today.

Now I want to go back to another story about All Blacks culture. At the end of 1994 Craig Dowd broke a leg. We went to what became pretty widely known as a tough camp in Taupo in February 1995. Craig had been back training for a while, but the leg was still pretty sore. We were doing these '150s' and at this particular time two players – there's a bit to this story – two players struggled. Then Craig Dowd was struggling, and we had people like Richard Loe and 'Fitzy' on either side of 'Dowdy' getting him through the 150s, an arm each, helping him through. He refused to not do it. That was the team culture.

Later that year, we were just about at the stage of selecting the World Cup squad and had had our last camp with the wider group in Christchurch. It culminated in an exhibition match in Greymouth, where Jonah Lomu was really dragging the chain. Brian Lochore, Colin Meads and I sat Jonah down and said, 'Look, if we were naming two trial teams tomorrow to play for the 26 to go to the World Cup, because of your fitness we could not select you and Sean Fitzpatrick.' Now, these guys have all got jobs, okay, and were also on these rigid training programmes that they were doing at about six in the morning and this sort of thing. Sean and Eric Rush came to me and said, 'Right, we have worked out what we are going to do with Jonah. Sean's taking three days of the week and I'm taking three days of the week,' said 'Rushie', 'and we are going out to pick up Jonah and take him running.' I said, 'Yeah, but hang on. This is going to interfere with your own training, because he is not going to be able to run.'

'No, no. We are doing this on top of what we do.'

They wanted him, we all wanted him, but he had to realise that he had to do the work.

Maori influence

I was brought up in a family and a society where the only thing different between a Maori and a Pakeha was they were a bit darker. We treated them exactly the same, and I have played with Maori rugby players all my career and it made absolutely no difference. I think some of the stories about them having flair and not being good at the hard work – I didn't buy into that. They might have had a bit of flair, but so did Graham Thorne, so did other players I played with and against. As a coach, the Maori aspect never influenced me in any shape or form. Maori players whom I coached were as disciplined and committed as anyone else, so it was never a consideration.

Polynesian influence

The Islanders, on the other hand – I saw the tremendous benefits of those athletes and I will admit from the outset that I had had limited experience with them at the time I took over the All Blacks. Earle Kirton taught me plenty about how to get the best out of them, but what I already had recognised was that they had this dynamic fast-twitch muscle fibre that made them explosive rugby players. In certain positions, they were definitely an asset. Earle taught me how to get the best out of them psychologically, for which I am eternally grateful.

When you had such great individuals as Michael Jones, there couldn't be any feeling that they might be somehow second class. Eroni Clarke, Inga Tuigamala, these players that were in my teams, were very fine individuals as both players and people, very much a part of the team and liked by all the other players. So there was never anything there that wasn't good for the team. When Jonah Lomu came along, we had to make Jonah some allowances in certain areas to get the best out of his phenomenal talent, but that had nothing to do with his culture or his race. It was simply who Jonah Lomu was, and the All Blacks as a group were totally supportive and accepting of him.

TECHNOLOGICAL INFLUENCE

There were ongoing and very significant technological changes in the way we analysed our games and reacted to what we found. The keeping of stats and tackle counts is an innovation that has improved in complexity all the way. I add one word of caution here: I would never let it creep beyond my expertise and knowledge of the game. I used statisticians, they fed the information to me, but I regularly checked that it was accurate by looking at it myself. However, it is not possible for a coach to get right into the realms of all this data-gathering.

I first got introduced to this by Kevin Roberts, who was CEO of Lion Nathan at the time. The league clubs that his company was associated with in Australia were a little bit ahead of rugby in this regard. I got quite a lot of the feedback on what they were doing from him and we developed that. For someone who hasn't coached and doesn't have a really in-depth knowledge of rugby, it's an area that can feed you false or misleading information. I always had to keep those checks in place so that what I was getting was accurate.

CHAPTER ELEVEN
WAYNE SMITH

People will rise to a challenge if it is their challenge. They won't necessarily rise to someone else's challenge.
– Wayne Smith, on his driving philosophy about personal meaning being a huge part of playing the game well

Wayne Smith's career as a first five-eighths in the late 1970s through to the mid-1980s was distinguished. Born in Putaruru on 19 April 1957, he played for Canterbury (where he was later a mainstay of their great Ranfurly Shield era) before making his international debut for the All Blacks in 1980, ultimately playing 17 tests amid his 35 All Blacks caps. Yet, in recent years, many more people recognise him primarily for his coaching abilities.

After seeing out his playing days with two years as a player-coach in Italy for a small club near Venice (a good challenge in a foreign-speaking land), Smith's first major coaching role was for the Crusaders in the Super 12 competition of 1997. He led them to consecutive titles in 1998 and 1999, was appointed assistant coach of the All Blacks in 1998 and technical adviser in 1999. He was then appointed All Blacks head coach after the 1999 World Cup – a position he lost in late 2001, at a time when he was publicly kicking and questioning himself over a Bledisloe Cup defeat. He went on to coach Northampton in England until being appointed backs coach in early 2004 by then All Blacks coach Graham Henry, who had followed John Mitchell in the interim. After the successful win in the 2011 World Cup, Smith's winning touch continued when he took a new role as assistant coach for the Chiefs, helping head coach Dave Rennie to guide them to consecutive Super Rugby titles in 2012 and 2013 – the first times the Chiefs had held aloft the trophy.

Smith sets out his philosophy of coaching in two books, *Developing Decision Makers*[1] and *Athlete-centred Coaching*,[2] in which he stresses the need for an international coach to create an athlete-centred philosophy, rather than the traditional, prescriptive, coach-centred style used in the past. He has been noted for 'his ability to form a team culture that is more successful than that produced by traditional rugby approaches'. Wayne's coaching philosophy has a strong emphasis on empowerment principle. He wants players with the ability to persist, be relentless and not give up; players who will take responsibility for their preparation and performance. He believes in traditional values and the importance of the whole person, not just the rugby player. [3] He has a belief that the principle of honesty with players is extremely important.He believes also that coaches need to be constantly learning and developing. A key component of a coach's development and enhanced performance is self-analysis. It is also important to get feedback from players.'[4]

In *Athlete-centred Coaching*, Wayne alludes to the importance of a core group of leaders, emphasising the need for 'the best support staff you can get . . . great people all going in the right direction'. His development as a coach is what he calls a 'global methodology' of combining the analytical New Zealand approach with what he learned in Europe about players instinctively making decisions on the field.[5]

Here, Wayne Smith reflects on his time as All Blacks coach.

PRIDE IN SELECTION

I like using the word 'journey', but coming from a small place like Putaruru [rural Waikato] you never dreamt or thought you could make it. You're not brought up to think that you could be a national player in a form of big business; however, there were a couple of people in town, Jim Graham [DJ Graham's brother, a former Waikato representative rugby player] and his wife, who were influential from my perspective. They say the journey is more important than the destination, but it was Ina Graham [Jim's wife and national netball administrator] who inspired me when I was a young player by saying, 'You could be an All Black one day.' This was an unusual statement in rural, small-town New Zealand where I seldom thought much beyond making it within my own community. It was one of the things that triggered me to think bigger and more globally. So, whilst the journey is, of course, massively important, dreaming of where I wanted to head allowed me to follow my bliss. When encouragement comes from people like that, who have national significance, you start thinking maybe I should aim for it.

I was small and not really built as a rugby player, so it was always difficult to imagine myself getting to that point. In any career, you have to have your breaks. When I finished university in Hamilton, I decided I would go to teachers' college, and had to select between Christchurch and Auckland. I looked at the playing roster and All Black Dougie Bruce had just retired down in Christchurch while Mike Richardson [established Auckland Number 10] was playing in Auckland, so I decided to go to Canterbury. I was going to go to the Christchurch Football Club, but there were 97 players just in their trials. I didn't think I would get a trial, let alone make the team. My cousin (the late Don Berry) worked at the Belfast Freezing Works and he rang me to say that the local club had a tough forward pack, but were always looking for backs. I trialled for them and made the senior team. Belfast RFC became my beloved lifelong club on the back of this chance phone call. I've only ever played for two clubs in New Zealand, and I was lucky that Putaruru and Belfast had similar values, with humility and working-man values being at the core of both.

I was lucky to make Canterbury through a series of opportunities, then had a really good year for Canterbury and got an All Blacks trial the next year in Hamilton, which was my 'home' town. I had a lot of school friends watching me play. I was in the 'Possibles' team against Bruce Robertson's backline, and we had 'Lachie' Cameron and Tim Twigden outside me. We played really well and won the game. In those days you went under the stand where they named the team straight after the trials, which was pretty brutal. It was the most surreal moment in my life, because here I was back home, basically, where I hadn't made it, getting named in the All Blacks team, with my family there and friends from school. Just the naming itself was the greatest moment of my life, then there was the All Blacks jersey. I remember getting an All Blacks jersey the night before and sticking it on the bed and basically sleeping with it. Playing my first game and all those things are incredible memories, but the trial, the naming of the team and what that meant to me at the time really keeps standing out.

Selection as All Blacks coach

It was a different process [to being selected as a player] because coaching doesn't really reflect your goals. It's hard to aim to be coach of this team or that team, because so much of coaching progress relies on winning, which is a meeting of luck, opportunity and ability. I began coaching because I wanted to continue to be part of a team, part of the weekly contest. My body wouldn't let me play any more, but I felt I could get a similar enjoyment out of coaching. The important thing is to just coach, enjoy it, keep learning, stack the experiences up and put the players first. Then, if you do a good job and the team wins, you might go up the ladder. I never set out to be an All Blacks coach, but as I began coaching I had some success and that got other jobs. It snowballed and then I joined the Crusaders, and the Crusaders won, and the next step all of a sudden – you're looking at perhaps being the All Blacks coach. I wanted to be a great coach, I wanted to be the best I could be, wanted to be the best in the world at it – and I've always been like that, but I never sat down and thought, 'I want to be the All Blacks coach, that's my goal.' Even if I had limitations, I wanted to work at it and try and be the best in the world, so that's what I did, without ever really aiming for the outcome of being an All Blacks coach.

My first role with Graham Henry, from 2004 to 2009, was as 'attack' coach, which included coaching the backs. For the end-of-year tour in 2009, we changed roles and I was in charge of 'defence', which had been Ted's [Graham Henry's] role. 'Shag' [Steve Hansen] did the attack and Ted took over the forwards. I also ran the counter-attack off both turnover ball and kick receipts as, strategically, it is an area hugely aligned to defence. I then retained this role through to RWC whilst Graham took over 'attack' (engaging and aligning the players beautifully) and Steve swapped back to the forwards after the 2009 tour. Making this point fits in with my belief that coaches have to be open to learning, thinking and improving themselves. We swapped roles at the end of 2009 because we were getting stale, locked in our own little silos and felt that a change would challenge us and interest the players. We took the view that we are continually pressuring players to improve, so we had to walk the talk ourselves.

RITES AND RITUALS
The haka

There is a big difference between the haka as it was done in my day and the way it is performed today that comes down to knowledge, understanding and education as to what it means. In my day, it was something you did as a tradition in the All Blacks and, whilst I was proud to do it, I always had my mind on the first kick-off or the next play I was going to make afterwards. We weren't taught to do it the way that it is done today. Today, for any player that comes into the All Blacks, there is an induction period, and part of that induction is learning both haka, 'Ka Mate' and 'Kapa o Pango'. Understanding what the movements mean, the grounding, the link with your ancestors and the Earth, and how important it is to our culture. There is a big difference between doing that then playing the game and doing what I did then playing the game. It is for the better. The challenge today is to not let the haka get on top of you and affect your first few minutes. We have had to put a bit of time into ensuring that the haka is something that grounds us and helps us with our first 10 minutes, rather than overhyping us and hurting those first 10 minutes.

The back seat of the bus

Our leadership model is based on the back-seat tradition and it is one of the positive legacies we will leave behind. It was the binge drinking and bad social behaviour arising from that which was a negative and has (largely) been stamped out. We tried to normalise having a beer as part of rugby's tradition, and the leadership group is a big part of guiding and controlling that. Many of my favourite memories in rugby revolve around a quiet beer following a test match win and the social cohesion that created. We tried to take the model and apply it to our leadership group. Selection of that group generally is done according to experience, but it is on merit as well. Most of our leadership group by default consists of our most experienced players, because they are also our best players and one of the first jobs in the leadership group is to be the best player on the field in your position. So that's pretty similar to how the back seat was established.

Leadership within a team grows from a belief that people rise to a challenge if they see it. Our players play a massive role in every part of All Blacks life. We have very few unilateral decisions made. In our team, decisions are done collectively through an alignment between management and players and that's led by the back seat or the leadership group.

Clearly there are game plans and strategy. We have little films, for example, about how we try and play the game and what our strategy is. Our moves within plays are animated on a programme. We get senior players, who can use that programme, taking new players through it and making sure they understand the moves and the plays. On the field, we generally put new players and experienced players in their position early on to ensure that they can discuss the game. They have 'relationship meetings' with the players who are influential on their role; for example, a number 8 would want to meet with his tighthead prop, his halfback and his co-flankers. They would room with one of them and encourage relationship meetings with them to talk through his role in the game.

There is also the element of values and cultural rules. We have an
'All Blacks 24/7' policy, the 'non-negotiables', the behavioural things
that every player has got to adhere to, knowing what breaching those
conditions means.

There is the cultural side. We have guys who teach the haka. We have
put a person like Hosea Gear or Piri Weepu, for example, with a new
player to teach them the haka, what it's about, what it means. We try and
turn it into a grounding haka rather than an over-arousing haka, and
teach some basic stuff about Maoridom's place in New Zealand society.
How cultures have been factored in is still an important part not only
of New Zealand life, but All Blacks life. We have an induction in the
area of the All Blacks' legacy: what that means, what the All Blacks have
achieved, what they've been about for over 110 years, what standards are
expected, the need to establish your own legacy. When you're handed
your jersey, you understand you are only in it for a short time and your
responsibility is to hand it on and for it to be better than it was when you
got it. So these are some simple concepts.

Gilbert Enoka [All Blacks mental skills coach] is an integral part of
our coaching and management team. He's filmed all our processes from
2004 to today, and he will sit down with a player and take him through
some of the past, from when we had Tana Umaga as captain and how
he talked about the All Blacks, the jersey and the silver fern, to how we
have progressed through that to today's induction. They will get a huge
history lesson. It is a very involved process and takes a lot of time. It is
something that has made the team special, and we have always said that
we want this team to be one that players never want to leave, that they will
die for. That is part of the feeling of significance – huge significance –
of being part of the group.

The 'dirt-trackers'

I always felt the term 'dirt-tracker' was a negative part of All Blacks
culture. I say that with respect, but the word itself isn't very positive. The
traditions that arose with it – getting as drunk as you could the night
before the game, big steak and eggs for breakfast after a training session,
just don't fit today's culture. We have changed the name 'dirt-trackers' to
'backboners', because they are the backbone of the team. How they go
during the week often determines how your team goes and they can set
the scene at training. If they are showing desire and huge commitment

as a player who is not possibly going to be involved, then the rest of the team feed off that. We have a policy of 'all ready to play'. If we have got 26 squad members – the number we have for the Tri-Nations, then all 26 are ready to play. They prepare, they train, do pre-game preparation and mental routines. Everything that they do when they play, they do as backboners, so that if someone is to pull a calf or hamstring or twist an ankle in warm-up, the backboners are out there warming up and able to fit into the reserves or into the playing team. That has happened three times in my career from 2004 until now. It's a positive policy and the players feel a more integral part of the team in that they are all treated the same, whether they are a starting player or a squad member.

VALUES AND BELIEFS
Pride in winning
Everyone who comes into the All Blacks understands that's what they are about. The expectations that we are going to win have been created by the success of the All Blacks since 1905. Without those huge public expectations and self-expectations, we would not have anywhere near the record we have. It's a real positive thing. It puts pressure on, but we think it's a 'positive pressure'. Every player who comes in understands that the bottom line is, as an All Black, you have to win. We won 89 games out of 103 during our eight years together and since 2004 we have only lost two in a row twice, which says something about when we do lose – how teams don't want to strike the All Blacks in their next game. We lost two in a row in 2004 (when this management group first started), in Australia and then in South Africa, at the end of the Tri-Nations; and did it again in 2009, twice against South Africa [one in South Africa and one in New Zealand]. Every other time we have lost, we have won the next game. That says something about mindset, desire and hunger to be successful. It's the thing that's been the common thread through the All Blacks since 1905.

LEADERSHIP
Coaching
It's all very well to have technical expertise and tactical understanding as a coach, but it is *how* you coach that is critical in my role. Modern rugby players are a different generation. They need logic so that they know why

they are doing something, and they want instant gratification, instant feedback. They are a different group to those we have had in the past. The areas that we have needed to work on as coaches are developing our ability to grow self-awareness, understanding and problem-solving with these young guys coming through.

They don't have to use No. 8 wire like New Zealand has had to in the old days, so we have also got to create our own No. 8 wire mentality. As coaches, we have had to become questioners. Instead of instructing all the time – technically or tactically – we use a lot of 'what' questions so that you get descriptive answers. 'What did you see in front of you?' 'What's your reaction to that?' You are getting a player to understand what he saw and what he did, building up a situation of awareness within the player. We randomise our training so that we don't use block trainings very often (by that I mean going out and doing 50 lineout throws). Tiger Woods doesn't go out and do 50 drives: he simulates the game of golf, he drives and then gets an iron and hits a chip and then he might play out of a bunker or out of a divot mark. That's what we try to do in a rugby sense.

If we have a scrum, we go back from the scrum to a ruck. We might turn the ball over and say we have got to go quickly into defence, trying to get players to adapt all the time. We act out game-like conditions. Our trainings have become more about decision-making than the game itself, and that has been really positive. We recreate and simulate pressures of the game and try and simulate the stress that they are going to come across. We throw them unpredictable events. We might go on to a training field assuming that Australia is going to do such-and-such against us: we'll unexpectedly throw in something else that they do and get the players to solve that problem. We might take a player off, yellow-card a player, so that we have got to play with only 14, and we might make them play on their own goal-line and give them a target to get out of the goal-line and into the opposition half, get possession back. We are saying, 'How are you going to do that?'

That is the skill that we have had to develop as coaches and, for us, it's a new way to coach. We have had to be open to understanding what needs to be done, and to seek to upskill ourselves so that we can deliver.

As a player, particularly near the end of my career, I did a lot of coaching. Coaches often said, 'Hey Smithy, take the backs away and work some moves.' That helped me a lot to understand the roles of different players, the moves, and what the outcome of the moves was.

If the move worked, do it again, if it didn't work, who was tackling who? Who was free? Right, let's hit that player in the next play. That understanding really helped me as a coach strategically.

I had a couple of great coaches at the end of my playing career, BJ Lochore with the All Blacks and Alex Wyllie and Doug Bruce with Canterbury. They were pretty special coaches and everyone in those teams were lucky to have them. Deserving of special mention are Kieran Keane and Gary Hooper who I played with in great Canterbury teams. They were outstanding thinkers of the game and also shaped a lot of the way I think about rugby. Likewise, [the late] Laurie O'Reilly (coach of Canterbury University and the New Zealand women's team, and Commissioner for Children) was another mentor who had considerable influence on me as a teacher of rugby. Mental skills trainer David Hadfield once told me, 'In five years, you'll be the same person you are today except for the people you meet and the books you read.' I've always tried to meet the right people and read the right books to help me in my life and profession.

I guess the biggest paradigm shift I had in my thinking about rugby came when I played and coached in Italy, where I was exposed to a French model of coaching used by Pierre Villepreux and André Buonomo – guys who used a more global methodology of coaching. In New Zealand we came from an analytic coaching methodology – put your hands here, your feet here. We built up a model of technique that turned into a skill. The French tended to throw the ball in the air and play while they looked at movements. They might have the defence starting outside the field and then coming into the field as they threw the ball up, and the attack having to come back at the defenders, hold them, and then pass into space.

The French coaches who mentored me believed that skill development is secondary to decision-making. Skills were no use if you didn't know when or how to use them. Conversely, New Zealand coaches traditionally believed in building the skills first and decision-making second. The French way of thinking is different – it's about adapting your skills to fit each situation. I think there is merit in both approaches.

When I came back to New Zealand and coached the Crusaders, I had married the two worlds. I retained some of our analytic aspects of coaching, but I incorporated much more of a 'game sense' approach. I have been a real advocate of playing small games, working on decision-making, situation awareness, understanding game strategy so that players become self-directed and independent in their ability to solve problems out on the field. They are the ones playing the game, they need to be solving problems and working out how to play it.

We do a lot of work as coaches on analysing opponents. For example, if we were playing England, we would look at their last six or seven games. I would look at a certain area, Graham Henry would look at another area, Steve Hansen would look at other areas. If you added up our hours together, we would probably have done 100 hours combined for the team. We believe that the coaches have to do that work, not analysts. We cut our own clips. We believe you need really good background knowledge of what you are going to be up against. Of course, you can't do 100 hours of work with players on strategy, so you have got to boil it down to maybe 15 minutes of clips and try to establish the priorities, involving the players in that process so that you are not covering everything in the week.

We have a process early in test week where on Monday morning we strategise with the leadership group. We have a defence group and a forwards group and, following that meeting, they come together and incorporate that strategy into their areas. We present back to the team on Tuesday morning. We create scenarios at training that reflect what our collective (leaders and coaches) priorities are for the week and then we briefly meet to check that we have covered what we wanted to cover. We then re-establish what we need to achieve Thursday morning in a walk-through before we feel we are ready for the last big team run for the week on Thursday afternoon.

Then, Thursday afternoon, it all comes together in the game plan. During the game we get live stats coming in so we keep an eye on how we are going in those areas that we were going to attack. We have different roles to play, and the coaches in the box. Post-game we start the next morning about 7.30 a.m., in front of our computers, analysing the game. We normally align the debrief with the preview for the next game.

Collective leadership

When we joined the All Blacks in 2004, Graham, Steve and I felt there were some dysfunctional and destructive traditions within the group. There was a lot of drinking at 'court' sessions with subsequent behavioural issues that could have brought us down. Tana was captain, and in the traditional leadership model that we inherited, he was responsible for all the leadership and decision-making on behalf of the team. That didn't allow for the contribution to our campaign by some great intellects we had in the team. It also encouraged social loafing – an attitude of 'she'll be right – I'm here to play, not analyse opponents, help with game strategy and police team behaviours'.

Following a disappointing Tri-Nations, we (the coaches) got together with BJ Lochore and Gilbert Enoka to discuss our thoughts about the negatives we encountered within our team and potential solutions. This involved not only changing the landscape but trashing some traditions and behaviours for ever.

There were several things there that became a blueprint for success for the next few years. One of them was that we had to get away from the Industrial Revolution leadership model where one boss was leading and the rest were just being workers. We decided that we needed a group of leaders to support the captain. It took a paradigm shift – it meant that we didn't want to do a lot of leadership training with guys and then not select them. We almost needed to pre-select the leadership group to ensure that they were in the team, almost guarantee that they were going to be picked for the team, which was different for the All Blacks.

On the 2004 end-of-year tour we started the leadership group. We had three or four sessions before getting together for the tour, taking players through some basic barriers to leadership. We all worked hard on being able to speak, being able to present, making sure we had structure in what we were saying, how to give feedback to each other. We had peer assessments where we were able to give brutal facts about each other to each other. We were able to put our ego aside and do it for the team. We brought in a lot of things that helped grow us all, as leaders and coaches, as well as players. We had a guy from the Ministry of Education, Ian Culpan (ex-rugby player and fine educator) who assisted us by discussing the differences between Generation Y and Generation X. What were the differences? What would that look like in terms of our environment? We went through quite an education period for a couple of years and soon found that everything we did as a team had more alignment, a common framework. The better the understanding we had, the more empowerment the players had and the better we played. The better the leaders led, the better we played. The better they played, the more we won.

If you were to look at one thing since 2004 that has been hugely influential in the All Blacks having an 86 to 87 per cent winning ratio, it's the leaders. Theirs is the greatest impact on the team, the way they play within the development of that whole programme. One thing we have learnt is that every six months or so we need to change it: we don't change the core, but we experiment around the fringes. That has been important in keeping things fresh and not letting players take things for granted, ensuring no complacency is coming in. We adhered to Ric Charlesworth's philosophy that you need to 'comfort the troubled and trouble the comfortable'. You need edge to win. Getting overly comfortable is your enemy!

The leadership model means the management and players dual-manage the team. There are very few unilateral decisions. There's that recognition that the players out on the field are the ones who have to be able to understand the game and solve problems out there and if you believe that, then you've got to feed it through every area of your environment.

At one stage, players completed online reviews of their game. They were simple and beneficial. Players had to rate their own performance and identify what went well, and prioritise their work-ons for the following week. We coaches also added our thoughts to the reviews, which then created conversations about how they were going (what we call one-on-ones). This created self-direction. Players had to get on the computers, view their footage, assess their game and not just rely on coaches to do it. In everything we do, we try to create independence and self-reliance. The leadership group, over the years, has learnt to be more demanding and have a bigger impact at training. They have an influence on how we train and what the priorities are for the week, and to be effective they have got to represent the team, rather than just themselves.

We fell into a trap early on in our leadership training of players where we were implementing what they wanted and what was right for them; they weren't thinking about what was right for the rest of the team. Now there is a much better understanding and more advocacy about what's actually needed. 'I might be right, but the bulk of the team aren't quite right, so we need to work on that.' We haven't got all the answers by any means, but we keep developing; it's evolution rather than revolution. We come up with ideas and new ways of operating. I guess we are also making ourselves redundant, and that's what great coaching should do.

Going back, there have been the odd behavioural problems, but they have been pretty few and far between in the All Blacks side. I've been involved for a long time now – as a player in the 1980s, in 1998–99 as a technical analyst, in 2000–01 as head coach, then 2004 through to 2011 as an assistant coach – and I've seen a steady improvement in behaviour. Back in my day, luckily there wasn't huge reporting of some of the behaviours that we had: 'What happens on tour stays on tour.' It's not like that today. People are looking for breaches, looking for scandal, but there is an acknowledgement of that by the players.

I've noticed with our players today that they are more likely to attack the issue and fix it up. Jimmy Cowan is a great example. He came through a period where drinking, nightclubbing, getting into the odd scrap was part of the game. I remember ringing him when he had been away with the Junior All Blacks in Australia and been sent home from that tour. I think wrongly sent home – and the people involved would have said wrongly, at the time, because it was for a pretty minor misdemeanour. Anyway, I rang him and said, 'What happened, Jimmy?' He said, and I'll always remember this, 'I shouldn't have been out, Smithy.' I said, 'But how bad was it?' He said, 'It's irrelevant, Smithy. I shouldn't have been out. I should have been home back in the hotel getting ready for the game.'

That was a refreshing attitude. In the past, players would have made excuses or diminished the extent of the behavioural breach. Jimmy had brutal honesty. That didn't mean he fixed up his issues immediately – he still had some scrapes after that. However, eventually he fronted the media (and the nation) to reveal the extent of his problem and stated 'Only I can fix it' – and he did.

He established a precedent for other players to follow. Players who have had problems in their Super 15 rugby environments have come into our environment and followed that example. That is through role modelling, through Jimmy Cowan and his history. It's through Brad Thorn, Richie McCaw, Daniel Carter, Keven Mealamu, Mils Muliaina: they have been our leaders and if we have any trouble with people who come in, we make sure they room with people like that. They then understand the standards. You may be picked to play for New Zealand, but you are not an All Black until you reach these standards. We have done that better than in any other team I have been associated with. There are always going to be breaches, because young rugby players, by definition, are risk-takers. It's an aggressive game and you need that element of aggression and risk-taking to be any good at it, so sometimes that comes out off the field, too.

POLITICAL INFLUENCE

There was more when I was playing than as a coach. The Springboks, the Cavaliers tour – there was a period there where differences of opinion existed between players who just wanted to play and those who wanted to force change. I never played in the 1981 Springbok test series, but I went on the Cavaliers tour. If I had my chance again, I wouldn't go. There was a group of us all at the point where we were going to go because we just wanted to play footy. The decision that David Kirk and John Kirwan made was the right one, and I always admire what they did, and wish I had had the strength of character or the moral sense to make that decision not to go.

Since I've been back, we've had a succession of pretty good rugby boards, good chief executives, and that's tended to take a lot of the political stuff out of the game. Once you go merit-based in selecting your administrators and the people on the board, then you tend to take some of the parochialisms and the little political biases out of the game.

SOCIETY AND CULTURE

There is an understanding within the team that you are an All Black 24/7 and that embraces things like alcohol use, the way you treat people and the way you treat women. How you are as a person beyond being a player is really important and you can't hide that. You will get found out if you're not that person. I've seen some real improvements, not just with attitudes to women, but to people in general, which includes sponsors. There are a lot of commercial requirements for these guys now, but in the early years of professionalism there was a prevalent 'hand out' attitude, rather than 'hand up'. Today we have a 'hand up' attitude.

That change to the 'hand up' attitude has really helped us. Players have become more acceptable, more intelligible in their speaking and ability to network. Whenever I go to functions, I'm really proud of who they are and how they are. Of course, there are always going to be exceptions. I would like to think that the leadership group would deal with a lot of those before they come to us, and we very seldom have to deal with any behavioural issues within our environment. There have been some outside our environment which, if you believe in the All Black 24/7 philosophy, is effectively within our environment – so we have to deal with those sometimes.

DIVERSITY

We have taken the view that we really haven't got Fijians, Tongans, Samoans, Maori or Europeans: we have just got All Blacks as rugby players. There are different attitudes, and that became apparent to us in about 2006, when we were doing some work on the haka, about our country's culture, and what has been important. We got the Fijians, Samoans, Tongans and Europeans to speak, and it was amazing to hear the differences in attitudes. The Pakeha boys talk about the plough, the tractor, sheep, going down to the pub and that sort of thing, and the Polynesian boys are talking about Mum, sister, family, church: totally different mental models and value systems. Most of our Polynesian boys are third-generation Kiwis, however, and guys like Victor Vito, as an example, was head boy at his school and doing study in Classics and English Literature at Victoria University. We have got a second- and third-generation Polynesian group who have targeted education as a key, and they are a really advanced, coachable group of young men.

The attitudes of Pakeha to Polynesian players in the team have changed. You have to acknowledge that, because there's much more understanding of their values, who they are and where they come from, and that's been positive in the group. Once upon a time, you'd see the Polynesian boys from one franchise sitting together and the Pakeha boys sitting together elsewhere. There is very little of that now and that's come about through acknowledgement, working to overcome it, rather than just ignoring it. I'm sure there's never been racism or anything like that within the team, but there have been differences in acknowledging other cultures and that is important.

CHAPTER TWELVE
GRAHAM HENRY

As a young man growing up in Christchurch, Graham Henry had two sporting passions: rugby and cricket. He would briefly represent Canterbury in first-class cricket as a wicketkeeper, but it would be years later, in coaching, and in the national winter code, that he began to leave a lasting mark.

Born on 8 June 1946, Henry began his science and physical education teaching career at Christchurch Boys' High School in 1971 and then moved on to Auckland Grammar in 1973, before being appointed deputy headmaster of Kelston Boys' High School in 1982, then headmaster in 1987. After a deep involvement in First XV rugby and coaching Auckland (which he would do from 1992 to 1997), he resigned from Kelston to become a full-time rugby coach in 1997. With Henry, Auckland won the National Provincial Championship for four years in a row (1993–96). He also coached the formative Blues team, winning the inaugural Super 12 title in 1996, repeating the feat in 1997 before losing the final in 1998.

After being overlooked for the All Blacks' head coaching position in 1998, Henry left New Zealand to coach Wales. Nicknamed 'the Great Redeemer' after guiding that side to 11 consecutive victories, he was appointed coach of the British and Irish Lions on their ultimately troubled 2001 tour of Australia. He left Wales in 2002 after a record 10–54 defeat to Ireland in the Six Nations and returned to New Zealand, where he was appointed technical advisor of the Blues for their successful 2003 Super 12 season.

Henry was finally appointed All Blacks coach following the Rugby World Cup semi-final loss in 2003, choosing Wayne Smith and Steve Hansen as his assistant coaches. They were nicknamed 'the three wise men' by media. Despite being heavily criticised for a 'rotation policy' in World Cup year, and despite the All Blacks' 18–20 loss in the Rugby World Cup quarterfinal against France in the cauldron of Cardiff later that year, Henry was controversially reappointed for a further term: the first unsuccessful All Blacks World Cup coach to be reappointed. He would eventually step down as head coach on his own terms and in style, following the All Blacks' gripping 8–7 win over France in his adopted home city of Auckland in the 2011 Rugby World Cup final. By then he had become one of the most successful rugby coaches of all time, having coached the All Blacks to 88 wins in 103 tests for a winning percentage of 85.4 per cent.

PRIDE IN SELECTION

It was a huge pleasure for me to be able to do the All Blacks job. I was very privileged but, in saying that, it fulfilled a lifetime ambition. I thought I'd burned my bridges at one stage, by coaching Wales: I was told by NZRFU officials that I'd never coach in this country again. [Indeed, after Henry left to coach Wales, the NZRFU adopted the so-called 'Henry clause', stating that a person was not eligible to coach the All Blacks if they had coached a national side overseas. It was later revoked.] So to get the opportunity was a privilege for me. I'd coached teams every year since about 1973, at every level – well, most levels. To coach your own country's international team, the All Blacks, is something special. I coached Wales and I coached the Lions, but it's not the same as coaching 'your own' country. It's something I'd worked hard for, and I just couldn't be more thankful.

I was lucky. There was limited competition for the position at the time. It's about doing the hard yards, and I had a track record that proved that I could coach [top-level] rugby. The Auckland team won four consecutive national championships, the Blues won the first two Super 12s, and Wales, they had improved, achieving a 59 per cent record during my time. When I came back from Wales, I assisted the Auckland team and the Blues again in three championships, and they won those three championships, which was helpful to me at the time. It just put me back in the mix. It could have made a difference – the Blues and Auckland around about that time had struggled, and it was just circumstantial that they won three championships on end and that John Mitchell's All Blacks team didn't win the Rugby World Cup in 2003.

He had a good record, John, but he didn't endear himself to those who make decisions. Rightly or wrongly, that didn't help him, obviously, while I happened to be 'Johnny on the spot'.

RITES AND RITUALS
The black jersey and the silver fern

The black jersey and the silver fern probably doesn't mean as much to me as perhaps the guys who have played in the jersey, like Wayne Smith, for example. He's hugely passionate about that. I'm hugely passionate about the legacy that's been built up over the last 110 years. Every year the team is very focused on trying to add to that legacy, they respect the history. I'm very proud that the team has indeed added to that legacy. There's a lot of information given to current All Blacks on what the team has done over the last 110 years and preserving and adding to that legacy is one of their major motivations when they put on the All Blacks jersey. The team won three Grand Slams in the time that I was involved, which makes it four in total by All Blacks teams. We've won five Tri-Nations, kept the Bledisloe Cup and won the 2011 Rugby World Cup.

Also, the players conducting themselves well as young men was important, so that we didn't tarnish the name of the All Blacks. These young guys didn't always make good decisions, but improved – it's a continual work-on. A good framework is in place, which is really controlled by the players themselves. They run their own off-the-field social situation; they give very clear guidelines and support each other. In recent years, we've got better as the players have become accustomed to the guidelines that have been set. We as management have agreed with the way it's been driven, we agree with the guidelines, and the leadership group of the All Blacks controls it.

The haka

The haka is very meaningful and a lot of work's gone into it. This particular team has produced its own haka. We've got two now, and they take performing either haka and understanding the meaning of them particularly seriously. It's a very important tradition of All Blacks rugby in New Zealand. Whether it helps us play better football, that's questionable, because it does take some focus away from the start of the game. However, it's part of our legacy, a very important part of New Zealand culture.

In the test in which the haka was performed inside the changing room, the issue was the Welsh in that particular game had wanted control of when the haka was going to be performed. We didn't agree: it went against tradition. We had not done that in 100 years of games versus Wales.

VALUES AND BELIEFS
Pride in winning

Winning is everything for me and that's why I coached. We just can't afford to lose; winning is part of what we're about. The success rate of the All Blacks prior to professionalism was around about 70 per cent: since professionalism it's been 80 per cent. Most people would pick that we were more successful in the amateur times, but we're actually much more successful in the professional era. Again, one of the major drivers of this team is wanting to add to the legacy and winning rugby games is how you do that.

Memorable losses

I have said before that it's like a death in the family, but I got criticised for that. It can't be that bad – but it is a major. You've got to handle it. It focuses people, and it's part of the game.

LEADERSHIP
Collective leadership

Conrad Smith, Brad Thorn and Keven Mealamu were part of the leadership group leading up to Rugby World Cup 2011:

An All Black who is in his first or second campaign is considered a 'new All Black' and those guys would help him with his induction into the team. That's taken particularly seriously, it's done well and the young players get a lot out of that. It's done by those with 50 test matches or thereabouts, who have been through it themselves and know what they'd have done differently when they were 'new'.

We had a policy, one of the few policies that we have had, that everybody prepares to play: whether they were in the 15 or the 22 or 30, there was no differentiation. We made that change because we found that those who weren't in the final 22 were inclined to be a bit too relaxed later in the week, and it's been very good since. We had situations where a player got injured in a warm-up for a test match and we'd had to bring in somebody who wasn't in the 22, either into the team or into the reserves – that's another reason everybody prepares to play. We used to call them the 'dirt-trackers' [Wayne Smith called them 'backboners'], but now they're also called 'the spark plugs' because they ignite the others. We wanted them to set a standard for the rest of the 22, be inspirational that week, train well and inspire the others. If the test players have quality opposition, the test team prepares better.

There have been huge changes overall in coaching brought about by professionalism; however, the previous era's players were 'professional', even though they were amateur. When I was coaching Auckland in the early 1990s, the Grant Foxes, Zinzan Brookes and Sean Fitzpatricks were just as professional as the players are today. Obviously, because they had another job and so on, it was a bit different, but they took the game exceptionally seriously.

The game has changed from a coaching point of view primarily because you've got many more people working alongside you doing the job. When I coached Auckland, I coached every aspect of it apart from the scrum and the lineout, perhaps – I had a forwards coach assisting me. When I coached Wales, even in the professional era, I had a part-time scrum coach, but apart from that, I coached all aspects of the game.

In the All Blacks, Henry had two assistant coaches and two specialist skills coaches (for kicking and scrummaging). This allowed him to concentrate on small aspects of the game that otherwise may have been brushed over.

There's a greater onus on players to perform because they're getting paid. So, there's a lot more concentration now on things like nutrition, hydration and recovery, doing everything to win, doing it correctly. There's no room for any grey area. A 'train to win' attitude – you expect that when you're playing for your country. In the amateur days, there wasn't the same emphasis on nutrition, hydration and recovery, and that is understandable.

Travel is also a factor, which is managed by making sure players sleep at the right times and putting strategies in place to try to adjust them quickly to changing time zones, particularly when the team is going to South Africa, the United Kingdom or Europe.

At the same time that there has been a gradual improvement in everything surrounding the game, there's also been more emphasis on game plans. When you've got more coaches doing the job, there's a greater analysis of the opposition and of how you're playing yourselves. I spend a lot of my time researching where the game is going. You're always searching for improvements – and that was my job. The players haven't got time to do that because they're at the coalface preparing to play.

There's an emphasis on training to win with regard to the whole area of conditioning, strength, hydration, recovery and diet because if you can get one per cent improvement here, one per cent there, that can assist in making you a winning combination. One of the reasons the All Blacks have been pretty successful is their fitness levels have improved enormously – we could then play at a high intensity in the last 15 minutes when other sides were falling over. That is critical.

The leadership of the team is vital. We put a lot of emphasis on the senior players and coaches, and between the captain, vice-captain and me, and the alignment between senior players and the other players, so that we were all on the same page about the game we were trying to play. Constantly tyring to improve and add new dimensions to our game has been a big plus, because if you're constantly playing the same style of game, you're going to get done by the opposition, they are going to work you out. So you've got to be constantly trying to improve what you're doing by adding new elements. That's important.

If there were new things to add, Richie McCaw, Daniel Carter and senior members felt good about that. Their response was never, 'We can't do that.' The alignment between what I might have been suggesting and what 'Smithy' and Steve [Hansen] might have been suggesting and the likes of Richie, Daniel, Andrew [Hore] and Mils [Muliaina] was hugely important. The leadership group was passing that to the players. The leaders' standards, leading by example, was also critical.

The social environment within the All Blacks is quite different from what it was eight years ago – exceptionally different. They don't have 'court sessions' any more, which used to be a ritual throughout New Zealand rugby. The last time we had a court session was the first year that I was involved in the Tri-Nations. Some of the boys enjoy a drink [drinking was a large component of court sessions]. They have their own 'rugby club' [Club All Black] now, which is a huge acquisition in the overall frame of what we have been doing. The boys come along in their individual club jerseys, whether it be Auckland Marist or Christchurch Football Club, and they might have a beer or they might have a Coke. There are usually two or three speakers at every 'club night' who talk about their club at home, the All Blacks who have come from that club and why their club's important to them. We have life members of this Club All Black and honours boards: all the players are on the honours boards with the number of test matches they've played, how many Tri-Nations they've won, how many Grand Slams they have won, etc. That's been a major development in the social scene, one which has some relevance to the grassroots of rugby, but also a lot of fun and a lot of laughs.

In terms of player leadership, we had an on-field senior leadership group and an off-field leadership group. Mealamu, Smith and Thorn mainly controlled the off-field, and they were the ones who set the parameters on a Saturday night. They might have said, 'Tonight, fellas, we'll be in bed by two and there won't be any drinking. We won't be in the hotel, but we'll meet and have a chat in the team room.' Or, 'Tonight the curfew is two and we're going out to this place, make sure you're on the bus to get home by this time.' So there was flexibility from week to week, depending on the circumstances, but it was not flexible on the night. The boys have been outstanding at setting the social scene and that's driven by the senior players.

The on-field leadership group of McCaw, Muliaina, Hore and Carter would meet with the coaches on a Sunday night to look at the week ahead and make sure they were all on the same page. We would discuss whether there was anything new we needed to introduce, or anything from the past game we weren't happy with, that we needed to improve on. Tuesday lunchtime we'd meet again to make sure we'd covered the things we wanted to cover in those first two days' review and training. Wednesday was usually a day off, then we would have our walk-through training on the Thursday and the running training on the Thursday afternoon.

Some of the bigger changes made placed emphasis on this leadership and its alignment with management. We didn't meet a lot, but we really emphasised that need for alignment. I would spend, even during the Super 15, some time with Richie and Daniel talking game plans so that when we got together in the All Blacks, we were already quite a way down the track. Them driving the standards of the All Blacks on and off the field is very important. Richie as captain has been outstanding, but he still continues to try to grow as a captain. He's obviously world-class and is very inspirational. The boys respect him and he leads from the front; he's got his finger on the pulse.

Getting back to Club All Black, that was a real positive as far as pulling all the guys together; it's really significant to have fun together. We could drop in the odd serious thing, but we mentioned the game on the weekend in a relaxed environment, so it was not all heavy. [Current head coach, with a laconic sense of humour] Steve Hansen is the club captain and he's good at it, he adds to that situation.

If I had coached the 2011 All Blacks the way I coached Auckland in the early 1990s and the Blues in the mid-1990s, they wouldn't have put up with me. They couldn't have handled it, because you were a lot more demanding, a lot more authoritarian than today. Quite frankly, you have to change with the clientele; you have to change with the players. These players have grown up in a different society, under a different educational system and couldn't relate to an authoritarian coach and a 'demanding' coach.

I can remember coaching the Auckland Grammar School First XV in the 1970s. Authoritarian coaching was appropriate in those days, but today they'd shoot you. Coaches, if they're going to have longevity in the game, need to be able to change. It's become consensus management, where communicating with everybody in the group is a bigger factor, combining everybody's ideas to produce something that is special. How it is going to be in 2020, I don't know, but I think that's the way you have to do it these days – we wouldn't survive if we went back to previous styles.

When we involved more of the total team in decision-making, it was a long-winded process. Today we rely on decision-making by the full-time management (the coaches and the manager), sports psychologist and the senior players. That group makes a lot of the decisions, but there's opportunity for the other guys to put forward their ideas, and they may be incorporated.

Outside of our leadership group, there was a strategy group, a defence group. Wayne Smith had the backs, and Steve Hansen had the forwards. Most of the team were split between those three groups so that they could have a significant role. The obvious people in the strategy group are your numbers 8, 9, 10, the captain and the fullback. Wayne would have the 6s and 12s and two or three others, maybe the halfbacks, too, in the defence group. The forwards are the forwards. They are given opportunity to lead, for example Kieran Read calling the lineouts, Tom Donnelly doing defensive lineouts, Anthony Boric doing the kick-offs, Tony Woodcock doing the scrums, Richie McCaw and Daniel Braid perhaps doing the breakdown.

Although they may also have a leadership role in the big picture, most of them have a leadership role in a minor part, but a very important part, of the game. Tony Woodcock was not in the leadership group, but he ran the scrum and he did it well, he was superb. Kieran Read was not in our leadership group, but I would say he is the next long-term captain of the All Blacks. His leadership is significant, he's number 8, he calls the lineouts. He's good at it and, because he's got a responsibility with the lineout calls, that takes him into other areas in the game. Players add to the total group by their self-sufficiency and their leadership.

POLITICAL INFLUENCE

There are some very good things that have happened to the team in the context of politics. Nelson Mandela's presence at the Rugby World Cup in Johannesburg, which was the 10th anniversary of Freedom Day in South Africa, was significant. The greatest man who ever lived? He was certainly highly inspirational to the South African side and the 80,000 people at Ellis Park. That's not political influence, but just a contextual situation that was memorable.

SOCIETY AND CULTURE

Alcohol

When the new management group first got together in 2004, a lot of the players had obviously come from previous All Blacks teams and brought the social/cultural things that they thought were part of the ritual of being an All Black. Although alcohol had been part of the scene for a long time, parts of that weren't what we thought was acceptable.

They are professional athletes: in the team right now, probably a third of them don't drink. Some of them have times when they don't drink – they might say, 'I'm not drinking during the Tri-Nations', and they are very disciplined in that. The leadership setting the social scene has a significant impact on how much they drink, because it becomes team protocol. But they don't say, 'You can't drink.' There may be a night they don't drink, but there is no rule that says the All Blacks can't drink at all. We just set the scene to what is appropriate for that particular night and what we have ahead of us.

Attitude to women

No women are allowed in the hotel on the hotel floors that we are staying in. In recent times there have been significant problems, which have derailed some sports teams. You can't afford to have that situation so we have strong protocols in that area.

Management were allowed to have their wives on tour, and they toured quite a bit with us, but players were not allowed to have a woman in their room even if it was their wife. If their wives or partners came over, they usually stayed in another hotel close by.

Multiculturalism

Naturally guys tend to gravitate to the people they know. We liked them to get to know everybody, to connect with everyone in the team. It may have been a provincial thing or an ethnic thing, but generally speaking, they were pretty good at mixing. If you looked at the leadership group in the All Blacks when we had Mealamu, Hore, Thorn, McCaw, Carter, Smith, Muliaina – you have a couple of Samoans in that group, but there was no thought behind that selection. We just picked who we thought were the best people. They used to be selected by the players, now they are selected by the team management. One of the key reasons the All Blacks are playing pretty well is the spirit in the group; they enjoy each other's company.

CHAPTER THIRTEEN
LEADING THE LEGACY

DR ANDY MARTIN

THE ALL BLACKS CAPTAIN

When we reflect on the leadership themes evident throughout our interviews with seven captains across the amateur and shamateur eras, and then with our four coaches in the professional era, how do we position the 'winning legacy' in a contemporary All Blacks leadership context? What did Richie McCaw inherit? How has the current All Blacks captain utilised the great legacy in his own era, and own development?

Sean Fitzpatrick was the professional era's first captain, achieving 92 caps – 51 as captain. Fitzpatrick and a number of senior players were already, as John Hart indicated, 'very professional. They were the leaders, they led by themselves.' Fitzpatrick himself noted that the 'notion of letting down their teammates, their country and themselves was a consistent theme . . . That thought drove me to be tougher on myself, push harder and work more intensely.'[1]

Laurie Mains argued that Fitzpatrick became a great leader, and had been installed as captain to help develop the culture of the team following the 1991 RWC loss. Highlights of Fitzpatrick's captaincy were a first series win in South Africa in 1996 and an unbeaten season in 1997. However, the subsequent retirement of Fitzpatrick and a core of other senior leaders (Zinzan Brooke, Frank Bunce and Michael Jones) significantly impacted on the strength of the All Blacks: five test losses followed in 1998.

We have seen that the All Blacks are expected to win every time they take the field. Maintaining the record, which has been phenomenal over the years, requires a collective player effort centred on performance-based standards and continuous improvement. Defeat and the circumstances that brought it about are rigorously reviewed. In a learning culture, reasons for defeat are analysed with a view to eliminating any failings: a knowledge-based approach so that the defeat will not be repeated. Very rarely have All Blacks teams lost more than two games in a row.

Collective captaincy

Team leadership has moved beyond the traditional 'one captain' style to a more shared-influence process. Previously, the leader-centric, specialised role reinforced the notion that the characteristics or behaviours of leaders were seen to have a significant impact on the attitudes, behaviours and performance of followers. Over the past decade, since Graham Henry, Wayne Smith and Steve Hansen came in as All Blacks coaches, the development of a collective leadership approach and a learning culture has been a significant shift. Collective leadership is still an emerging field, but the All Blacks' leadership in a performance-driven environment has proved its effectiveness.[2]

Rugby is now more than a 15-man game with a sole leader responsible for standards. Before the 1990s, players could be replaced only if they were injured; now players can be substituted during a match. The entire squad of 23 train in the expectation that they will take the field at some point.

The All Blacks coaches have taken this a step further, training an extended group of about 30 players, all of whom are good enough to contribute to the overall team performance. Those who are not starting, variously called 'dirt trackers', 'spark plugs' or 'backboners', put pressure on those that are, so that everyone's contribution is important.

Policies have also been established for the induction of young players – policies that communicate and reinforce the All Blacks' identity and culture; what it means to be an All Black and to perform every week. It is accepted that players will make occasional mistakes, on and off the field, but those who repeatedly offend and who do not perform at the necessary level will not have a long tenure as an All Black.

Part of this player induction is learning both haka, 'Ka Mate' and the newer 'Kapa o Pango', created and introduced during Tana Umaga's era. The haka is unique to New Zealand in world sport and All Blacks now take pride in understanding and performing it to an excellent standard. It represents, defines, and is an important part of New Zealand and All Blacks culture. All Blacks culture acknowledges different characteristics among different groups, yet transcends ethnicity: everyone comes together under this common team culture.

Changes in the leadership approach since 2004 are testimony to these coaches' ability to recognise the need for change and find a successful solution. Henry pointed out the importance of alignment between the coaches, the captain and senior players under the new model. 'The leadership of the team is vital.' The captain provides the bridge between coaches and team. This process began during Tana Umaga's tenure as captain (2004–2005) and has continued under the current leadership of Richie McCaw (and, when McCaw has been unavailable, Kieran Read).

Where does the captain, as a leader, fit into this leadership hierarchy? The captain carries the most visible responsibility for the team's performance. He must also command his own position and, in so doing, set the standard for the team. The captain's vision for the team and the coaches' needs to be aligned, but the biggest strength of a captain is that he is trusted to make effective decisions and adapt, especially at pressure times during a game. A consistent feature of successful All Blacks teams is that the captain is supported in his decision-making role by a core of senior players, whose input is encouraged. Yet the influence of his unique position cannot be understated, as on-field decision-making is required at all times and the difficult calls often occur when things aren't working according to plan.

Professionalism in practice

Professionalism is not just receiving money to play sport. In the All Blacks' environment, it is an individual and collective commitment on the part of players to ensure that their every action, on and off the field, is focused on delivering the best possible performance on game day. As the interviewees have noted, even during the amateur era, the All Blacks prepared in as professional a manner as possible. The All Blacks have stayed at the forefront of innovation in rugby, otherwise individuals and the team would fall unacceptably behind. For example, the size, strength and speed of forwards and backs have increased over the past 20 years, increasing the physical challenges and pressures to perform. Physical conditioning and recovery are increasingly important; consequently there is significantly less after-match drinking than in previous eras. In addition, there is now a lot of analysis using sophisticated technology; for example, players can now see an individualised video analysis of their game when reviewing their match performance. They also have a wealth of data to mine on opposing players.

While technology helps inform and improve individual and team preparation, it does not in itself guarantee that a team will perform well in a match. The pride in winning, in the jersey, and preserving the historical legacy remain significant factors and, over the past decade, through 'Club All Black' these have become increasingly embedded in the psyche of the players. These values, and ultimately results, have been achieved through a collective team leadership process in which Henry, Smith, Hansen, Umaga, McCaw and senior players have played a prime role.

Richie McCaw

First selected as a 20-year-old at the end of 2001, McCaw has been highlighted here as an exemplar of the embodiment of these themes. Like other All Blacks, he has played with a determination to win and not let down the players who have worn the jersey previously. After establishing himself as a peerless and instinctive player in his position, he was appointed as the All Blacks' full-time captain in 2006.

Although McCaw led his team to many successes, he discovered that captaincy required more of him. Failures – notably the 2007 RWC campaign – spurred him to personally reflect and adapt, which then saw him grow as captain. This ability, with a resultant long tenure, has meant his experiential knowledge has increased exponentially, to a point where he is now regarded as a world-class, inspirational leader. He has appreciated the demands of the professional era on and off the field, and set standards of performance and leadership that challenge others – providing huge footprints for other players to follow.

Developing decision-making

Despite stinging media and public criticism following the All Blacks' elimination to France in the 2007 RWC quarterfinals, McCaw's captaincy was retained. After a 13–3 lead at half-time, the All Blacks had camped for much of the second half of that sudden-death match in the French 22 and the collective decision-making was poor. They had tried to force a try as pressure mounted, when a dropped goal would have sufficed. Only as time ran out were some (woeful) attempts made by players, but they were unpractised in setting up the ball for such a specific, high-pressure moment – the execution of a long-range dropped goal. They lost 18–20.

Had lessons not been learnt from the extra-time dropped goal by Springbok Joel Stransky, which resulted in South Africa beating the All Blacks in the 1995 World Cup final? Or Johnny Wilkinson's winning dropped goal in the 2003 final? McCaw commented that when 'decision-making becomes muddled, clarity is lost and accuracy is compromised'.[3]

Years earlier, after the All Blacks' 1999 RWC semi-final loss to France, there had been a shift in coaching focus towards empowering and improving player decision-making. The 1999 loss (31–43) had also arrived despite a 24–10 lead early in the second half. The players had either been unable to action or ignored coach John Hart's half-time team talk 'to pin the French to the corners and not give them a chance, lock them out, lock the game up'.

Then the French ran riot, scoring three tries and 33 unanswered points.

Poor decision-making amid a lack of understanding of how to close out a game reared its head again in the deciding matches of the 2000 and 2001 Bledisloe Cup series. Australian captain John Eales stepped in as a substitute kicker and converted a penalty in the final seconds in Wellington in 2000, while loose forward Toutai Kefu's last-gasp try won the bragging rights for Australia in Sydney in 2001. What is often forgotten about the Wellington match is that, just minutes before the end, the All Blacks were leading and near the Australian try line. Rather than holding on to the ball for the win, they kicked to the corner, aiming for another try. The ball was lost, then kicked up field for an All Blacks lineout – which resulted in a turnover and a penalty to Australia. The rest is cup history.

The NZRU introduced coaching programmes at all levels that help facilitate 'developing decision-making in rugby'.[4] Wayne Smith has been at the forefront of this development of player empowerment, 'using a questioning approach and a Game Sense sort of approach',[5] incorporating video analysis to enhance players' individual understanding and collective performance. This approach assisted McCaw's decision-making as captain, which matured markedly to the point where he spearheaded the team to a tight victory in the 2011 RWC final in Auckland.

Whilst the nation held its breath over the slender 8–7 lead going into the last few minutes, McCaw's decision-making came to the fore as the All Blacks held on to the ball tenaciously – forcing the French into a penalty which finally resulted in the trophy returning to the All Blacks 20 years after the inaugural event. As Sir Colin Meads pointed out, McCaw had received a lot of the blame for the loss in the 2007 RWC, however, 'Richie is now a very good captain, but he's grown into it. It doesn't just happen.'

During the 2011 World Cup, McCaw had played the last three key matches after having fractured a bone in his foot, evoking memories of his predecessor Andy Dalton – whose injury had ruled him out of participating in the inaugural 1987 tournament. As he wrote up his experiences, McCaw recalled the thoughts running through his mind at the time: 'The forgotten man, the original captain Andy Dalton . . . sits in the back of my head, ready on playback every time my foot flares. *Don't let that be me.*'[6]

McCaw's determination earned him the sobriquet 'Captain Courageous', for a desire to win that not only surmounted the pain barrier, but saw him play outstanding rugby despite a fundamental injury. Against Australia in the semi-final he was a dominant player, making bone-crunching tackles and then getting to his feet almost instantaneously to tackle the second recipient ball-carrier. It was inspirational leadership by example: the whole team responded by dominating the Wallabies.

McCaw has successfully redefined the openside flanker position despite following in the footsteps of many highly regarded All Blacks who wore the same number. Kel Tremain was the first loose forward to score 100 tries in first-class games and was a great player of his generation, with tremendous anticipation and lethal scoring skills close to the line. Ian Kirkpatrick was an outstanding runner with the ball and also scored over 100 tries in first-class rugby. Waka Nathan, BJ Lochore, Graham Mourie and Michael Jones are just a few of the other outstanding loose forwards New Zealand has produced through the years, yet arguably Richie McCaw has become recognised as our greatest loose forward of all time – he is certainly the most capped. He has had the ability throughout his career to secure possession at the breakdown as well as to adapt to the constantly changing interpretation of the laws of the game in a seamless way.

Statistics describe the longevity of his success at top-level rugby. In 2010 McCaw played his 100th Super Rugby game, made a record-equalling 94th test appearance for his country and became New Zealand's most capped All Blacks captain, having led the side in 57 test matches. He has been named the IRB International Player of the Year a record three times and in 2011 became the first All Black to reach 100 caps. A year later, he also became the first rugby union player to notch up 100 winning tests, having lost only 12 games in his glittering career at that time. By the end of 2013, McCaw had 124 New Zealand caps (second to Colin Meads' 133 games) and had been captain 87 times.

Leadership into the future

In 2013 fellow loose forward Kieran Read was named captain of the All Blacks in place of McCaw, who was on an elective sabbatical. Sir Graham Henry has suggested that Read is also the likely next long-term captain of the All Blacks. On 15 June 2013 Read played his 50th test, coincidentally the All Blacks' 500th, in the second match of the series between New Zealand and France. Read also claimed rugby's top individual honour as 2013 IRB Player of the Year.

Steve Hansen was appointed All Blacks coach after Henry stepped down, following the 2011 RWC win. Hansen was named IRB Coach of the Year for 2012 and 2013, during which time he recorded a 94.6 per cent winning record. His teams have won nearly all their matches – the exceptions to

date being one draw (18–18 with Australia, October 2012) and one loss
(38–21 to England in the final game of the 2012 end-of-year tour). His All
Blacks went undefeated in 2013, winning all 14 matches – the first team
from any country to win all their test matches in the professional era.

The team's final test of that year was a significant illustration of its
commitment to winning. As our interviews have demonstrated, the margin
between victory and defeat can be very small at test level and there is never
any room for complacency – as the lower-ranked but disciplined Irish side
showed them.

The All Blacks' 22–19 second test win against Ireland in 2012 had been
sealed only by a Dan Carter dropped goal in the final seconds. In 2013 the
win also came only in the closing seconds. All Black Ryan Crotty had scored
the last try in the left-hand corner, which Aaron Cruden had to convert for
the win. His first attempt missed, but was declared invalid as the referee
called the Irish for breaking early. Cruden nailed the second attempt to
maintain a 108-year unbeaten record for the All Blacks against Ireland.

The significance of the All Blacks closing out this win was that they had
shown calm self-belief in their decision-making under both scoreboard and
psychological pressure. No one wanted to be in the first All Blacks side to
lose to Ireland. Earlier, the Irish had led 19–0 after 18 minutes, and held a
22–17 lead going into these dying stages. The All Blacks decided to move
the ball some 60 metres up the field to enable the try, winning in the fine
margins that decide success and failure at this level.

Other test nations are once again trying to close the gap on the All
Blacks. It is only through the learning culture of continual improvement
and change that the All Blacks will be able to position themselves for a third
RWC victory, come 2015. The final section of our book presents an analysis
of how those All Blacks can continue their legacy of winning.

PART IV

A STUDY OF WINNING

Success is like anything worthwhile. It has a price. You have to pay the price to win and you have to pay the price to get to the point where success is possible. Most important, you must pay the price to stay there.
— *Vince Lombardi*[1]

KEEPING ON WINNING

We have tried to answer one central question about the All Blacks: why does this team keep on winning? In the introductory section we discussed the historical and cultural factors behind the All Blacks success. New Zealand was one of the few countries in which rugby became a national sport and from the outset there was a wholehearted commitment to winning with a player-driven culture of innovation. Rugby became a central feature of New Zealand's national identity, with a broad cross-section of support throughout New Zealand society. The sporting public demanded success from its rugby teams at school, club, provincial and national level. Tom Johnson gave a personal example of the impact of this sporting culture on his own life, and how it influenced his playing and administrative career.

The emphasis placed on winning resulted in teams being intensively trained from an early age, particularly in schools and club rugby. For the selectors of New Zealand national teams, this meant that, for the most part, they were able to select players with a high degree of technical and tactical competence in their position. At the highest level, however, mastery of the fundamental skills is only the beginning, for most opposition teams will already be competent in these areas. It is the mental side of the game, particularly the leadership of players, in a physical game such as rugby that separates teams at the highest level. As we have seen, the organisational culture of the All Blacks has been at the heart of their success.

Edgar Schein expressed the connection between organisational culture and leadership as 'usually the result of the embedding of what a leader has imposed on a group that has worked out . . . culture is ultimately created, embedded, evolved, and manipulated by leaders'.[1] He also regarded leadership and organisational culture as flip sides of the same coin and stated: 'Leaders will explore the many mechanisms they have available to them to reinforce the adoption of their own beliefs, values and assumptions as the group gradually evolves.'[2]

As the interviews in this book demonstrate, there have been strong elements of both continuity and change in the organisational culture of the All Blacks since 1950. In this concluding section we begin with a summary of the key themes that have emerged. Tom Johnson asks in what ways, if at all, the All Blacks' organisational culture may be applicable outside a sporting context? In particular, he asks what we can learn about leadership from analysing the All Blacks' culture and what will be required for the team to keep on winning. Following Tom's chapter, Geoff Watson discusses the historical context in which rugby developed in New Zealand.

Winning the Rugby World Cup for a third time is the challenge the All Blacks will face in 2015. If they are to win, they will need to do what no other All Blacks team has done: win a World Cup away from home. This is not, however, entirely unprecedented in the history of New Zealand rugby, as Farah Palmer captained the Black Ferns to the Women's Rugby World Cup crown three times away from home. The Black Ferns later won a fourth consecutive World Cup in 2010, in London. Farah will give her perspective on how this was achieved. Much of the material in this book might be subjective, being focused primarily on the perspectives of the players and coaches as to what factors shaped the culture of the team and its on-field performances. Persuasive as these viewpoints may be, they still need to be grounded in demonstrable truth.

In the final chapter of the book, Hugh Morton asks, 'How good are the All Blacks?' with reference to cold, hard facts. He demonstrates that allusions to a 'culture of winning' are no idle boast. They can be verified by statistical analysis of data going back more than 100 years. All Blacks teams know they will win more often than not, indeed they will prevail, on average, seven times out of ten. This does not guarantee victory in any given match, but it gives confidence that, if they perform to their usual standards, the odds and facts are in their favour.

CHAPTER FOURTEEN
WINNING WAYS

DR TOM JOHNSON

KEY SUCCESS FACTORS

We have examined the culture of the All Blacks since the 1960s through the perspectives of 11 leading players and coaches. Everyone has had differing experiences, but some common themes are apparent. First, there has always been a genuine pride in being selected for the All Blacks and in coaching the All Blacks. The symbolic artefact of the All Blacks, the black jersey with the silver fern, has maintained its capacity for inspiring players and instilling pride in performance. The haka has evolved significantly as a ritual, having been peripheral between the 1950s and 1970s, but taken far more seriously from the mid-1980s to the point where it is now one of the first things new All Blacks are taught.

There has been an uncompromising focus on winning and a commitment to maintaining the heritage of All Blacks success. In earlier eras, this sense of pride was sometimes implicit, and on other occasions it was an explicit part of All Blacks culture. Recently, it has become more formalised with incoming players receiving a formal induction in which the All Blacks legacy is spelt out to them. The conscious appeal to the history of the All Blacks has been maintained in recent times by initiatives such as 'Club All Black' in which All Blacks celebrate their connection to their local club by speaking to team members about its heritage and wearing club regalia.[1] This serves to remind players of the wider constituency they represent.

For some teams, an unrelenting focus on winning might be intimidating for new players but, for the most part, the single-minded dedication to winning has been an asset to the All Blacks team. Their legacy of success gives confidence to the team that they are likely to succeed when they take the field. Arguably, it has instilled a self-belief in some inexperienced All Blacks teams that has seen them achieve victories where other teams would fail.

Self-belief, coupled with a refusal to accept defeat (often even to contemplate it as a possibility), means that fear of losing has generally acted as a catalyst for success, rather than being the cause of failure. One often-stated truism in sports psychology is that teams should focus on getting their processes right rather than fixating on a result.[2] Arguably, the All Blacks achieve both. There is an ever-present quest for constant improvement in all elements of preparation: technical, tactical, mental and physical, while simultaneously being driven by an internal drive to win. This core characteristic of the All Blacks is reflected in the academic literature on leadership. Edgar Schein states that 'organisational cultures will vary in strength and stability as a function of the length and emotional intensity of their actual history from the moment they were founded'.[3] The history of the team has had a profound influence on the culture of the All Blacks because it imbues in players a sense of responsibility that they are part of something much bigger than themselves. It is all the more effective because it is not something that is imposed on players from the top down. Rather, the responsibilities of being an All Black are instilled in players by their peers. This influence of senior players is noted by Sir John Kirwan, who represented New Zealand between 1984 and 1994: 'When I first made the All Blacks, the older guys were pretty tough on me, as they were for all newcomers. They said, "You know, if we lose on Saturday, it's your fault" . . . They said, "It's the man in the jersey, not the jersey" . . . That's the whole attitude: take the responsibility first . . . and while that might sound particularly hard, it's actually true.'[4]

The core values of the team – a pride in winning, a willingness to be adaptable, an unquestioned acceptance that the collective good of the team is paramount – have endured despite massive changes in the economic and cultural character of rugby and, at a wider level, New Zealand society.

The transition towards professionalism posed significant challenges for rugby, but at the All Blacks' level they have largely been managed by adapting the core assumptions of the amateur era and grafting onto these the more formalised leadership processes developed during the past decade. The leadership group has superseded the informal 'back of the bus' group of senior players who previously set the standards for the team. This culture, both unchanging and evolving, has encompassed players from all ethnicities. It has developed protocols around drinking alcohol which place recovery as a priority rather than using alcohol as a tool for socialising and letting off steam, as happened in the amateur era.

As Schein argues, an organisation must be prepared to change or modify the way it does things to continue to be successful. The key to maintaining a winning culture has been to use a language and approach that resonated with the values and beliefs of players, thus making the objectives clear cut, and the strategies to achieve the objective likewise easily understood. Pride in the legacy, selection and winning is linked to a learning culture and collective leadership involving coach, captain and senior players.

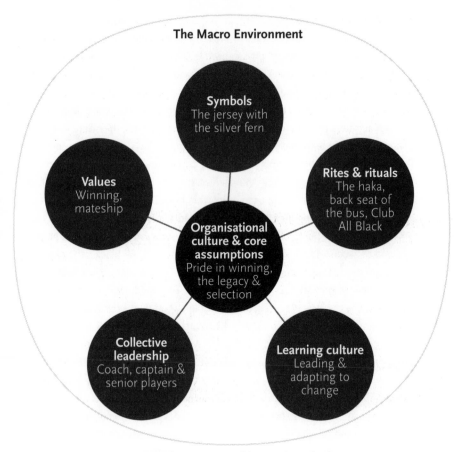

FIGURE 1: Developing a successful organisational culture

- Adapting to the macro environment – political, economic, socio-cultural, technological (PEST).
- Core assumptions – winning is paramount, pride in selection, representing your country, wearing the black jersey and fern, maintaining the legacy. Core assumptions are embedded things as part of instinctive or tacit knowledge.
- Symbols (the jersey with the silver fern) and rites and rituals (haka, back seat of the bus, Club All Black) are artefacts that help reinforce, by symbolism or by process, those values and core assumptions.
- The learning culture and learning leaders – the flip side of culture, they influence the adoption of values (beliefs, attitudes) and encourage a culture of learning that adapts to the macro environment accordingly.

Perhaps the most challenging element of the All Blacks maintaining their winning record in the professional era is keeping their competitive advantage over their opponents, who are often better resourced financially. Achieving this has required both humility and innovation. The team recognised they needed to develop a learning culture. The learning leadership was an admission that they didn't know everything and the commitment to a learning culture was to maximise the use of the collective knowledge of their key players.[5] It requires players and coaches alike to be ruthlessly honest in assessing their performance, and astute analysis to make the micro-changes that will continuously improve a team's performance.

The crushing 18–20 defeat against France in the quarterfinals of the 2007 Rugby World Cup prompted an intense re-examination of the All Blacks' approach, including the unprecedented step of an external review of the team.[6] It is the intellectual acuity of the players and coaches that, historically speaking, has been New Zealand rugby's greatest strength. As Crocombe, Enright and Porter pointed out in their 1991 book *Upgrading New Zealand's Competitive Advantage*, the All Blacks' consistent position at the top or near-top of international rugby was due to their unparalleled rugby knowledge, with new ideas readily accepted. Other teams could match New Zealand in terms of climate, rugby facilities and overall playing numbers, but the ability to be both innovative in their own right, combined with a pragmatic adoption of overseas tactics when they proved superior, has been a consistent feature of New Zealand rugby.[7]

LEARNING CULTURE AND LEARNING LEADERSHIP

We have highlighted how All Blacks leadership has developed a strong team culture that is strategic and geared to handle future change. The following sections introduce specific models and methods, which form the theoretical foundation of leadership development in both sport and business organisations. Because we are living in an increasingly complex and fast-paced world, we do not know precisely what the future holds for us, what tomorrow may bring, except that it will be different and difficult to predict. Amongst the many reasons for this are the effects of the information age, the development of knowledge-based organisations, globalisation, increasing multiculturalism, and inevitably the impact of rapid change.

Schein believes this means organisations and their leaders have to become perpetual learners. However, whilst culture is a great stabilising influence and a conservative force that endeavours to make things predictable and meaningful, it confronts leaders with something of a paradox. If strong cultures are by definition stable, focused, and the basis for effective and successful performance, they are hard to change. Technical advances, competitive activity and other macro-environmental forces mean for organisations to survive and then flourish, they must be prepared to change, or they will not compete. For strong cultures with an adherence to the status quo, a law of diminishing returns can set in if the culture resists change.

The Icarus paradox is a neologism used by Danny Miller to describe a phenomenon he observed in successful businesses that fail abruptly, after a period of apparent success.[8] Businesses bring about their own downfall through these successes by being overconfident and by becoming complacent. Berman, Down and Hill's intensive research on NBA basketball teams in the United States found that, with successful teams, ultimately there came a period of knowledge 'ossification', unless the team was rejuvenated with the appointment of a new coach and/or the infusion of new players.[9]

The All Blacks of the 2004–11 era are an example of the phenomenon of a learning leadership and a learning culture. They were a team that, through collective leadership, brought about change that produced exceptional results, culminating in the winning of the 2011 Rugby World Cup. This was the coaching era of Graham Henry, Wayne Smith and Steve Hansen. Based on the results of the 2012–13 period, this success has been continued by the new head coaching leadership provided by Steve Hansen.

Identifying the problem

Schein, in his advocacy of modern organisations developing a learning culture, also expresses the importance of cultural analysis and reflection as a necessary part of the learning process. In 2004, the All Blacks' coaching leadership considered, after rigorous evaluation, that leadership of the team was one-dimensional, based on pioneer American consultant Frederick Taylor's scientific management theory of one boss and one best way of doing things. This was not a criticism of Tana Umaga, who was captain at the time and a great player who gave of his best as captain: it was recognition that there had to be better ways of leading and achieving the strategic goal of winning.

Solving the problem

Change came during the 2004 Tri-Nations when the coaches, together with mentor Sir Brian Lochore (to whom they threw all their ideas) came up with a number of solutions. This is a good example of problem-solving, which is such a critical part of the culturalisation process. Their solutions became a blueprint for success for the next few years.

A leadership group of senior players was then selected, which was a very different, proactive approach from the past selection of All Blacks teams. Through better alignment, understanding and a common framework, the more empowerment the players had, the better they played. The team developed a philosophy of confronting problems, even though problems cause discomfort. The leadership group did not necessarily like discomfort, but it helped keep an edge. The leadership model had changed to one of dual management, both players and coaches 'managing' the team. There were very few unilateral decisions made. The All Blacks learnt to be more demanding, representing the team, rather than just themselves.

DEVELOPING A LEARNING CULTURE

To recap, organisational culture was defined by Edgar Schein as: 'A pattern of shared basic assumptions learned by a group as it solved its problems of external adaptation and internal integration, which has worked well enough to be considered valid, and therefore to be taught to new members as the correct way to perceive, think and feel in relation to those problems.'[10]

There are a number of consistent factors related to the All Blacks that have endorsed Schein's theory of organisational culture: artefacts and creations, rites and rituals, espoused values and embedded core assumptions.

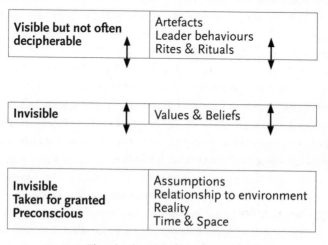

FIGURE 2: Three-level model of organisational culture[11]

Artefacts are the visible, tangible things that represent the first level of culture (seen, heard, touched). They include language, technology, creations, myths, legends, stories, clothing, symbols and are often difficult to decipher. Examples from the All Blacks include the coaches' and captains' behaviours, the black jersey and silver fern, the haka, stories, myths and legends, and the historical winning record.

Espoused values and beliefs are objects, qualities, standards or conditions that satisfy needs and/or act as guides to behaviour. Values are global when it comes to desirable end states or modes of behaviour that underlie attitudinal processes. Behaviour is the manifestation of a person's fundamental values and corresponding attitudes. All Blacks values include pride in selection, pride in the jersey, the need to win and the need to preserve a legacy.

All organisations and teams, when they begin, are faced with the problems of initial survival and adaptation to the external environment and the problems associated with the integration of their internal processes. Both sets of problems involve leadership activities and shared experiences. Shared basic assumptions are the deeply embedded, taken-for-granted behaviours, which are usually unconscious, but constitute the essence of culture. These assumptions are typically so well integrated in the group dynamic that they are hard to recognise from within.

Every new group, as part of its adaptation to the external environment, must develop a shared concept of its mission, goals, strategies, measurements of success and failure, and the correction mechanisms to be applied. The organisation or team must handle its internal relationships with an agreed common language, boundaries for inclusion and exclusion, agreement on how power and status is handled, the development of norms of friendship, acceptance of how rewards and punishment are meted out and how ideology and religion is handled. There must be shared assumptions about truth, reality, time and space, human nature and relationships.

Leaders must have a commitment to 'learning to learn'

Leaders must learn how to handle change in the external environment – and then, how to affect the contingent change in internal relationships whilst ensuring the organisation adapts well to the external changes. As the All Blacks prove, the key to learning is to get feedback and to take the time to reflect, analyse and assimilate the implications of what that feedback has told you. Leaders need to be prepared to try new things around the periphery of the team or organisation, without disrupting the successful core activities. A learning culture must value reflection and experimentation, and must have the resources to do so.

Leaders must have positive assumptions about human nature

Learning implies a desire for survival and improvement, so if leaders start with an assumption that their followers are lazy, it will inevitably become a self-fulfilling prophecy. The team or group will fail as environments change and become more turbulent while technological and global trends cause problem-solving to become increasingly more complex.

Leaders must believe that the environment can be managed

Change in today's world is rapid and can be turbulent compared to previous generations. Leaders must therefore reflect the shared assumption that the environment is, at least to some extent, manageable. Schein contends: 'The more turbulent the environment, the more important it will be for leadership to argue for and show that some level of management of the environment is desirable and possible.'[12]

Leaders must make a commitment to truth through pragmatism and inquiry

A learning culture must contain the shared assumption that solutions to problems will be derived from a deep belief in inquiry and a pragmatic search for truth. Dogmatic, dictatorial or autocratic leadership that prevailed in past years just won't work today. Likewise, wisdom and truth do not reside in one source of knowledge or in one method. The All Blacks of the 2004–11 era collectively solved problems and created strategies and tactics through experimentation, practice, and the contributions by all leaders and team members. Such is the influence of television on top sport that the matches played by international sides are videoed and analysed over and over again for the purpose of improvement.

Leaders must have a positive orientation towards the future

Leaders should be thinking far enough ahead to assess the consequences of different courses of action, but they must also think in terms of the near future to assess whether or not their solutions are working. In rugby terms, for All Blacks leaders and the coaches of Super Rugby or provincial teams, it is about not only planning for the future in terms of resources and results, it is also about ensuring success in the short term or near future.

Leaders must have a commitment to full and open task-relevant communication

A learning culture must accept that information and communication are central to its potential success. Everybody within the team or organisation must be able to communicate with everyone else, but with an acceptance of telling the truth being preferable to any obfuscation. It must be acknowledged that interpersonal openness can cause cross-cultural problems if certain sensitivities are affected. To overcome such barriers and to achieve the open and full task-relevant communication, team members must learn to trust one another, which only comes through the members learning to tell the truth at all times.

Leaders must make a commitment to cultural diversity

Schein states: 'The subcultures in a multicultural task group must value each other enough to learn something of each other's culture and language . . . Creating diversity does not mean letting diverse parts of the system run on their own without coordination.'[13] New Zealand rugby had a bicultural beginning and, like most areas in the world, New Zealand has since become a multicultural society.

Leaders must make a commitment to systemic thinking

Schein believes the learning leader must believe that the world is more intrinsically complex, non-linear, interconnected and over-determined, in the sense that most things are multiply caused.[14] The All Blacks leaders in the 2004–11 era were fully cognisant of the need for systemic thinking and an alignment in all the activities resultant from their learning leadership processes.

Developing learning leadership

Culture creation is usually driven or brought about by the enthusiasm of the leaders. The culture comes from three sources:
- The beliefs, values and assumptions of the leaders
- The learning experience of group members
- The new beliefs, values and assumptions brought in by new members.

Because organisations don't form spontaneously, the direction of the leader(s) is vitally important. Leaders may create the idea, possess the vision and believe the risk is worthwhile. In sporting organisations, the team or group is selected to perform a task of winning, which creates a ready-made group, but that doesn't obviate the need to establish the culture. In business, it is the founding group that raises the money, sets the objectives and goal and takes the risk so that the history of the organisation commences.

Leaders embed and transmit culture

Initially, leader values and assumptions are taught to the group through a process of socialisation, aided immeasurably if the leader is charismatic and confident. The primary embedding mechanisms used by the leader include what the leader pays attention to and measures.

DEVELOPING STRATEGY

Professors Jennifer Chatman and Sandra Cha argue that culture boosts organisational performance when it is strategically relevant, is strong, and emphasises innovation and change.[15] Culture 'works' when it is clear, consistent and comprehensive, particularly during challenging times. Organisational success hinges not on how brilliant, or unique, a strategy is, but on the alignment between culture and strategy, and how clearly employees understand, and how intensely they feel, about their culture.

The reason strong cultures enhance organisational performance is because they improve performance by energising employees or team members – by appealing to their higher ideals and values, and getting them to focus on meaningful goals. Such ideals excite team commitment and effort. Strong cultures boost performance by shaping and coordinating employees' or team members' behaviour. Clearly stated values and norms focus the team members' or employees' attention on organisational priorities that then guide their behaviour and decision-making. They do not require a formal control system.

Strategic management is important because it helps organisations identify and develop a competitive advantage – a significant edge over the competition – in dealing with competitive forces. This is where there are many similarities between a business organisation and a sports team or organisation. The strategic management process involves establishing a vision and the mission ('where you want to go'),[16] and undertaking a resource analysis, a 'SWOT and PEST' analysis ('where have we come from'): strengths, weaknesses, opportunities and threats; political, economic, socio-cultural and technological. Formulating strategic plans focusing on growth, stability or retrenchment requires feedback and ongoing evaluation.

LEADING CHANGE

Change management is one of the most fascinating areas of modern management because change is constant and all leaders are confronted by, at times, complex problems to resolve. The need to change occurs when the leadership perceives some problem(s) that need resolving, rather than a need to modify the culture: 'There is nothing more difficult to carry out, nor more doubtful of success, nor more dangerous to handle than to initiate a new order of things.'[7]

Social psychologist Kurt Lewin's 1947 model is a good one to explain the three stages of change in an organisation. The first stage is unfreezing: creating the motivation to change through disconfirmation. The second stage is one of learning the new concept or standards for change to be introduced – this transformation means the group or organisation must unlearn something, as well as learn something new. The third stage, refreezing, is about internalising the concept into the organisation and the relationships within it. The learning will not stabilise until it is reinforced by actual results.

It is important, firstly, to understand the difference between change and innovation. Change is any alteration to the status quo while innovation is introducing something completely new. To change in more than minor incremental ways, the group must experience enough disequilibrium to force the cognitive processes to experience anxiety. Schein defines the process as having three parts:
- Enough disconfirming data to cause serious discomfort and disequilibrium
- There must be a connection between the disconfirming data and important goals and ideals causing anxiety
- Group members must see the possibility of solving the problem, learning something new, without the loss of identity – a safety factor.

SUMMARY

Culture is more specific than vision in that a good vision engages employees emotionally, by setting up motivating, overarching goals to which they can aspire. Culture operates at the level of daily beliefs and behaviour to translate abstract visions into useful information about how to behave and what decisions and trade-offs to make. In business, an effective culture is closely related to business strategy. Strategy focuses on the specific business objectives such as your target market, the products or services you offer, and how you compete. In sport, it's about winning or improving performance. You cannot craft an organisational culture until you fully develop and articulate your business strategy; strategy must come first.

The first criterion for using culture as a leadership tool is that it must be strategically relevant. It is somewhat ironic that the less formal direction given to employees and/or team members when leading through culture about how to execute strategy, the more ownership they take over their actions and the better they perform. It requires encouragement to becoming perpetual learners and problem-solvers. There is a need for less formal rules to enable full delivery of strategic objectives.

Team members must understand the ultimate strategic goals, and the norms through which they can be successfully achieved. They must care about reaching those goals and what their co-workers will think of them if they don't. Strong norms increase members' clarity about priorities and expectations – and their bonds with one another. Culture empowers employees/team members to think and act on their own in pursuit of strategic objectives, increasing their commitment to those goals.

The second criterion for using culture as a leadership tool is that it has to be strong. What makes culture strong? It has two characteristics: high levels of agreement among group or team members about what's valued; and high levels of intensity about these values. If both are high, a strong culture exists, and if both are low, the culture is not strong at all. Chatman and Cha described three key managerial tools for leveraging culture for performance:
- Recruiting and selecting people for culture fit
- Managing culture through intensive socialisation and training
- Managing culture through the reward system.[18]

Socialisation is the process by which an individual comes to understand the values, abilities, expected behaviours and social knowledge that are essential for assuming an organisational role and participating as an organisation's member. Organisational cultures that are strategically relevant, strong, and emphasise innovation and change can be a powerful force that clarify what is important and coordinate members' efforts without the costs and inefficiencies of close supervision.

Managing culture requires creating a context in which people are encouraged and empowered to express creative ideas and do their very best, while selection, socialisation and rewards should be used as opportunities to convey what's important to organisational members: 'Culture "works" when it is clear, consistent, and comprehensive . . . Organisational culture is too important to leave to chance; use your culture to fully execute your strategy and inspire innovation . . . It is your primary role as a leader to develop and maintain an effective culture'.[19]

Leaders are instrumental in embedding culture in organisations and will explore the many mechanisms they have available to them to reinforce the adoption of their own beliefs, values and assumptions as the group gradually evolves. As the organisation succeeds, the leader's assumptions become shared. The most enlightening fact on leadership to emerge from our interviews is the formal system used by the 2004–11 All Blacks teams. This was a development from different styles of leadership in the past, and recognition of the importance of the previously informal leadership by key players. The leadership of the team (captains and coaches) had accepted the need, in a fast-moving world, to develop a learning culture as recognition of the fact that nobody had the capacity to know everything. So, there was a new commitment to continuous learning and the development of individual problem-solving. The success of these moves is endorsed by the results of the All Blacks between 2004 and 2013.

The management leadership of the All Blacks, particularly during the amateur period, was, by contrast, conservative, traditional and lacking in innovative processes. Whilst there have been periods where glaring mistakes have been made, such as the loss of the 2003 World Cup hosting rights, there have also been successes – again, an example being securing the rights for 2011. New Zealand's winning ethos has always been maintained by at least one sector of its leadership responding positively to the challenges the team confronted.

CHAPTER FIFTEEN
A HISTORY OF WINNING

DR GEOFF WATSON

THE HISTORICAL CONTEXT

By virtue of winning over 70 per cent of their matches, the All Blacks' achievements are at the forefront of New Zealand's sporting history. This chapter firstly explores the reasons rugby became so closely linked to provincial and national identity in New Zealand. It then seeks to explain why winning was so important to so many people, and examines historical factors which assisted in maintaining the winning record.

HISTORICAL FACTORS IN ALL BLACKS SUCCESS

New Zealand is one of the few countries where rugby is the national sport. By specialising in a code which was (and is) a minority sport in many nations, New Zealand has, by accident or design, gained a competitive advantage. Historically, there are only three tier-one nations in which rugby could be regarded as the national sport: South Africa, Wales and New Zealand. In each of these countries, it became the code most closely linked to nation-building.[1] In South Africa, rugby was the chosen sport of the white minority, both Afrikaner and English, and became an expression of Afrikaner nationalism.[2] In Wales, as David Smith observed, an 'educated, urban and professional middle class' keen on promoting the sporting values of public schools found a ready constituency among the growing Welsh industrial working classes.[3] It was only in New Zealand, however, that rugby became the main team sport of both the settler and indigenous peoples and was played throughout the country.

In South Africa black and coloured peoples had little access to rugby, despite some early pockets of interest – and those who did play were restricted to segregated competitions.[4] Moreover, while rugby was strong in South Wales, Martin Johnes suggests football gained support there during the interwar period and the association game was well established in North Wales.[5] In the long term, the nationwide presence of rugby in New Zealand, with its 26 provincial unions and its ability to develop elite players from all peoples, particularly Maori and Pacific Islanders, are important factors in the continued strength of the game. In order to understand how and why this came about, we need to understand the historical context in which the game emerged in Britain before it was transplanted to New Zealand and other countries.

IMPERIAL CURRENTS: THE TRANSFORMATION AND EXPORT OF SPORT IN VICTORIAN BRITAIN

The Victorian era saw profound changes in the form and character of sport.[6] First there was a transition from localised varieties of games to the formal codification of sport by national authorities. Football, previously played according to localised rules (and frequently banned by rulers), became divided into three principal codes: the Football Association (FA), established in 1863, oversaw the emergence of a game primarily characterised by dribbling and passing; the Rugby Football Union (RFU), established in 1870, administered a handling-dominated game; the Northern Union (now known as Rugby League), founded in 1895, initially followed Rugby Union rules, but later developed its present form of 13 players per team and a distinct 'play-the ball' method.[7]

These sports proved popular with the public, especially industrial workers in the cities, and with improvements in railways and working conditions, professional sporting competitions with scheduled home and away fixtures emerged in the form we see today. Yet although the Victorian era saw the emergence of the professional sportsman, amateurism became the dominant ideology in sport. It was applied in different ways in different codes, but its key principles were that sport should not be played with the expectation of gaining material reward; that players should respect opponents and officials alike; and that sport should be played in an entertaining manner. In practice, however, amateurism was an ideology that allowed the middle and upper classes to determine the conditions under which the working classes were admitted to sport.[8] Arguably, the RFU's insistence on retaining rugby's amateur status worked to New Zealand's advantage because the game remained a niche sport in many countries such as Argentina, the United States and Australia. Had New Zealanders chosen to adopt a code which became professional in the nineteenth century, such as football, as their national sport, it is unlikely they would have enjoyed the success they have in rugby because they simply would not have had the resources to compete.

These changes reflected underlying movements in the relationship between sport and society. During the Victorian era, sport began to be linked to promoting social values. Previously a form of recreation, it came to be seen as training for life – something which taught the value of teamwork and the unconditional acceptance of authority.[9] Beginning with Thomas Arnold's tenure as principal of Rugby School between 1828 and 1842 – it should be noted Arnold himself had little time for games, but many ex-pupils of Rugby School were keen sportsmen and went on to become headmasters, teachers and clergy – these values were inculcated in British public schools and universities. With the significant expansion of the middle classes in this period,[10] demand for this type of schooling, with its focus upon games, increased and consequently the constituency of sport expanded.

By the last quarter of the nineteenth century, sport had gained the support of the educational, religious – in particular, the notion of 'muscular Christianity' which saw sport as a means of spreading the Christian message among the urban working and middle classes – and commercial establishments, particularly the owners of large workplaces, and publicans. The rise of the middle classes was especially significant. Any code with pretensions to being a national sport needed their support. If a sport's catchment was concentrated among the upper classes, it had money and influence, but not numbers. If its support was concentrated in the working classes, it would have numbers, but not money and influence. However, if a sport had support from significant sections of the upper, middle and working classes, then it would have money, numbers and influence. The reason football became the 'people's game' in Britain was because of its cross-class appeal.[11] In England, rugby began as a game played by the upper and middle classes, but by the late 1870s its appeal extended to working-class communities in Yorkshire and Lancashire. Players from these regions dominated the successful England teams of the early 1890s, but when disputes over proposals for 'Broken Time' payments (where players who had to take time off work to play a match would receive reimbursement for lost wages) resulted in the formation of the separate Northern Union the strength of English rugby declined significantly.[12]

As we shall see, rugby in New Zealand gained a foothold among the urban middle classes, from which it extended its appeal to the working classes. Related to the above, sports teams became seen as a representation of their communities, something especially evident in the way the British male working classes supported their football teams in all codes. By extension, the sporting prowess of a group, be it school, province or country, was seen as a reflection of its physical and moral development.[13] The suggestion that sportspeople are, and ought to be, role models (a popular albeit problematic notion) can also be traced to this period. These sporting values and the games through which they were inculcated were transplanted throughout the British Empire, including New Zealand.[14]

FORMATION OF RUGBY IN NEW ZEALAND CIRCA 1870–1904

What were the key characteristics of the New Zealand society into which rugby was established between 1870 and the early 1900s? First, it was a period of massive population growth. Between 1840 and 1911, the population of New Zealand increased tenfold – from between 60,000 and 100,000 in 1840 to 1,058,308 in 1911.[15] The vast majority of these newcomers were of European ancestry, the European population increasing from 254,928 in 1871 (one year after the earliest recorded rugby game in New Zealand) to 1,005,585 in 1911. In some places and in some times, single males comprised the vast majority of the European population. Many of them were transient, moving to where the work was, and in rugby terms this meant that a number of clubs established in rural areas folded after a few seasons' existence.[16] Some have interpreted the rise of rugby as a consequence of the appeal of such a physical game among these men, but this view must be qualified by the fact that the early impetus for rugby came from towns where, by the 1880s, the gender balance tended to be more even.[17]

Secondly, it was a period of rapid transformation, both in the environment – vast tracts of which were being converted from wilderness into pasture – and in the nature of society, which became more centralised and specialised.[18] Much of this environmental transformation came at the expense of Maori who, in the space of just over half a century, went from exercising sovereignty over most of New Zealand to having most of their land alienated and their population reduced from approximately 100,000 in pre-European times to 42,113 in 1896.[19]

Thirdly, it was a society which valued 'progress', which was generally equated with population growth, improvements in communication and the formation of new settlements.[20] The ability of a town to offer recreation to its citizens was a measurable yardstick of progress. *The Manawatu Herald* of 15 April 1879 commented: 'The town of Ashhurst appears to be growing rapidly. One of the latest signs of civilisation is the formation of a [rugby] Football Club.'[21] Greg Ryan cautions that the allegedly rapid progress of rugby has been overstated.[22] By 1904 there were approximately 7000 registered adult players, a relatively modest figure.[23] Given that New Zealand's population has expanded fivefold since 1901, the equivalent figure in today's terms would be 35,000 players – far fewer than the 149,978 players actually registered in 2012.[24]

The game developed unevenly throughout New Zealand, being strongest in the main centres and larger towns, but what can be said is that it did develop in a more systematic way than other sports, and that many New Zealanders developed an emotional investment in rugby, which gave it a resonance beyond the sporting arena. The commitment to progress fostered another self-perceived virtue: pragmatism. Visitors to New Zealand during the era of the Liberal government (1891–1912) remarked that the extensive changes introduced – including compulsory arbitration of labour disputes; acquisition of large estates and a generous loan scheme to small farmers; granting women the right to vote and the world's first old-age pension – were not discussed in philosophical terms, they were simply presented as doing what was necessary and just.[25] During New Zealand's transition from the disorder of early 'frontier society' and conflict between Maori and Pakeha to a more ordered, centralised society, rugby was a symbol of collective effort. It is possible that the collective nature of rugby also resonated among Maori. Clubs such as the Aotea Sports Club near Dannevirke, which was founded in 1902, provided a visible symbol of Maori survival.[26]

Why was it that rugby became established as New Zealand's leading team sport between 1870 and 1904? To adapt a well-known rugby phrase, it had on its side the three Ps: patronage, provincialism and populism. Patronage refers to the support rugby obtained from the political, commercial, religious and educational establishment. Provincialism denotes the way in which rugby became the leading expression of provincial identity in New Zealand after the provincial governments were abolished in 1876. Populism refers to the capacity of rugby to provide social recognition to its players and communities.

Patronage from the educational establishment was a significant factor in the rise of rugby. It was not always the dominant sporting code in New Zealand. In the formative years of colonial society (1840–70), cricket was the first team sport established. The earliest inter-provincial matches occurred in 1860, while horse racing was undoubtedly 'the people's choice' when it came to popular recreation. Relatively speaking, rugby was a latecomer among football codes in New Zealand.[27] The Christchurch Football Club, established in 1862, played a version of football closer to Eton rules and Victorian rules (which had been introduced into New Zealand by miners coming from Victoria in the 1860s).[28] Crucially, rugby became the code of choice among the educational establishment. The earliest recorded game of rugby occurred on 14 May 1870 at Nelson, when Nelson Town played Nelson College. Although not many students went to secondary school – there were only nine secondary schools in New Zealand in 1870 – many of those who did became keen exponents of the game and formed clubs so that they might keep playing after they finished school.[29] Moreover, ex-pupils of rugby-playing schools in England also played a leading role in forming clubs.[30] They were keen proselytisers of the game, willing to freely devote their time to play and administer the sport. It was via schools of this type, such as Te Aute College, which won the Hawke's Bay senior championship in 1883 and 1884, that many prominent Maori players, such as Tom Ellison, entered rugby. By contrast, football was unable to gain a foothold in schools and remained primarily an adult, urban sport until the second half of the twentieth century, while rugby league, founded in 1908 in New Zealand, was actively barred from schools.[31]

If schools provided the foundation for rugby, inter-provincial rivalry was the catalyst for clubs to adopt its rules. Rugby received a significant boost when Auckland embarked on a national tour in 1875. Canterbury and Otago adopted rugby rules to meet the visitors, and it became the game of choice for young men wanting to represent their province. As Geoff Vincent has observed, after the provincial governments were abolished in 1876, sport became the principal everyday expression of these otherwise arbitrary entities.[32] Association football, compared to rugby, had infrequent provincial matches – the earliest recorded inter-provincial match occurred in 1890, 19 years after the first inter-provincial rugby game; and between 1892 and 1900 only four provinces (Auckland, Canterbury, Otago and Wellington) contested the Brown Shield.[33] Rugby therefore offered greater opportunities for provincial representation and for the social and peer esteem this provided to young men. Arthur Swan records at least 30 representative matches between 1871 and 1880. From the 1880s, rugby also offered the opportunity to compete against touring teams and occasional overseas tours. Canterbury and Wellington were the first provinces to found provincial rugby unions, in 1879, and by 1890 there were 18 provincial rugby unions.[34]

In addition to patronage from the educational establishment, rugby also received approval from New Zealand's commercial, religious and 'popular' establishment. The involvement of the urban middle and working classes provided the principal constituency of rugby from the 1880s. It would be an exaggeration to say New Zealand was classless, indeed rugby became established at the same time as the so-called 'long depression' was heightening concerns about class privilege in New Zealand (especially the concentration of large quantities of land in the hands of a few owners), but what can be said is that people from all classes played rugby, and in some cases played alongside each other.[35] Also significant is that rugby gained support among both the 'reputable' and 'disreputable' elements of society. As in Britain, churches supported the game as an expression of 'muscular Christianity' and many clergymen, such as the Reverend C.C. Harper, took an active role in the game. Jock Phillips argues rugby underwent something of a 'civilising process' in the 1880s and 1890s, the support of the establishment turning it into a respectable game in response to criticisms that it was promoting 'larrikinism'.[36]

The working classes were not excluded from rugby, however. Indeed, many workplace-based teams were formed, such as those based around railway workshops, thereby incorporating the section of society the historian James Belich refers to as 'crew cultures'.[37] Consequently, Phillips observes, rugby developed an 'official culture' reflected in high-minded statements about the game promoting civilised, manly values, and an 'unofficial culture' in which rugby provided its participants with an opportunity to partake in a physical game followed by drinking and 'smoke concerts'.[38] More than other sports it became integrated into folk culture in New Zealand, developing its own rites and rituals – including songs such as 'On The Ball', written by Edward Secker in 1887.[39] This unofficial culture was enthusiastically supported by publicans, who saw patronising rugby as a fruitful way of ensuring custom of their premises. For many years women were excluded from rugby as players, a proposal for a women's touring rugby team in 1891 falling through after considerable public criticism. However, they were present as spectators from the outset.[40] Although not couched in such terms at the time, long before a national union was established in 1892, a pathway for players was established, comprising school, club and provincial rugby.

Populism was the third pillar of rugby's success. In its political manifestation, populism is a brand of politics whereby a politician and/or party present themselves as representing the interests of the people against a privileged elite.[41] In New Zealand, a narrative emerged in which rugby was 'the people's game' and in which the underdog New Zealander took on the world, overcoming the obstacles of small population and geographical isolation. In his analysis of sport in New Zealand, Belich identifies a New Zealand sporting 'populism'.[42] By this he means that sport, in particular rugby, offered a means of advancement to both individuals and groups. At an individual level, a male seeking to make a name for himself could gain esteem as a player, coach or administrator in rugby. At a collective level, sport was a means for communities and, at an international level, New Zealand, to enhance their peer esteem. Belich's notion of a 'populist compact' whereby New Zealanders expected governments to provide everyone with an opportunity to prosper – to 'get on' in the phrase of the day, so that those willing to work hard would be rewarded – is applicable to the expectations rugby followers expected of their administrators.[43]

At a practical level, the importance attached to victory meant that New Zealand rugby, while not immune from selection quirks, was generally meritocratic. Provincial teams generally picked their best available players, irrespective of social class or ethnicity, to give themselves the best possible chance of victory. Rugby gave New Zealanders a common point of reference, functioning as a conversation-starter for people otherwise unfamiliar with each other. It attracted support from outside its own pool of players – for example, 6000 to 7000 spectators watched a match between Kaikorai and Alhambra in Dunedin in 1890.[44] Scott Crawford has observed that rugby was one of the few areas where a generally Calvinistic New Zealand society displayed outward emotion.[45] Many New Zealanders developed an emotional investment in rugby, irrespective of whether they played the game. Consequently, the rugby-minded sporting public was a large constituency. They may not have understood the finer points of the game, but they knew good rugby when they saw it and decried poor performances.

The integration of rugby into an emerging New Zealand national identity was another expression of populism. Historian Richard Holt, citing Clifford Geertz, argued sport is 'a story we tell ourselves about ourselves'.[46] Crucially, in rugby, unlike cricket, a narrative of New Zealand success emerged from the outset. Between 1884 and 1904, New Zealand touring teams (including the 1888/89 Native Team) won 114, lost 25 and drew six of their 145 matches, a winning percentage of 79. Touring teams to New Zealand between 1882 and 1904 won 26, lost 37 and drew five of their matches, a winning record of 38 per cent, and only once in four international games in New Zealand between 1884 and 1904 was a New Zealand national team defeated by a touring opponent.[47] By contrast, New Zealand cricket teams were often comprehensively defeated by international teams, winning three, losing seven and drawing one of 11 international matches between 1894 and 1903, while touring teams in New Zealand between 1863 and 1904 won 81, drew 33 and lost only 10 of 124 games.[48]

When New South Wales, the first rugby team to tour New Zealand, visited in 1882, 'It was expected our sides would not be a match for the visitors', yet the tourists won four and lost three of their matches, including two comprehensive losses to Auckland.[49] When a New Zealand team toured Australia in 1884, they won all eight of their matches, scoring 167 points and conceding only 17. Despite being selected eight years before the formation of the NZRFU, the team was unambiguously referred to as 'the New Zealand football team' in newspapers, and reports of the tour noted the strength of the game in New Zealand.[50] An account of the first match against New South Wales, won 21–2 by the visitors, noted that 'with the exception of Robertson and Braddon, all the New Zealanders learnt their football in New Zealand'.[51] The success of the team boosted an emerging feeling of national prowess. The *Auckland Star* approvingly reproduced statements from a *Sydney Telegraph* article of 14 June 1884 which proclaimed a 'natural affinity between the climate of New Zealand and the robust character of this outdoor sport. It has taken hold of the youth of the colony.'[52] Objectively, such statements might be disputed, but what was important was that they were widely perceived to be true.

Maori participation was of significant symbolic value because it provided a national story of rugby as the game which united classes and races.[53] Certainly, there were some high-profile Maori players in rugby's formative years. Jack Taiaroa and Joe Warbrick were star players from the 1884 team. The 1888/89 Native Team, the majority of whom were Maori, also performed very creditably. Given that they were selected from a relatively small pool of players and played against the best players in British rugby (because they toured prior to the 'split' in 1895), their achievement of winning 49 of 74 games in Europe bears favourable comparison with the 1905 team.[54] Tom Ellison, who played in the Native Team, captained the first New Zealand team selected by the Rugby Union in 1893 and Davy Gage captained the New Zealand team against Queensland in 1896.

Beneath these high-profile examples, however, the extent of Maori participation in rugby is difficult to determine. Greg Ryan has observed that the vast majority of identifiably Maori representative players in the late nineteenth century came from a small number of schools, particularly Te Aute College.[55] Moreover, because most Maori at the time lived in rural areas, where the development of rugby was spasmodic, their opportunities for participation were limited. University of Otago's Dr Brendan Hokowhitu, a specialist in Indigenous Studies, suggests rugby was a 'contradictory site where Maori have both gained and lost mana'.[56] On the one hand, Maori gained recognition for their skills as rugby players[57] and, as we shall see, played a leading role developing the New Zealand game. On the other hand, in coming under the control of the Rugby Union, they could not control their destiny. Later, the game became linked to tribal identity, with leaders such as Sir Apirana Ngata and Wiremu Ratana encouraging games as a means of promoting Maori identity.

Maori participation in rugby also played an important role in developing the key rituals and symbols associated with the New Zealand national rugby teams: the haka, the silver fern and the All Blacks uniform.[58] Performed in Maori culture on occasions of social significance, versions of the haka in rugby can be dated back to at least the 1888/89 Native Team and possibly the 1884 team.[59] Until the 1980s, performances of the haka were generally restricted to touring teams and different teams performed various versions of the haka until the 'Ka Mate' version, associated with Ngati Toa, became standard.

The use of the fern dates back to the 1884 team, which wore a gold fern with their blue uniforms, but it was the Native Team who were the first New Zealand team to wear a black jersey with a silver fern. Tom Ellison instigated the NZRFU's adoption of the black jersey with a silver fern as the uniform of New Zealand national teams and also authored the first canonical text in New Zealand rugby: *The Art of Rugby Football*, which was published in 1902. While the name 'All Black' is often said to have originated during the 1905 tour, Ron Palenski's research makes it clear that the name is of New Zealand origin, being, in lower-case form, initially associated with Wellington teams of the 1880s and, in a national context, with the New Zealand team that played New South Wales in 1893.[60]

PREPARATION, COMBINATION, INNOVATION AND ADAPTATION: ACCOUNTING FOR THE SUCCESS OF NEW ZEALAND TEAMS

The success of New Zealand teams was often attributed to their physical conditioning, teamwork and scientific approach to the game. Social historian Geoff Vincent notes that Canterbury players in the 1870s were exhorted to train hard so that they might be in peak condition to represent their province – and those perceived to be slacking in this regard were publicly admonished.[61] Australian newspapers commended the 1884 team for their well-developed physiques and training, comments which were endorsed by William Milton, the team captain.[62] For many years, an alleged distinction between New Zealand and British rugby was that, whereas the British played rugby to keep fit, New Zealanders would get fit to play rugby. The primacy of the team was a feature of New Zealand teams from the outset. Match reports on the 1884 team commended their 'most unselfish' play and the quality of their passing and backing up.[63]

Significantly, New Zealand rugby was a site of innovation from its earliest stages. At a time when many New Zealanders still referred to Britain as 'home' and adhered to the form of cricket, football and hockey as played in England, rugby was a place of experimentation. Tom Ellison and J. Morris Mackenzie asserted the British team that toured in 1888 and the opponents the Native Team encountered on their tour of 1888/89 (with the possible exception of the Yorkshire and All England teams) revealed little that was new, aside from the possibilities of back play after heeling the ball out from the scrum.[64]

Observers of New Zealand rugby identified the development of specialist positions, especially the 2-3-2 scrum with its 'wing forward' and the five-eighths system, as a key element in its success. Ellison, in *The Art of Rugby Football*, observed: 'The placement of each man in a particular place is characteristic of the New Zealand style of play, and goes a long way to account for our present proficiency.'[65] The 2-3-2 scrum, comprising two hookers in the front row, three middle rankers (called pivot and pivot supports) and two back rankers, was a distinctive feature of the New Zealand game until it was outlawed in 1931. The eighth forward, the wing forward, who followed the ball through the scrum and then harassed the opposition halfback, was another New Zealand innovation.

Ellison may not have originated this position – references to it appear at least as early as 1884,[66] but he is credited with refining its role in relation to the 2-3-2 scrum formation. Introduced during the 1892 season, he recalled it required 'two months' hard drilling at the gymnasium' before his teammates grasped the concept. Morrie Mackenzie, citing W.G. Garrard, credited the Alhambra club from Otago with developing the five-eighths role[67] – a player positioned between the halfback and the rest of the backs (who were generally referred to as three-quarters) – and asserts the superiority of this system was demonstrated when Alhambra, Dunedin's champion club, defeated Christchurch's champion club Merivale 7–1 in October 1890. Later, historians of rugby in New Zealand would emphasise these innovations were player-driven. Mackenzie described the pre-1905 period as 'a vigorous pioneering age when men's minds were highly receptive to change, experiment and innovation'.[68] Because there 'were no old hands' they 'had to coach themselves', so were 'not cursed with outworn traditions'.

1905 AND BEYOND: REINFORCING AND REINVENTING WINNING RUGBY

So far, we have alluded only briefly to what some perceive as a crucial foundation story of New Zealand rugby: the so-called 'Originals' 1905 tour of Britain, Europe and North America. This is because recent scholarship has confirmed that the key features of New Zealand rugby – the playing formation of the 2-3-2 scrum, wing forward and five-eighths system; specialist positions, connection to community, provincial and national identity; key rituals and symbols such as the haka, black jersey with a silver fern and identifying name 'All Blacks' and a pattern of winning – were evident prior to the tour.[69]

The tour was significant in that it was the first officially sanctioned New

Zealand team to tour Britain and that they gained a measure of respect from sections of the British media. Even here, however, the legacy of the team is more complex than legend allows. Greg Ryan and Caroline Daley have demonstrated that the All Blacks were criticised as much as they were praised, especially for their allegedly rough play, the 'obstructive' nature of the wing forward (the position occupied by their captain Dave Gallaher) and their purportedly overzealous emphasis on winning and playing to the letter of the law.[70] The legacy of the tour was also a mixed one. Certainly Premier Richard Seddon and William Pember Reeves, New Zealand's Agent General in Britain, seized on the performances of the team to extol the virtues of New Zealand's purportedly healthy lifestyle. Seddon also associated himself with the team for political benefit. On the other hand, the £8908/10/4 profit the NZRFU received from the tour served as a catalyst for the introduction of rugby league into New Zealand because it highlighted how profitable rugby league was in comparison to the daily allowance of three shillings the players had been receiving whilst on tour.[71] The significance of the tour lies in the way that it reinforced the standing of the game of rugby and its link to national identity. While the strengths of the team – the high level of fitness and skilled play by backs and forwards alike – were already part of New Zealand rugby, the team displayed these skills to a wider audience and gained extensive publicity for them.

Whichever reasons are advanced for All Blacks success, the notion that they prevailed because they had a preponderance of farmers has little foundation in fact, as Lincoln University historian Greg Ryan has demonstrated.[72] The 1905 team, lauded for demonstrating the virtues of New Zealand manhood, included only three farmers and Ryan's research has demonstrated that the vast majority of All Blacks have come from New Zealand's urban areas. There have been periods, such as the 1960s, when a number of long-serving forwards were farmers (when farming was a relatively profitable, state-supported activity), but even in these periods the forward packs were statistically as likely to include urban professionals as they were farmers.[73] It is true that many distinguished players have come from rural areas, and that a number of players have grown up in country areas and small towns before moving to the city and being selected for the All Blacks. Arguably the most significant factor in the social composition of New Zealand teams is that they are a merit-based team drawn from a cross-section of society.

The core qualities of successful All Blacks teams? Collective leadership by senior players; specialisation and teamwork; dedication to physical fitness; pride in the team's history; a commitment to winning; and an unquestioning acceptance of the primacy of the team over the individual have remained central to All Blacks teams since their inception.[74] Sir Terry McLean's comment on the 1968 All Blacks team is representative of many such observations: 'Within the average All Black team . . . there develops, from the mere act of creation . . . a boundless pride of team. At the necessary times, discipline within this group is never demanded, it is a willing contribution by every man to the team ideal.'[75]

Tellingly, Sir Colin Meads, popularly portrayed as epitomising the uncomplicated and physically uncompromising farmer purportedly characteristic of New Zealand rugby, emphasised the intellectual skills of successful All Blacks teams. Accounting for New Zealand's defeats against South Africa in 1970 and the British Lions in 1971, he did not assert there was any lack of 'mongrel' in the team, rather he expressed concern at a 'decline in the capacity of New Zealand players to think about the game', pointing out that the best teams he had played in during the 1960s were full of thinking players.[76]

While these qualities help explain the winning record of the team, they do not guarantee victory in and of themselves. The playing record of the team has fluctuated. For many years South Africa could rightly lay claim to rugby's 'world crown', remaining unbeaten in a test series from 1896 to 1956, when they were beaten by New Zealand. There have also been periods of lower success rates, such as 1926 to 1935 when they won fewer than 50 per cent of their test matches; 1946 to 1950 when their winning ratio was 50 per cent; and the 1970s when their winning percentage was around 65.[77] For the most part, however, their winning percentage has remained at over 70 and, for the past decade, has exceeded 85, a remarkable achievement in the era of professionalism.

PLAYING UNDER PROTEST: THE CHALLENGES OF SOUTH AFRICA AND FEMINISM

From a historical perspective, the most remarkable characteristic of rugby is its enduring status as a central feature of New Zealand's national identity, despite massive changes in wider society. While it has retained the support of at least a working majority of the New Zealand public, its position has never gone unchallenged. The sporting-minded public is an engaged constituency who will withdraw their support from the game when they are dissatisfied. The three most significant challenges rugby has encountered are the controversy surrounding sporting contact with South Africa; the criticism of rugby as supporting and promoting male chauvinism, conformity and homophobia; and the professionalisation of the game.

Whereas present-day matches between New Zealand and South Africa are politically uncontroversial, All Blacks versus Springbok clashes in the 1970s and 1980s divided New Zealanders to an unprecedented degree. Contact with South Africa posed two significant questions for New Zealand rugby. First, was it worth compromising New Zealand's pride in the All Blacks being a truly multi-racial, merit-based team in order to take on South Africa for the mythical world crown? Secondly, was it worth compromising New Zealand's self-image as a good international citizen by continuing to play against South Africa in the 1970s and 1980s, after world opinion had largely turned against such contact? For the best part of 70 years, New Zealand's rugby administrators answered both questions in the affirmative, omitting identifiably Maori players from New Zealand teams who toured South Africa in 1928, 1949 and 1960, and continuing to play against South Africa despite increasing protest from 1960.

The racial issues of playing South Africa were evident from the outset. When South Africa first toured New Zealand in 1921 and played a New Zealand Maori team, controversy occurred after a South African correspondent asserted the actions of European spectators cheering on the Maori against 'members of their own race' had disgusted the South Africans.[78] Seven years later, two first-choice All Blacks, Jimmy Mill and George Nepia, were excluded from the 1928 team to South Africa. There were further protests when South Africa toured New Zealand in 1937, when some Maori opposed welcoming the team, and when Maori players were omitted from the 1949 team to South Africa. However, it was the decision to exclude Maori players from the 1960 team which promoted mass protest amongst significant sections of Maori and Pakeha communities, the Citizens All Black Tour Association (CABTA) gaining over 150,000 signatures in support of its 'No Maoris, No Tour' stance. Public opinion turned against compromising with South Africa and a proposed tour of South Africa in 1967 was cancelled when it became clear Maori players would not be included. Three Maori players and one Samoan player were included in the 1970 team which toured South Africa, but by the mid-1970s world opinion on sporting contacts with South Africa was changing.

Rather than demanding South Africa change the way it selected its sports teams, the anti-apartheid movement demanded South Africa itself be isolated from sport until apartheid was abolished – 'no normal sport in an abnormal society'. Protesters in New Zealand were becoming more militant. The proposed South African tour of New Zealand in 1973 was cancelled partly on security grounds and partly because South Africa would not agree to hold multi-racial trials. When the All Blacks toured South Africa in 1976, New Zealand became subjected to vigorous criticism and more than 20 African and Arab nations withdrew from the Olympic Games in Montreal.[79]

Against this background of mounting international criticism and increasing domestic tension over race relations, the 'Springbok Tour' of New Zealand in 1981 resulted in unprecedented levels of violence, with more than 150,000 New Zealanders taking part in protests against the tour.[80] As we have seen, the rugby community was itself divided, with then captain Graham Mourie declaring himself unavailable to play against South Africa, as did mainstay centre Bruce Robertson. When the NZRFU proposed another tour of South Africa in 1985, it was stopped by an injunction brought by two lawyers reportedly linked with rugby clubs who successfully argued that the proposed tour was contrary to the NZRFU's own constitution, specifically their obligation to foster and promote rugby. The response of some players was to arrange a private tour of South Africa under the name 'the Cavaliers' in 1986, an action which further divided New Zealand rugby.

When South Africa played the All Blacks at Eden Park in 2013, there were no political undertones and it is easy to forget that just over 30 years ago that ground, and its surrounding suburbs, were the site of pitched battles between police and protesters. For many of the interviewees in this book, South Africa was a defining moment in their rugby experiences, forcing them to make choices which risked alienating them from their rugby peers and the wider community.

Changing attitudes towards South Africa reflected wider changes in society. By the mid-1960s and early 1970s a new generation, often university educated, were challenging society's values in a variety of areas, including women's rights, New Zealand's participation in the Vietnam War and attitudes towards the environment. Rugby, as the sport most closely identified with the 'establishment', came under increasing criticism. Former All Black Chris Laidlaw's 1973 book *Mud In Your Eye* criticised the conformist culture of rugby and the excessive expectations parents placed on young players. All Blacks, once venerated, were increasingly seen as representatives of a racist game.[81] While some women continued to support their children playing the game, others challenged expectations they would provide a laundry and taxi service for players and the sexist attitudes reinforced by rugby's popular culture. As players and supporters, women remained very much on rugby's periphery. Wives and partners of players tended to be excluded from after-match functions until the 1980s when, partly as a result of pressure from two wives of leading players, Trecha Haden and Pip Dalton, the NZRFU adopted a more inclusive approach.[82]

Historically, the attitude of the NZRFU towards women's rugby has been at best ambivalent and at worst outright discouraging. There were occasional games of women's rugby prior to the 1980s, but it was not until 1980 that the first inter-provincial women's match occurred. Even then, it was not until 1992 that the NZRFU accepted responsibility for women's rugby in New Zealand.[83] Despite the success of the Black Ferns team at international level – they won four successive Women's Rugby World Cups in 1998, 2002, 2006 and 2010 and won 90 per cent of their international matches between 1989 and 2012 – resourcing of women's rugby has been limited in comparison to the men's game.[84] Indeed, the NZRU (formerly the NZRFU) scrapped the 2010 women's National Provincial Championship on financial grounds, despite the Black Ferns having a far superior record in World Cups to the All Blacks. The inclusion of rugby sevens in the 2016 Olympic Games has, however, benefited women's rugby, with the leading women's sevens players being contracted by the NZRU in 2013 – the first time any women rugby players have been professionally contracted.

CHANGE AND CONTINUITY IN THE PROFESSIONAL ERA

Rugby was one of the last team sports to become professional and this has posed significant challenges for the game in New Zealand. Rugby formally became professional in 1995, but commercialism had been an increasingly prominent element of the game since the 1980s. The Rugby World Cup, first hosted by New Zealand and Australia in 1987, highlighted the commercial potential of rugby. This made the game an attractive acquisition for Rupert Murdoch's subscriber television network, which became the dominant provider of live sport during the 1990s when it acquired the rights to British association football and American football, among other sports. On the positive side, the money from Sky Television enabled the union to retain its leading players and lessen the chance that they would be enticed to rival codes such as league, which had recruited a growing number of All Blacks during the late 1980s and early 1990s. On the other hand, it soon became evident that the NZRFU could not match the remuneration overseas clubs could offer its players, and a growing number of players chose to play overseas. Moreover, although the newly formed Super 12 (now Super 15 or Super Rugby) competition was initially very popular among fans, its spectator appeal has fluctuated and many New Zealanders were concerned that the competition was undermining the 'traditional' backbone of the game, the National Provincial Championship (NPC) – although this in itself is a relatively recent competition, having started in 1976.

In contrast to the amateur era, when All Blacks held full-time jobs and, sporting skills aside, were everyday members of society, professionalism changed the perception of All Blacks and leading rugby players. They were now paid at a level far higher than the average wages of their peers and were increasingly depicted as celebrities whose private lives were discussed in women's magazines as well as the sports section of newspapers. The gap between the salaries of leading players and the average wage in New Zealand reflected wider trends of growing inequalities in society, and the more individualistic culture encouraged by economic liberalisation and 'user pays' policies in education and health.[85] To some degree, these changes made professionalism more legitimate to the public because they promoted the notion that individuals were entitled to be rewarded for their talent. Somewhat paradoxically, the negotiating power of rugby players has been greatly strengthened by the New Zealand Rugby Players' Association, which has successfully used collective bargaining to improve players' incomes and employment conditions at a time when the union movement as a whole has experienced a significant decline in numbers and influence since the Employment Contracts Act was instituted in 1991.[86] When the All Blacks threatened to boycott the 2003 World Cup unless their demands for better bonuses were met, the NZRFU acceded to their request and there was no significant public backlash against the players.

At a playing level, professionalism was a mixed blessing. On the one hand, the All Blacks had long prided themselves on their essentially professional approach to training and playing. Indeed, it was their perception that they were being expected to produce professional performances while receiving no income from the game that drove player opposition to amateurism.[87] On the other hand, some characteristics of the amateur era – notably binge drinking after games – were unsuitable for the professional era because players were now playing rugby for 10 months every year. Moreover, the practices of the amateur era – visiting schools and engaging with communities – came to be seen as good business practice and players were expected to be role models off the field. With players now receiving much higher incomes and media taking a much greater interest in their off-field activities, indiscretions which had previously gone unreported were now public fodder.

The professional era coincided with significant changes in the ethnic composition of New Zealand. In 1951, 93.3 per cent of New Zealanders were classified as European, 5.96 per cent as Maori and 'other' peoples (Asian and Polynesian) comprised only 0.74 per cent of the population.[88] By 2013, Europeans comprised 74 per cent of the population, Maori 14.9 per cent, Pacific peoples 7.4 per cent and Asian 11.8 per cent.[89] The composition of the All Blacks was also changing. By the early 2000s, Maori and Pasifika players comprised 56 per cent of the players in Super 12 franchises and 57 per cent in NPC teams[90] and at least seven of the 15 players who started the 2011 World Cup final for the All Blacks were of Maori or Pacific Island ancestry. The All Blacks have adapted their team culture to some degree in response, introducing the 'Kapa o Pango' haka in 2005, but for the most part the culture of the All Blacks is a pan-ethnic culture in which the ultimate loyalty is to the team.[91]

Given all the challenges professionalism posed, the ability of the All Blacks to maintain a winning percentage in excess of 80 per cent in the past decade is a phenomenal achievement. The combination of highly talented players and skilled coaches has played a significant role in this, but arguably it is the collective commitment of players and coaches to a shared set of values, a pride in the heritage of the team and an uncompromising focus on winning that has separated the team from its competitors.[92] Interestingly – some would say notoriously – the success rate in World Cups (two wins from seven tournaments) has been much lower than might have been expected from this overall winning percentage. Paradoxically, the style of rugby that is effective in winning most games – sophisticated interplay between backs and forwards and a premium on skill – is not necessarily best suited to a tournament in which an emphasis on defence and tight forward play is often effective in critical semi-final and finals encounters.

Despite receiving extensive criticism, crucially the NZRU has got the big decisions right in the professional era. By insisting on the central contracting of players, and requiring players who want to play for the All Blacks to reside in New Zealand, the NZRU has ensured All Blacks coaches have unfettered access to their players when they want them for training camps and games – as opposed to what happens overseas, where players are contracted to clubs and the national union must negotiate with clubs to release players for national duty. With the winning of the 2011 Rugby World Cup in New Zealand generating arguably the greatest feeling of sporting nationalism since the 1956 Springbok tour (certainly in rugby), and the game on a sound financial and administrative footing, New Zealand rugby has seldom been in a stronger position than it is at present.

CHAPTER SIXTEEN
WINNING BLACK FERNS

DR FARAH PALMER

PRIDE IN SELECTION

According to Anna Richards in the 2002 *Black Ferns World Cup Media Guide*, the first New Zealand selection for women's rugby was in 1989 and the players had to pay their own way. In 1991, all the players who were considered to be in the squad were sent letters advising them how much money was required to go to the World Cup in Wales. A team was selected from those who could afford the trip.

By the time I was asked to attend the trials in 1995, the NZRFU had sanctioned the team, and fully funded trials occurred over one weekend at the Royal New Zealand Police College in Porirua. The team was announced in person at the end of the weekend and I remember it as if it was yesterday. We all filed into the lecture room and took up seats next to those we had befriended or had known prior to the intense weekend. An official from the NZRFU then made his way to the podium and proceeded to name the team from number one through to number 22. I had no expectations and was enjoying the experience of being there as 21 of the names were called out, which all seemed a mumble to me anyway. But when my name was mentioned – the last name to be called out, as the reserve hooker usually has the number 22 jersey – my hearing suddenly improved. I couldn't believe it. I was in shock, and remember getting an elbow jabbed into my ribs from someone sitting next to me as it all started to sink in. I had just been named in the New Zealand women's rugby team! The realisation was followed by an awkward moment of people consoling those who didn't make it, and celebrations for those who did. I was elated, surprised, shocked, in disbelief, had butterflies, became instantly nervous, and was exhilarated all at once.

Everyone who didn't make it was then asked to leave the room, and we were given our first official talking to as a 'team'. As soon as we were allowed out of the room I rang my parents (and this was in the day when you had to queue up in front of one of the pay phones). I exclaimed through tears of joy and overwhelming emotion that I was 'an All Black'. My parents couldn't digest what I'd just said, so they said, 'That's nice, dear.' Neither I nor my family really understood the enormity of it all at that stage. I was on a bit of a joyride and everything was new to me. Having never been in an 'elite' team or environment before, I didn't know what to expect or what was expected of me. But being selected will always be a special moment, and it still brings back the same emotions reminiscing about it now.

Being named each time after that was still a thrill, but it was never as unbelievable as that first time. Being named in 1996 was amazing because I was selected as the only specialist hooker in the team, and being named in 1997 was significant again as the games were against England and Australia, in front of a home crowd. It was around 1997 that the trials changed from a one-off weekend to a series of trial games and, from then onwards, after all the trial games were completed individuals were contacted by one of the coaches to receive the good or bad news over the phone. The surprise element was gone a little – and that social anxiety was also minimised – but it was still nerve-wracking waiting to hear whether you'd get the good or bad news.

Being named the captain in 1997 was another key moment for me. It was at this stage that my father really got emotional when I told him. I was asked to be captain after two years in the team (and only one year as a playing member) so I thought, 'You're not ready for this', but my heart said, 'Go for it' – so I did. I decided these opportunities don't come up that often, and if the selectors and coaches felt I had what it took to lead the team, then I would do my best to honour their belief in me. Of course I was on a huge learning curve regarding captaincy, and made many mistakes along the way, but I believe my core values and behaviours reflected those of the New Zealand women's rugby team at the time. I wasn't the flashiest player, but I was hard-working, diligent, respectful, tough and passionate about playing. I was lucky that some of the other key players who could have fulfilled that role were injured at the time – I may have been the third or fourth choice!

Induction

I can't remember being inducted officially into the team back in 1995. I was so overwhelmed by the whole experience that I probably didn't even notice. Overloaded with sensations, emotions and information, I was like a possum in the headlights that first year. I remember being introduced to everyone as a rookie and then being allocated to laundry duty, a special treat reserved especially for the newcomers to the team. It was a great way to bond with the other rookies and to earn your stripes as a member of the team. Each additional year you were in the team, you got to dish out the same punishment/initiation to the next lot of newcomers and you'd always hear the more experienced players saying, 'We had to do that too when we were rookies, so no use complaining!'

New players knew just to keep their heads down and do as they were told. Don't question (well, I didn't), follow instructions, be well-prepared, well-informed and well-presented. Team-issue clothing was often three sizes too big for us all for the first few years, when we were allocated leftovers from the men's teams. We had XXL shirts and pants, and most of us had to roll our pants and sleeves up several times, plus tuck our shirts in just so that we didn't trip over them. The smaller players got first choice of the team-allocated gear, then it was first in, first served for the rest of us. As a new player, you knew there was a pecking order, so rookies got the most ill-fitting gear. Many of my jerseys and tracksuits from 1995 to 1997 were far too big, but that didn't detract from how special they were to me.

Setting team values and goals

In terms of setting the values and expectations of the team, we had a series of rituals. These included the first official gathering as a team, which was quite ceremonial and formal. The coaches and manager would lay down the law at this meeting, and give us a sense of what they expected from us. On the second or third day of our time together, the players would have a players' meeting where the management were often excluded. We would come up with a set of values and expectations regarding attitudes, behaviours and team goals. The captain and senior players tended to coordinate these.

The values and expectations didn't vary much from year to year, but how we came up with them did. We would use metaphors, acronyms and symbols to help us to visualise our team values. One year we had value cards that were laminated and given to each player for the entire tour. If you lost your value card, you had to be punished in some way. Punishments are another set of rituals altogether. Another year, we had a piece of rope to depict how important each strand is in making a rope/team strong. Another time we had a piece of No. 8 wire lovingly hammered to a piece of native timber by one of the players. It was to epitomise the can-do attitude and rural history associated with New Zealand and rugby, and a 'shut the gate' theme that we had in 2006.

World Cup themes

In World Cup years we put a lot of effort into theming our campaigns. In 1998 we chose 'professional on and off the field' as our team motto for our first IRB-sanctioned World Cup. In 2002 our theme was 'BTB' (Better Than Before, and Back To Back wins) and 'shut the gate' for 2006.

In 1998 we had wanted to set the standard – demonstrate why we believed we were the best at this game in the world, and that we had high expectations of ourselves on and off the field. This meant our trainings were intense, we prepared properly for games, were focused when we went into the arena, always presented ourselves in a unified and professional manner in terms of dress standards and behaviour, and conducted ourselves in interviews and at after-match functions to the highest standards. I remember we were the only team at the tournament with water bottles on hand at all times, and who ate bananas and complex carbs within 30 minutes of a game. Many of the other teams treated the 1998 tournament in Amsterdam as a carnival – and were surprised when the Black Ferns refused to participate in a casual tournament a couple of days before a World Cup match, involving playing against locals with beer kegs on the sideline to ensure players were replenished with alcohol when necessary!

We probably came across as a bit aloof and arrogant, but this was a serious business to us. We wanted to be friendly and approachable, but not to the detriment of the game. We were there to uphold the standards expected of a New Zealand rugby team, irrespective of our gender. We were there to continue the legacy associated with New Zealand rugby. We all loved playing rugby, representing our country in our national sport, and being considered elite athletes. Individually, we probably did rebel a little from gendered expectations, but then New Zealand had more relaxed gender expectations of women. Being active, strong, mentally and physically resilient and innovative were admired traits in both men and women in New Zealand, especially in rural, Maori and Pasifika cultures.

The BTB theme in 2002 had been all about creating a change in mindset after a loss to England in 2001 that had been completely devastating for the team. The loss was the first in 10 years and we didn't like it one bit that we were the ones to wear it. Our coach, Darryl Suasua, along with some of the senior players, decided that a change of team culture was necessary. That change involved focusing on the positive (being 'Better Than Before'), rather than focusing on the negative (not losing). In 2001 we had been so worried about maintaining our winning streak and upholding some of the more negative rituals associated with the team that we stifled our creativity and personalities. If we could win the 2002 World Cup, it would be 'Back To Back' wins. So the BTB acronym represented both a process (Better Than Before) and an outcome (Back To Back). Of course, there was always humour in all of these value sessions. BTB also stood for more 'Beautiful Than Before' or 'Bigger Than Before' (suggesting we wanted to get stronger and more powerful) and, because the tournament was in Barcelona, Spain, which was rather hot, 'Blacker Than Before' also applied! We never took ourselves too seriously. We gave out BTB badges to anyone 'caught' being better than before in whatever they did (training, playing, general behaviour). We had a leader's jersey which was yellow and given to the player who had most depicted the values of BTB. We encouraged more input from the whole team in terms of getting words of inspiration and direction from different individuals in the mornings or prior to games or trainings. We set positive goals, rewarded positive behaviour and tried to encourage everyone to express themselves more freely.

My last World Cup was in 2006 and that theme was around the components of a gate and the farming concept of always shutting the gate once you've passed through it. It was to keep us focused on one game at a time, to help us avoid thinking we'd already made it to the finals. Just because we'd won the last two World Cups didn't mean we were unbeatable – we'd learnt that lesson in 2001. The gate theme was also a reminder for us to have periods of being focused and relaxed. We took two poles all the way from New Zealand to Canada to represent a gate: when we passed through these poles at training, we switched on. We didn't talk or think about anything else but rugby. Prior to passing through these symbolic gates, we could talk about other stuff women like to talk about (what was on TV the night before, something funny someone had done the previous evening, music we enjoyed listening to – whatever), but when we passed through that gate, we were 'rugby heads'. This proved quite awkward early in the tournament because family members who had travelled to Canada to support us would often meet up with us at the training/playing fields and expect us to interact with them, but we'd have to ignore them and focus on warming up and training. Afterwards we'd explain to them why we may have seemed a bit rude. We also had a 'passport' that each of us got stamped after every game we played at that World Cup. It was a nice way of ticking off each step towards the final. The No. 8 wire aspect of the gate theme was about being proud of innovation and ingenuity and can-do attitude. We needed to be innovative and to solve problems as they arose on the field without relying on being told what to do. Our coach at the time, Jed Rowlands, was big on us all being skilful and intelligent players who could problem-solve and create without being completely reliant on the management/coaching staff.

The Black Ferns name and jersey

There were different rites you went through as a member of the Black Ferns. The first was being named in the official squad. The second stage was to get named in the playing 22 – this meant you would get a black jersey. The third stage was to get named in the starting XV, receiving a jersey numbered somewhere from 1 to 15. The receiving of the jersey before a test was a hugely significant and emotional ritual in the team.

Each coach did this differently. Some would meet with players individually to give them their jersey, then explain to them why they were in the team and what their job was for that game. Some would arrange for someone significant to present the jerseys prior to travelling to the venue. Either way, it was pretty special to get your first black jersey, and then first starting-test jersey.

Even though the jersey has changed slightly over the years, we still refer to it as a black jersey. It is why we, as a team, agreed that the name 'Black Ferns' was the name we wanted to be called. The fern because it is something associated with female sports teams in New Zealand, and black because this is the colour associated with representing our country in sport, and in particular rugby. At the time we didn't know that black ferns (or black tree ferns) were nga mamaku, a native tree considered the matriarch of the forest in Maori culture, but that has also become a wonderful meaning associated with the team name.

The rookies reminisce

Another rite for players is for the rookies to stand up one at a time in front of the team and share their thoughts, memories and emotions regarding their first game. This can be a quite emotional but also an intimately funny time for the team, each player expressing herself in a unique way. Some players are shy and don't want to say much, so I used to interview them; they'd come up with the funniest responses, unscripted and honest. They'd all highlight something a little different about their first game as a Black Fern, whether it was the haka, the anthem, a tackle they made, a try they scored or seeing their loved ones up in the stand.

Team milestones

During his tenure as coach, Darryl Suasua suggested to the NZRFU that there should be some way of recognising longevity in the team. For the men, this is recognised by giving players who have played 100 games a silver cap. In women's rugby we have far fewer games per year, so it would be unlikely for a player to get to 100 games. So, it was decided that 10 games would be acknowledged by receiving a bone carving pendant and 20 with a pounamu (greenstone) pendant.

The 'Cinderellas' or 'dirt-trackers'

The test team and the non-playing dirt-trackers, as they became known, had different rites. The phrases 'dirt-trackers' and 'dirty dirties' were inherited from men's rugby: the dirt-trackers usually got midweek games, taking the metaphorical dirt track rather than the main route to the black jersey. I remember the team tried to come up with our own, alternative term, but nothing seemed to stick. At one point they were called the Cinderellas, but I'm not sure that it stuck.

There were usually four players who were not named in the starting 22 and therefore not included in the captain's meeting the night before a test. These dirt-trackers were expected to help on the day of the test match and were assigned as assistants to the doctor, the manager, the physiotherapist and the trainer. They would often be the 'water girls' and ensure that everything around the team was ready so that the test team could focus on playing and performing. They would also have an intense workout with the trainer after the game so that they at least felt like they'd perspired and exerted themselves to keep up their fitness and feel part of the team.

No one is greater than the team or each other

I've found in women's rugby that hierarchies are not really encouraged, or explicitly promoted. Although the dirt-trackers were given these subordinate roles, the test players would also help out when possible and would not expect the dirt-trackers to do anything that was demeaning or that made them feel inferior. In women's rugby, everyone liked to keep the structure of the team relatively flat. On the bus, for instance, there were no rigid hierarchies about where people could sit. The coaches often mixed and mingled with the players and didn't have to sit at the front. There were some attempts to incorporate the 'back seat of the bus' culture into the team, but it didn't really work for us. We made an effort in the Black Ferns to eliminate egos, to make sure everyone felt they needed to prove themselves and that they all had a chance of making the test team.

We also tried to avoid cliques by rooming people together who didn't know each other well, or by changing roomies halfway through a tournament. While on tour, everyone had to say hello to everyone else in the team at breakfast and often we'd make this more challenging by having to say hello or good morning in a different language. The shy ones, or players who were terrible at remembering new names first thing in the morning, would come down really early so that everyone else had to say good morning to them. This gave them a bit more time to put a name to the face.

There was also an expectation that people would make an effort to sit with someone different at each mealtime, and whenever they were on the bus. We'd even set a task of getting players to find out as much as they could about someone else, without letting them know that they were the 'mystery pal'. There were lots of games, activities and rituals that were about breaking down barriers between players, keeping a level playing field, and keeping the team as united as possible. Of course there are always going to be clashes of personalities, or people getting on each other's nerves due to close proximity and the length of time we spent together. That is where having strong values kept the team focused on their goal, which ultimately was to perform well and win.

Other rituals were about sharing parts of our culture with the rest of the world, in a way that made us all proud to be New Zealanders and women. This included rituals like the haka that we performed before games, and waiata that we sang after our games.

Waiata and waiata-a-ringa

After the games we would mix and mingle with our opponents, exchange gifts (like pins or in some cases jerseys), share food and drink, and in most cases sing songs. Singing songs was a huge part of women's rugby, especially in the United Kingdom and North America. We heard many from our opposition teams that were a female take on traditionally male rugby songs. The words had been adapted, often in a way that emphasised the strength of women and the marginality of men. My experience of women's rugby in New Zealand (and the focus of my honours dissertation) was that this was not, however, part of the women's rugby culture in New Zealand. The songs or waiata associated with women's rugby in New Zealand tended to be associated with Maori culture and were more about values that were associated with our rugby, such as kotahitanga (unity), kia kaha (being strong), arohatanga and manaakitanga (caring and hospitality). We also had fun songs that we tended to sing on more light-hearted occasions.

We sometimes adopted songs we liked from teams we played against (such as the 'Banana Song' from the USA team), and each year someone would introduce a new one that the team tried to learn. We had Maori songs, songs sung in English ('The Gambler' was a favourite!) and Samoan songs. The diversity reflected the cultural diversity of the team, and no song suggestion was declined straight away. If an individual had a song they thought was appropriate for the team to perform, it was up to them to provide the words and try to encourage the team to learn it. If there was collective enthusiasm for the song and we felt we could sing it well enough, it would be sung at after-match functions to support a speech (similar to what happens on a marae).

Being able to sing in unison, in tune, strong and confident, was another way of our team demonstrating professionalism, pride and unity to our opposition. Of course, winning on the field was the most relevant way of portraying this, but the singing of songs after the match was also important. This was part of Maori culture in particular, and also a big part of Pasifika culture. There was one song, however, that tended to divide the team, and this was because it was catchy and fun to sing, but also a bit arrogant. One of the verses mentioned that we liked to 'ruck and maul and smash as a team' and 'don't mess with us, coz we're the bomb'. It was not really our style to sing a song like this after the game and, although it was easy for the team to sing, we didn't do it that often. Probably only when we played teams like England, whom we really enjoyed beating; or on the way home in the bus.

Singing was a significant way of sharing part of our culture. Of course this would start off with a hiss and a roar, but sometimes the opposition were also into singing songs and the after-match function would become a sing-off between the teams! The Spanish team were really into singing and once we ran out of songs that everyone in the team knew, while they had more to come. We ended up singing 'Oma Rapeti' – a song about a rabbit! We sang that song as if it was the most culturally important song in New Zealand, the Spanish were none the wiser and seemed impressed and we laughed about it all the way home.

Singing songs was a big part of the unwinding and celebratory atmosphere after trainings and games. That part of the team culture has died off more recently due to individuals listening to their own song choices via headphones and iPods, which I find quite sad. However, that is the nature of team sports: as the generational cultures change, so too do the tastes and rituals of the team. For many years in the team we had individuals – whether it was a player or member of the management – who could play the guitar and initiate the singing of old songs that everyone knew. They were the moments I cherished in a team, when we'd won a game and everyone was on a high and enjoying each other's company.

Performing a song to endorse a speech, however, is still a strong cultural practice. In 2002 we adopted a song that was specifically composed for us by Pania Papa, a friend of one of the Black Ferns players at the time, Regina Sheck. Pania explained to us that inspiration for the song came when she was travelling back to Tokoroa (the home town she shared with Regina) amongst the trees and the falling rain. She also referred to my explanation of the team, its spirit, passion, pride and aspirations to represent our country. Pania is a much sought-after composer in the world of Maori performing arts, yet she gifted the song to us as a team in acknowledgement of our mana as role models for our youth and for our families.

Pania was an excellent tutor, and made everyone feel comfortable and included in the process. There were Pakeha/European and Pasifika players in the team who were not familiar with singing waiata (songs) or waiata-a-ringa (action songs), but she did it in such an inclusive and non-threatening way that the team bought into the waiata-a-ringa wholeheartedly. She arranged for the team to break into mini-teams and come up with a series of actions to depict the meaning of that line, then each mini-team had to teach their action to the rest of the team. All actions were accepted without criticism and in no time at all the team had composed actions to go with all the words. It was an excellent demonstration of how distributed and empowering leadership can achieve a goal and sell a vision effectively.

This process was also indicative of how we liked to operate as a team – inclusive, creative and empowering. The song was simply titled 'Nga Mamaku' or 'The Black Ferns' and reflected the matriarchal nature of the botanical fern that stands tall and gains its sustenance from the wind, water and sun. The waiata-a-ringa also included meanings associated with pursuing the peaks of sporting success through unity and activity. It called for us all to stand tall with pride as women and Black Ferns.

The haka

The way the team has incorporated the haka underwent several transformations over the 10 years I was involved with the team. Initially, it was a basic copy of what the All Blacks were doing. Then we adopted a traditional haka performed by women of the Ngati Porou tribe before finally embracing a haka composed specifically for the team.

At the first unofficial World Cup Festival in 1991 I understand the New Zealand team performed 'Ka Mate', the All Blacks' traditional haka. I've seen one photo in a magazine of it being performed by one of the female players and heard a few murmurs that some felt it was inappropriate for the women's team to perform this haka. It is my belief that women can perform 'Ka Mate' – women feature quite strongly in the story behind it, so as far as I'm concerned women can perform it as well as men. The stance used by some of the women, however, was considered too masculine by some, which created the impetus for another haka to be adopted by the New Zealand women's rugby team.

When I entered the team environment in 1995, the haka taught to all of us was 'Ka Panapana', the Ngati Porou haka performed as a welcome by women. Our captain Lenadeen Simpson-Brown was of Ngati Porou descent and had sought permission from kaumatua/elders for the team to use it, with the original meaning modified for the purposes of the rugby team. The lines, 'Ka haere, ka haere taku pohiri, Ki te tai whakarunga, Hoki mai hoki mai taku tinana' and 'Ka haere ka haere taku pohiri, Ki te tai whakararo, Hoki mai hoki mai taku tinana' are a call of welcome and translate as, 'My invitation goes out to the Southern Sea! Come back, come back to my body! My invitation goes out to the Northern Sea! Come back, come back to my body!' This was a way of us connecting with our ancestors, family and New Zealand if we were playing overseas. Another line says, 'Kia huri au ki te tai whakatua Kupe, Ki te tai o Matawhero I motu mai, E ko te hoariri, Ki roto i aku ringa kutia rawatia, Kia pare tona ihu' which translates as, 'I turn to the sea which Kupe [the historic Maori explorer] raised up, To the sea which breaks at Gisborne [a place of significance to the Ngati Porou tribe]. The assailant in my arms is digging. He (or she) will be squeezed, choked, until their nose is flowing!'

For the people of Ngati Porou, this haka has many layers of meaning. For us as a team, this haka acknowledges the power of women, and of our ability to be both welcoming and strong in the face of a threat if necessary. We performed this haka before every game until 2002. Even as the captain at the time, I didn't understand the deeper meanings and nuances of 'Ka Panapana' because I didn't have a strong kapa haka upbringing and was not of Ngati Porou descent. I still felt proud performing it, and believed in the messages of the power of women, but I wasn't completely comfortable leading it, and neither was anyone else in the team at the time.

By 2006 and my third Rugby World Cup, I felt it would be culturally safer for me and the team if we had our own haka, rather than risk offending people of Ngati Porou descent because we were not interpreting the words, meaning or actions appropriately. I had been involved with Maori rugby for a few years now and knew Whetu Tipiwai well as the kaumatua of our regional representative team (Te Tini a Maui) and of the Maori All Blacks team. He had helped compose a haka for these teams. I felt this was what the Black Ferns needed.

Whetu was open to help, so to assist him the waiata-a-ringa used by the team in 2002 and composed by Pania Papa was used as inspiration. As captain I also gave him a bit of history about the team and women's rugby in New Zealand. The kupu (words) for the haka came to Whetu while driving over the Tararua Range, and in August 2006 he passed these on to the Black Ferns through me. At that point a group of players who had experience in kapa haka and tikanga Maori (Maori culture) were asked to come up with some actions for each line. Exia Edwards (née Shelford) in particular played a key role in this process, and together we performed a draft version of the haka to the team, once we'd explained the meaning and story behind it all.

Named 'Te Haka o Nga Mamaku', the haka of the Black Ferns is unique in that it starts with a karanga (call), which is an important part of marae protocol for which women are responsible. It also refers to the beginning of humankind according to te ao Maori (the Maori worldview), which involved three powerful women – Hineahuone, Hinetitama and Hinenuitepo. It suggests we gain our life-force from above (the heavens), below (the land) and that the team is like a gathering of clouds over a lofty mountain – as a team we gather momentarily to achieve a lofty goal, and then we disperse.

The haka then acknowledges that members of the team come from all corners of Aotearoa/New Zealand and neighbouring islands and lands. As women we stand tall and proud, with strength and prestige. When the challenges arise we will advance, stand united and do what we can to achieve success as a team.

In terms of values emphasised in this ritual, they are those of team unity, of pride in being from New Zealand, of our heritage, and of our strength as women and as a team. Our haka is now a legacy that is passed on. Each year as the team changes and adapts, so too will the haka. It is not stagnant and changes with the team dynamics, demographics and goals.

Humour

Humour is a big part of the culture of the Black Ferns, as I'm sure it is for most teams. If there isn't humour to defuse the tension, it can get pretty intense – so it is essential to make sure there is the right mix between intensity and focus and relaxing and having fun. There were several rituals incorporated into the culture of the Black Ferns to ensure we had a laugh or two. This included laughing at each other's misfortunes by having a 'dick of the day' or 'faux pas' award at a team session where everyone would nominate someone for the award. The trophy for doing the silliest thing, or making the biggest and most hilarious fool of yourself, varied from year to year. As each year progressed we had to up the ante, so in 2001 we decided that the 'faux pas' award would involve wearing a hideous pink towelling jumpsuit someone had got from a second-hand store. The suit was dreaded so much, however, that what ended up happening was no one doing or saying anything in case they were nominated.

When we consciously decided to change the Black Ferns culture from one that was focused on the negative (like mocking people publicly and not losing) to one that was more positive (catching people being 'better than before' and winning), we had a ceremony of burning the pink jumpsuit, which was met with such spontaneous joy and laughter that it proved a great way to symbolise the change in culture of the team.

A few years earlier, in 1998, we had shared a hotel with the Welsh women's rugby team and ended up socialising with them on a couple of occasions because we were not directly competing with them in the pool games – and it was highly unlikely that we'd meet them in the play-offs. They were more elaborate in their tomfoolery than we were and staged this huge kidnapping of our mascot at the time, Sheewee the Kiwi. They recorded the whole abduction and sent us the tape, which we duly played at a team meeting. There was our mascot with her arms and legs tied up and her mouth taped shut with sock tape. Standing next to her were two women dressed in black from head to toe with Welsh accents threatening to 'kill' the Kiwi if we didn't reveal our secrets and give them a black jersey. It was hilarious. As a way of getting them back, we arranged for a powhiri (welcoming/sharing ceremony) where we introduced ourselves (in Maori or English) and sung waiata for ages – while two of our players stole all their training shoes, which had been appropriately left outside. We said we'd return their shoes if they returned Sheewee. We had a bit of a stand-off for about two days. In the end, the coaches had to call a negotiation meeting where a 'treaty' was signed and a neutral area established where the exchange of shoes for Sheewee took place.

When the new 'Nga Mamaku' haka was introduced in 2006, we held 'Haka Idol' sessions. Exia and I were the judges and players had to perform the haka in front of us individually, or in small groups if they wished, in order to pass and be permitted to perform the haka before a game. It was a serious business, but also funny and a great way of giving some of the more culturally/ musically gifted players a chance to lead. We'd walk down the hallways of our accommodation and see groups practising before they'd ask us for an 'official' audition. It must have been nerve-wracking for some of the players, but they all did it – and they were so stoked to have passed and performed the haka with confidence when the time called for it.

We had many other ways of ensuring that we switched off and had fun when appropriate. There were mini-teams, and the coaches sometimes put on a show for the team a couple of days before the final. There were skits and games we played on recovery days which helped us to relax. There was never a dull moment, and although we were serious about winning (task cohesion) we also wanted to enjoy each other's company and have a laugh (social cohesion).

There were also rituals around deterring particular behaviours and attitudes in the team. If you were late, the coach and/or senior members of the team would come up with some form of punishment, which varied from polishing everyone else's boots to carrying each member of the team from the try line to the 22 in a fireman's lift. To keep everyone motivated in games that were not close, the team would be reminded that we had agreed to do one 'Hennie Muller' for every point that was scored against us. Hennie Muller was apparently a player who invented a hideous fitness drill. A 'Hennie' involved the team running a figure eight that is the length and width of the field, usually at quite a fast pace. It tends to be done at the end of a hard training run the day after the game. This was great motivation for tackling like our life depended on it if any team looked like scoring a try. As a result, we not only defended our winning record with conviction, but also kept our 'points against' record to a minimum.

VALUES AND BELIEFS

Formal value-setting started to happen when Darryl Suasua took over as head coach, and started to meticulously plan every aspect of the team's build-up and day-to-day schedule while on tour. In 2002, for instance, Darryl had arranged for a video clip to play as the team entered the Sport and Rugby Institute in Palmerston North for the first time as a World Cup squad. The room was dimmed, and there were exactly the number of chairs in the room as players in the team. Each chair had a red rose on it, and we all filed into the room in silence and darkness and took our seats. The video that had been composed specifically for this moment started with Lenadeen Simpson-Brown, the captain prior to me, doing a traditional karanga (call) to the team. Then ex-players were interviewed and asked about what being a Black Fern meant to them. They were quite emotional interviews.

This was followed by a clip from the movie *Dead Poets Society* where the teacher asks the young students to lean in and listen to what their predecessors would have said to them if they had the chance. He starts whispering 'carpe diem' to his students, asking them to 'seize the day'. The video then changes gear and shows clips of every single person in the room at the trial games that led to them being selected, with inspirational music from Kiri Te Kanawa playing in the background. At this point everyone in the room is laughing and getting excited, and pointing out when they see themselves or their friends/teammates do something amazing during the trial. The clip then changes to past Black Ferns tries and tackles at the 1998 Rugby World Cup. The closing clip has the voice of Robin Williams again suggesting we 'seize the day', with images flashing up of previous players, coaches and managers well known in women's rugby.

The final image is of everyone at the trials in a team photo with the question, 'If not you, then who? If not now, then when?' It was a very moving way of inducting us all into that Black Ferns team and it had a lasting impact on me personally – even though I was partly involved in the production of the video. I still use that video today when doing motivational speeches, because it was so meaningful to me and depicts the values and attitudes of the team that I cherished. These values were of pride in who we were and what we were doing; valuing a proactive, trailblazing culture; and celebrating our diversity and unity at the same time in terms of skills, backgrounds and experiences. Of course, that kind of thing didn't happen every year and every single time the team got together, but there was often more of an effort made in World Cup years.

Pride in winning

The legacy of winning was not just an All Blacks thing – it was a New Zealand rugby thing. The Maori team was expected to win, the sevens teams were expected to win and the Black Ferns were expected to win. Rugby is our national sport irrespective of gender, so we are expected to be just as skilled, knowledgeable, intense and excellent as the men. We are very proud of the winning legacy of New Zealand rugby and ultimately of the Black Ferns.

Everybody knew that our history was very fresh by comparison, however. We had become recognised by the NZRFU only in the early 1990s, although we all acknowledged that the first team had been selected in 1989 and the first World Cup (not sanctioned by the IRB) took place in 1991 in Wales. At that tournament New Zealand lost to the USA in the semi-finals, but after that we remained unbeaten for 10 years. The winning streak was broken in 2001 in front of a home crowd at North Harbour Stadium against our arch-rivals England with a runaway try from their winger in the dying minutes of the game: it was gut-wrenching. I was completely devastated, as were most of the team. I cried and cried in the changing rooms because I felt I had let the team down, let down the legacy, and failed to uphold the reputation of the Black Ferns as a winning team. In a strange way, that loss was a blessing in disguise. It indicated to us that we needed to tweak our culture a little and focus less on the fear of losing and more on the joy of winning. We also had to demand more from the officials and NZRFU in terms of resourcing, time together as a team, better competitions, fitness preparation and so forth.

Since my retirement the Black Ferns have lost a few other games to England, which I still find devastating even though I'm no longer involved with the team. It does feel like the team legacy isn't being respected, even though I know that the team and athletes themselves don't want to lose, just as much as we didn't want to lose. It has been suggested that the rest of the world is catching up with the Black Ferns now that professionalism and resources are being allocated to women's rugby in places like England, but those excuses just don't cut it with me. New Zealand has always proclaimed to punch above its weight when it comes to sport. So what if we have fewer resources? We still should have the most rugby-savvy population, and rugby is still our national sport. As long as the importance of winning and maintaining high standards and the expectation of excellence is reinforced within the team and within women's rugby at the lower levels, it shouldn't matter how much each player gets paid by their respective unions.

Maybe I'm just old school having come through women's rugby when it was amateur and having played the sport because we loved it and wanted to be a part of making history. Despite losing to England a couple of times, the team has continued to win the World Cup, which is the pinnacle event for the Black Ferns, so that is great to see. Overall the legacy of the Black Ferns is probably not perceived as being as invincible as it used to be, but they are still world champions, and still bring out the best in other teams.

LEADERSHIP
Coaching
In the early 1990s, Laurie O'Reilly was the coach and champion of the national women's rugby team in New Zealand. He was a lawyer who later became New Zealand's Commissioner for Children and without his passion for the team, his networks in the community (especially in the legal, human rights and rugby arenas), a women's team would never have got off the ground. His daughter played, so perhaps that is how he got involved, but he was certainly the right person to have in the role at that time. He did a lot to get women's rugby recognised by the NZRFU and, because of his high profile,

helped draw attention to women's rugby in general. When I started to play rugby, the NZRFU had finally accepted that women's rugby was here to stay and there was official support for a national provincial competition of some sort, from which a national team could be selected. When I made the team in 1995, Vicki Dombroski was the coach, and Darryl Suasua and Brian 'Chubby' Hayes the assistant coaches. Vicki was another champion of women's rugby and had written several letters to the NZRFU asking for women's rugby to be acknowledged by the national sporting organisation. JJ Stewart, a member of the NZRFU board at the time, ended up being an advocate of women's rugby and hence the first trophy for women's rugby was named the JJ Stewart Trophy.

In 1996 Darryl was the sole coach that took us to the Canada Cup (a quadrangular tournament held in Canada, 1993, 1996, 2000, 2005), along with one doctor and one manager. That year was a significant one for the team. Anna Richards, a legendary New Zealand player, explained that in the 1980s women's rugby was about having fun and being carefree, but acknowledged in 2002 that the attitude of that era would not produce a competitive team in the professional era.[1] Darryl realised this and was transformational in his leadership of the team. He instilled in us how important it was that we performed beyond expectations at this tournament, and that we present ourselves in a professional manner on and off the field at all times in order to win over the NZRFU officials, rugby supporters in New Zealand and the New Zealand public. We didn't want to just beat the other teams, we wanted to annihilate them and do it in style. Darryl did a lot that year to change some of the aspects of the team that he didn't approve of, so we had strict diets, a no-alcohol/coffee/tea/butter/junk food policy while on tour, and had to do a lot of PR and media work leading up to and during this tournament. He coached the team from 1995 to 2002, when Jed Rowlands took over.

Jed's approach was very different to Darryl's and it took me a while to adjust to. I must admit I struggled under Jed's leadership compared to Darryl's, but that may have had to do with my waning motivation (I had contemplated retiring after 2002), lack of form, and niggling injuries. Darryl's style was more involved in every aspect of the team and its culture, whereas Jed believed in empowering the players and having collective leadership. Both styles of player management and team leadership have their merits and I'm a great believer in having the right leader for the right context. Laurie was the best person to get a national team together in the late 1980s and early 1990s, Vicki did her part to get women's rugby recognised by the NZRFU, Darryl's leadership style helped to change the way women's rugby was perceived, and Jed's style allowed the players to become leaders in their own right.

Captaincy

My leadership role as I matured as a player and person also changed. As I said, I am not sure why I was selected as captain back in 1997. From my perspective, it was a combination of being one of the best in my position at the time, believing and living the values and behaviours expected of an elite athlete, having the interpersonal skills to get on with a range of individuals, having the confidence to fulfil the formal roles expected of a captain, being able to make decisions in the heat of the moment, and being able to bring a team together and inspire them when necessary. As I developed as a captain, I styled my leadership style to be more authentic to me, whereas initially I tried to replicate the leadership I had been exposed to from others as captains and coaches.

Initially I tried to adopt Lenadeen's more authoritarian style of leading, but I just didn't have the personality or mana to do that. I was too young, not only in age, but in terms of years in the team and life experience. I was still a student, had no children or 'real' job, and had only two years in the team under my belt. In hindsight, perhaps I was a really good 'first follower', because I was a great conduit with regards to reinforcing values, expectations, standards and attitudes within the team. As I grew in confidence, though, I asserted my ideas more. I resisted what I perceived to be homophobic attitudes that started to appear in the team environment, and made suggestions about what I felt the team should and shouldn't do in the short and long term. I started to play the political game more as my time as captain lengthened. I still have a letter that I sent to the NZRFU in November 1999, for instance, which outlined some concerns that the players had expressed to me. They were issues with regards to the black jersey, the issued gear, the transport, dress uniform, assembly information and allowance. As a student I must have had a lot of time on my hands and was also very idealistic and optimistic that I could change the world!

As my time in the team grew, I became more aware of the internal and external issues the team faced, and was more ready to stamp my own ideas on the team rather than being seen as only a mouthpiece for the coach. In 2002, for instance, I wanted to assert myself as captain so I led the haka, did the after-match speeches, often prompted the waiata, helped to decide the values and expectations of the team, and was the single person communicating between the management and players. That wasn't to say that no one else could lead, but it seemed the team was happy for me to take on these extra stressors in a year that was important to all of us, and they seemed to have faith in me that I could do all of this and continue to play to a high standard. I was probably at my physical and mental peak as an individual in 2002. At this stage I would suggest that my style was more like a manager on the field, but more like a transformational leader for women's rugby off the field, in terms of using my profile at the time to draw attention to the sport, the team and the issues I felt needed to be raised. I was not an authoritarian leader, more of a democratic one. I encouraged open dialogue and clear, two-way communication.

There were leaders of subcommittees in the team for social activities, food and nutrition, clothing and so forth. Each of these lieutenants was given a lot of control and leadership, but if there were any conflicts or debates, the decisions would often be left to the management team, which included myself as the player representative. I felt I had the support of the management team and the players, so it was a system that worked well at the time.

Collective leadership

My leadership style and preferences were challenged in 2003 when Jed took over from Darryl as the coach. From 2003, a more collective leadership model was adopted by the Black Ferns. This was probably due to the concurrent changes happening in the All Blacks with regards to leadership, and was also Jed's preferred style of coaching and managing a team. The benefits of a collective style are that the burden and responsibilities associated with captaincy can be delegated more officially, and that a more collective style of decision-making can occur.

There are definite reasons to have more leaders in a team. Of course, at the time I felt my performance as a captain so far was being questioned, and that all the hard work we'd put into the team's culture would be undone. It was difficult for me to adjust to this change after being in such a privileged single-leader role for so long. Luckily for me, Jackie Barron, our manager, left a copy of the motivational book *Who Moved My Cheese?* by Spencer Johnson on my bed. It made me realise that I had to embrace change, and that the new coach would have a new way of doing things: if I wanted to stay in my role as captain, I'd also have to adapt. That meant not being so black and white when it came to contraband in the team (i.e. alcohol and chocolate) and that the final decision was not down to me as a member of the management team, but more of a collective decision-making process with a selected group of players.

When it came to the formal roles of a captain, there were very few issues with this change from a singular model of leadership to a collective one – because the roles were delegated in an unofficial way anyway (i.e. others could lead the songs, the haka, the team talks), while on the field a collective style of responsibility was already operating. We had someone leading the lineouts, another the scrums, the first five usually dictated the attacking plays, and the second five the defensive pattern.

This continued under Jed's leadership. There were, however, issues with off-field communication under this new model. Initially there was confusion about who did what, who to listen to and, if there were any disagreements, who had the final say. We went through a bit of an adjustment period as the new leadership model was implemented, but we eventually got it right.

Perhaps because I felt my role as the standard-setter in the team was no longer as important in this collective environment, I let my standards slip. I was also struggling with motivation, injuries, maintaining expected fitness levels and a close and open relationship with Jed. I just didn't have the skills and attributes he valued (i.e. I was never highly skilled, more a hard-grinding, resilient player). Because I had let my standards slip on and off the field, I had also lost respect from the players and I struggled to understand what made the younger players tick. I was losing that prototypical and charismatic element that is necessary to be an effective leader in a team environment.

After getting lost a little for a couple of years, I decided to have one more go at getting in the team in 2006 – and at raising my own standards, gaining back some respect and leaving the Black Ferns legacy in a better state than I had in the last two years. I encouraged others to take the lead in the ceremonial aspects of the captaincy role. Someone else led the haka and waiata (usually Exia), and the co-captain, Rochelle Martin, did many of the after-match speeches. One of the most savvy players in women's rugby, Anna Richards, controlled most of the back moves and attacking plays during the games, so toward the end of my time as co-captain with Rochelle, I was more of a figurehead than someone with a lot of influence. That was okay with me as I still felt privileged to be a part of the team, and to be a part of the legacy that was the Black Ferns. I just hoped that, despite my momentary lapse in standards, I wasn't too detrimental to that legacy.

Communication

There was always strong communication between coach and captain and, later on, with the senior leadership group of players. The captain was often the conduit, indicating the team's temperament to the management and vice versa. This changed to a more distributed style of leadership and communication where there were several leaders who then reported to the management and to the team as a whole. Communication was by email and documents were distributed prior to the team gathering, and every day there would be a daily schedule that became a lifeline for knowing what was going on each day. There were also team play books and folders with all material that was handed out and created for the team to be kept informed. Verbally, communication happened at the first team meeting for the day, prior to trainings, on the bus to and from trainings/games, at post-game events, and there were also players-only meetings where we would bring up anything that was necessary.

There were times when we would communicate in our mini-teams (off the field), or mini-units (on the field). A lot of communication happened between friends and between roommates. Each day, the captain and/or another delegate from the players would attend the management meetings. This may be a stereotype, but I don't know any other way to be: I would suggest that as a female team, we liked to communicate and to know what was going on at all times. If, for some reason, information was not forthcoming from the management or senior leadership group about what the schedule or expectations were for that day, the players would start to worry and tended to take on the issues themselves personally. Being well-organised, well-informed and up-to-date was an essential part of the success of the Black Ferns.

Conflict and debate

In terms of conflicts, the team tended to get on well enough not to upset the culture or performance of the team, but there were some issues and events that did divide the team a little. The players tended to be divided on which leadership style they preferred – the micro-managing style of Darryl versus the more laissez-faire approach of Jed. Once again, players didn't feel strong enough about this to act against the wishes of the coaches at the time, because the desire to be a part of the team, and to be a Black Fern, was stronger than any individual's personality clash with the coaches. I'm sure there were times when players were not selected because they didn't reflect the values and expectations and skill set a particular coach was looking for – such is the nature of team sports and elite team selection. Each player had a choice to adapt or to no longer be a part of the team.

The formal team name had been up for debate in 1998. We had a team meeting and the players brainstormed different names because the North American press at the time was starting to call us 'Gal Blacks'. That seemed demeaning to us, so we argued whether we should be called the Lady Blacks or the Black Ferns. After a lengthy debate we decided that Black Ferns was the best fit, and announced this on New Zealand television's *Holmes* show. Of course we were not officially named the Black Ferns until the NZRFU had decided to endorse the name – providing their own version of what this brand would stand for and officially announcing the name at an acknowledgement ceremony at Parliament a few months later.

The official brand name was associated with several traits, attitudes and characteristics also associated with the All Blacks. The core brand values, however, were 'feminine' and 'respect'. Other key values and objectives of the brand were 'athleticism', 'excellence', 'inspirational'. Although we wanted to be considered rugby players first and 'feminine' second, we understood as a team that if we wanted to be embraced by the NZRFU, rugby fans and New Zealand society in general, we couldn't reject our femininity outright. Many of the players also liked to over-emphasise their femininity and sexuality off the field and spent what seemed like an eternity in front of the changing-room mirrors after the game and prior to the after-match function! Coming across as serious rugby players on the field, and feminine off the field, was important enough to most of the team that we had a big part to play in deciding what our 'Number Ones' (formal attire) would look like. We even put the likes of Melodie Robinson, one of our flankers, a previous Miss Canterbury winner, model, and these days television rugby broadcaster, in charge of helping to design it. Not all players were comfortable with wearing a skirt, but they did it because they knew this was an expectation within the team in order for the Black Ferns to be supported by the NZRFU, sponsors, fans and the public.

A closely related issue to the emphasis of portraying a 'feminine yet athletic' image was the issue of sexuality and homophobia in the team. Lesbianism and how to deal with it in a team environment was a sensitive issue. Research for my honours dissertation in the early 1990s suggested that women's rugby in North America developed, for the most part, out of the lesbian subculture, but in New Zealand it tended to emerge from within an already strong rugby structure that had been predominantly masculine and unchallenged. Initially, lesbianism in New Zealand women's rugby was not obvious. Later it was denied, then 'managed'. Attempts were made to squash its existence and now it is, for the most part, accepted, but I would argue it is not explicitly celebrated.

There is an ongoing conflict between those who feel lesbians in women's rugby are detrimental to the image (i.e. women who play rugby are 'butch' and therefore not 'real women') and development of the sport (i.e. parents fear their daughters will be turned into lesbians if they play or are preyed on by gay players). Others feel it is a non-issue and that heterosexual, bisexual and homosexual women play rugby – so get over it. Either way, I don't think we'll ever see the Black Ferns carrying a rainbow flag as a team, but it is great to see former player Louisa Wall go on to become a Member of Parliament and have a bill passed to legalise same-sex marriage. I'd like to think that the Black Ferns stood for challenging the status quo, giving women of all walks of life and sexual preferences a chance to excel in a sport, and resisting the urge to conform in a way that is going to disadvantage anyone.

PROFESSIONALISM
Gendered expectations

During my time as captain, which was about a decade, there were a few significant changes for the Black Ferns. They went from being a team nobody wanted to endorse or officially acknowledge, to the national darlings who won a World Cup in 1998 when the nation was still angry at the All Blacks for sustaining several losses in a row. In a terrible way, the All Blacks' demise helped us to shine more because the New Zealand press, public and rugby fans were looking for a success story – or at least for something to provoke the All Blacks into action. What better than a women's team winning at what was considered by most to be a man's sport? Of course, the spotlight didn't stay on the team for long. Once the All Blacks' winning percentages started to rise again, we were relegated down the priority list. But at least we were on the list. Once we received official acknowledgement from the NZRFU, and the IRB agreed to sanction the World Cup events, we had some stability.

From the late 1990s to the mid-2000s, women's rugby and the Black Ferns were at least resourced well enough to exist and to play internationals annually. There was a national provincial competition funded by the NZRU that peaked in the early 2000s with two divisions and more than a dozen provinces involved. By 2005, however, women's rugby at the lower levels was starting to haemorrhage.

This was probably due to a combination of factors. Women's rugby was no longer a novelty: it never received much in the way of media coverage to attract sponsors, so was a costly exercise for the NZRFU. It would always exist in the margins as a female element of a sport that is seen as a flag bearer of dominant masculinity in New Zealand. Provincial men's rugby had gone professional, suggesting women's rugby at that level would have to compete for limited resources at both the national and provincial/club/school level. Fortunately, throughout all of this the Black Ferns have continued to exist, but their budget has been limited at times and overseas tests are not guaranteed.

A recent sponsorship deal with AIG has thrown the Black Ferns a lifeline in that regard, with guaranteed games against England for three years. The future of the Black Ferns will always be determined by a mixture of the passion that women themselves have for playing rugby at the elite level and maintaining the legacy that was started back in the late 1980s, and the acceptance of women playing rugby by executives, sponsors, administrators, coaches and rugby fans. As a verse in the haka suggests, the Black Ferns legacy will continue as long as the women who represent the team are willing to fight for and uphold it in the face of resistance and apathy:

Tumai ra koe
Te mana wahine
Te Wharetangata
Nga Mamaku o Aotearoa
He tia he tia
He ranga he ranga.

You stand tall and proud
Women of strength and prestige
Who will bear the future
The Black Ferns of New Zealand
Let us proceed
Press on, press on.

CHAPTER SEVENTEEN
WINNING STATISTICS

DR HUGH MORTON

In his book *The Open Side*, Richie McCaw[1] says about coach Wayne Smith, 'Smithy's . . . big on stats . . . because he can interpret them in a useful way'. I can relate to that. When I meet people for the first time and tell them what I do, it often clams them up. With my attempts to revive the conversation the usual response is something like, 'Oh, I never thought maths and stats had anything to do with sport!' After a moment's reflection, however, they realise that there are plenty of sports statistics out there. The real problem is getting across the various messages that those statistics contain. For some time now, 'Smithy' obviously has solved that problem, and put his knowledge to good use. The question, then, is whether I can now extract some interesting information from the All Blacks' statistics. Can the All Blacks really be described as a winning team? Are other rugby teams as good as they are?

In layperson's terms, the meaning of 'winning' is usually obvious from the context, but in a book such as this it really needs more careful definition and interpretation. Being a sports statistician, an appeal to the numbers is my normal tactic, by asking simply, 'What should the numbers say to make the term sensible?' In this instance I'd say that the All Blacks, or indeed any team or individual, could sensibly be described as 'winning' if their win percentage is not just greater, but significantly greater, than 50.

If you take a look at very recent statistics, the All Blacks' test match records until the end of 2013,[2] you will find that, of the 512 recognised tests played, they have had 390 wins, 18 draws and 104 losses. This represents a winning percentage of 76.17 per cent.

Statisticians usually qualify such data by also providing what is called a confidence interval – like a margin of error – which is their way of saying that the real percentage (as distinct from the observed percentage) lies somewhere within that range, at least to a high (usually 95 per cent) degree of confidence. For the All Blacks, the appropriate 95 per cent confidence interval is from 72.33 to 80.01 per cent. Without question then, even at the lower end, their real winning percentage is obviously much greater than 50. Are they a winning team? I think it's indisputable.

Significantly, the All Blacks are better even than that: they are the 'winningest' men's rugby union team in the world! The team with the next best winning record is South Africa's Springboks, with a winning percentage of 62.47 and associated 95 per cent confidence interval of between 57.72 and 67.22 per cent. Therefore they, too, can be described as a winning team, but because these two confidence intervals do not even overlap, the Springboks at their best are most likely not as good as the All Blacks at their worst (that is, with 95 per cent confidence). Heady stuff! No doubt some readers with a Springboks bias will disagree, but the figures are facts and you can't argue with that.

Next on the list are Australia's Wallabies at 52.99 per cent, but although their confidence interval exceeds 50 per cent, they don't really merit the winning label. The British and Irish Lions are even further behind with a winning percentage of 40.35. If you'd like to see the figures for yourself, here's the whole table of win/draw/loss records for test matches played by these four teams.

WIN/DRAW/LOSS RECORDS OF THE TOP FOUR INTERNATIONAL RUGBY UNION TEAMS

Team	Win (%)	Draw (%)	Loss (%)	Total
All Blacks	390 (76.2)	18 (3.5)	104 (20.3)	512
Springboks	263 (62.5)	21 (5.0)	137 (32.5)	421
Wallabies	284 (53.0)	16 (3.0)	236 (44.0)	536
Lions	46 (40.3)	10 (8.8)	58 (50.9)	114

This high winning percentage by the All Blacks is not a new thing either. It goes back to the very start of their playing history. It is a fairly simple matter to examine the extent to which the All Blacks have retained their winning attribute over the years since. In this book the four epochs of particular interest are pre-1950, 1950 to 1969, 1970 to 1989, and 1990 to the present. The appropriate table of data follows.

WIN/DRAW/LOSS RECORD OF THE ALL BLACKS OVER TIME

Period	Win (%)	Draw (%)	Loss (%)	Total
Pre-1950	44 (62.9)	4 (5.7)	22 (31.4)	70
1950–69	57 (79.2)	4 (5.6)	11 (15.3)	72
1970–89	73 (71.6)	6 (5.9)	23 (22.5)	102
1990–	216 (80.6)	4 (1.5)	48 (17.9)	268
Total	390 (76.2)	18 (3.5)	104 (20.3)	512

Certainly there are minor differences in the percentages from one epoch to another, but the real question is whether they are significantly different – and if so, when might they have been? These questions can be statistically tested using what is known as a Chi-squared test, or contingency table test. It addresses the simple question: Is the real winning percentage the same (i.e. 76.2) throughout the whole time? Assuming it is, we can estimate, for example, that in the 1970–89 period when 102 matches were played, 78 wins (rounding up from 77.7) would have been expected, rather than the observed 73 – not a big difference. Likewise, we would expect 9.4 draws since 1990 from the 268 matches played – this time more than twice the number actually observed. By comparing all these observed and expected values throughout the table, which is what the Chi-squared test does, it turns out that these differences do indeed amount to significance, again with a high degree of confidence. The All Blacks' winning percentage has changed over time. We should therefore delve deeper into this.

Firstly, have the All Blacks always been a winning team? That is, has their win percentage always been significantly above 50? Clearly the pre-1950 epoch is the poorest and its 95 per cent confidence interval is from 57.28 to 68.44 per cent. Still, even then they were a winning team, and indeed have always remained so.

Next, if the differences are significant, can we discover just where the important differences lie? Indeed we can, by examining the differences between the observed and expected numbers of wins, draws and losses in the above table, together with their individual relative contributions to the overall Chi-squared test. When we do this, we discover that the win percentage was lower than average and the loss percentage higher than average in the pre-1950 period; and that there were too many draws in the 1970–89 period and too few in the period since 1990. Apart from that, any differences are within their margins of error.

With the kind of record the All Blacks have, many people have pondered why they have not won the Rugby World Cup more than twice out of the seven occasions it has been held. Gary Hermansson in his 2011 book *Going Mental in Sport* raises the question of whether the All Blacks are chokers, meaning that when a really big occasion arises they are not able to produce the usual winning outcomes. Whilst I can't really answer either of these questions, I will provide some figures derived from the preceding analysis which may assist you in forming your own opinion.

I will try to keep it reasonably simple. I'm assuming, first, that an estimated win probability of 0.7617 (76.2 per cent) applies throughout; and that the All Blacks have made it through to the last eight teams, the knockout stage of the tournament, as they always have. To win the Cup from there, they simply need three wins in a row, which has an estimated probability of $(0.7617)^3 = 0.4420$. Right away, this may be lower than you might intuitively have expected, but there's more! Taking part in seven tournaments, in which the estimated win probability at each is now 0.442, and using what is called the 'binomial distribution' of probabilities, we can calculate the probability of winning only two of them. This figure turns out to be 0.2220 (22.2 per cent) – half as much again. Putting this in context, the full binomial distribution of probabilities for the seven World Cups is as follows.

NUMBER OF WORLD CUPS AND PROBABILITIES OF THE ALL BLACKS WINNING THEM

0	1	2	3	4	5	6	7
0.0169	0.0934	0.2220	0.2931	0.2321	0.1103	0.0291	0.0033

Certainly three or four World Cup wins are estimated as more likely than two, but the expected number of wins is only three (rounded from 3.09). So, my view is that their World Cup record is poorer than might be expected, but not too bad. You may interpret these figures differently. Perhaps we are a little guilty of expecting too much from the All Blacks.

Rugby pervades the New Zealand sports landscape. From an early age our children are exposed to New Zealand's most popular game. Although the men's version of rugby union sits at the top of this tree, there are other closely related versions of the game and the All Blacks are not the only New Zealand rugby team with such an enviable record of success. Their female counterparts, the Black Ferns, have an even higher win percentage of 86.57 and, like the All Blacks, are also a winning team. Compared to the All Blacks, their international match record is presented in the following table.

WIN/DRAW/LOSS RECORDS OF THE ALL BLACKS AND BLACK FERNS

Team	Win (%)	Draw (%)	Loss (%)	Total
All Blacks	390 (76.2)	18 (3.5)	104 (20.3)	512
Black Ferns	58 (86.6)	1 (1.5)	8 (11.9)	67

As in the second table, there are some differences between the figures, but again the real question is whether they are significantly different. The Chi-squared test can once more be used to address this question. If the win/draw/loss percentages were really the same (448/579 = 0.7737 or 77.4 per cent, 3.3 per cent and 19.3 per cent, respectively, for both teams), we would have expected the All Blacks to have won 396 matches (rounded from 396.2) and the Black Ferns to have won 52 (rounded from 51.8). This time, however, these differences are significant, and on further testing I'm quite confident (95 per cent) in saying that the Black Ferns are significantly 'more winning' than the All Blacks themselves! The Black Ferns' 95 per cent confidence interval from 83.7 to 89.4 per cent does not overlap that of the All Blacks (72.33 to 80.01 per cent). Some may be surprised at this fact, but those who know the figures won't be.

So what can we conclude from all this? Without a doubt, the numerical evidence is unequivocal. The All Blacks are winners and have been since inception, and so too are the Black Ferns. Since they all come under the same umbrella, maybe it's the All Blacks brand that's the real winner here. No others in the rugby world come close.

NOTES

Introduction: A Winning Culture
1. Gilson, Pratt, Roberts & Weymes, 2000
2. Fitzpatrick, 2011, p. 144, p. 128

Chapter 1: A Life of Rugby
1. Fitzpatrick, 2011, p. 124
2. De Jong, 1991
3. Cushman, 1989
4. Sahlins, 1985
5. Taylor, 1985, p. 107
6. Taylor, 1985, p. 112
7. Sinclair, 1986, p. 147
8. Sinclair, 1991, p. 318
9. Laidlaw, 2010, p. 52
10. Mourie, 1982, pp. 27–45, p. 28
11. Mourie, 1982, p. 29
12. Romanos, 2002
13. Thomas, 2003, p. 9
14. Thomas 2003, p. 23
15. Thomas, 2003
16. Romanos, 2002
17. Thomas, 2003
18. Mourie, 1982, p. 82
19. Denis, Lamothe & Langley, 2001; Lemay, 2009
20. Schein, 2004, p. 22
21. *The New Zealand Herald*, 3 June 2008

PART I: A WINNING LEGACY
1. Thomas, 2003, p. 9

Chapter 2: John 'DJ' Graham
1. McLean, 1964, p. 237
2. McLean, 1964, p. 55

Chapter 3: Colin Meads
1. Veysey, 1974, p. 49

Chapter 4: Brian 'BJ' Lochore
1. Veysey, Caffell & Palenski, 1996

PART II: WINNING THE WORLD CUP
1. Thomas, 2003, p. 47, p. 50
2. McLean, 1977
3. Haden, 1983

Chapter 6: Andy Haden
1. Haden, 1983
2. Haden, 1983, pp. 206–221
3. Haden, 1988

Chapter 7: Andy Dalton
1. Cited in Russell, 1999, p. 40

PART III: WINNING THE WORLD CUP TWICE
1. Thomas, 2003, p. 9
2. Laidlaw, 2010
3. Laidlaw, 2010
4. NZRU estimate, 2010

Chapter 11: Wayne Smith
1. Kidman, 2001
2. Kidman, 2005
3. Kidman, 2001, pp. 37, 38
4. Kidman, 2001, pp. 43, 45
5. Kidman, 2005, pp. 189–191

Chapter 13: Leading the Legacy
1. Fitzpatrick, 2011, p. 116
2. Johnson et al., 2012, 2013a, 2013b
3. McCaw, 2012, p. 181
4. Parrant & Martin, 2010, p. 70
5. Kidman, 2001, p. 49
6. McCaw, 2012, p. 213

PART IV: A STUDY OF WINNING
1. Source: vincelombardi.com/quotes. html, 1 May 2014
2. Schein, 2010, p. 3
3. Schein, 2010, p. 235

Chapter 14: Winning Ways
1. Howitt, 2012
2. Kornspan, 2009
3. Schein, 2010, p. 3
4. Kirwan, 2010, p. 42
5. Johnson et al., 2012
6. Heron & Tricker, 2008
7. Mackenzie, 1960; Haden, 1983; Hokowhitu, 2005
8. Miller, 1990
9. Berman, Down and Hill, 2002
10. Schein, 2010, p. 18
11. Schein, 1981, p. 4
12. Schein, 2011, p. 168
13. Schein, 2011, p. 370
14. Schein, 2011, p. 371
15. Chatman and Cha, 2002
16. Bartol & Martin, 1998, p. 221
17. Machiavelli, 1513/1950, p. 21
18. Chatman and Cha, 2002
19. Chatman and Cha, 2002

Chapter 15: A History of Winning
1. Booth, 2000
2. Collins, 2009

3. Smith, 1981, p. 34
4. Odendaal, 1988
5. Johnes, 2000
6. Holt, 1989
7. Baker, 1988
8. Collins, 2009; Holt, 1989
9. Holt, 1989
10. Collins, 2009; Huggins, 2004
11. Murray, 1994
12. Collins, 2009
13. Holt, 1989; Murray, 1994
14. Mangan, 1986
15. McLintock, 1966
16. Ryan, 2005a; Swan, 1948
17. Macdonald, 1999; Ryan, 2005a
18. Olssen, 1992
19. McLintock, 1966
20. Belich, 1996
21. Akers, 1986, p. 12
22. Ryan, 2005a
23. Ryan, 2005b
24. NZRU, 2012
25. Siegfried, 1914
26. Watson, 2003
27. Phillips, 1996
28. Vincent, 2005
29. Turley, 2008
30. Phillips, 1996
31. Greenwood, 2008
32. Vincent, 2005
33. Hilton & Smith, 1991
34. Swan, 1948
35. Phillips, 1996
36. Phillips, 1996, p. 96
37. Belich, 1996
38. Phillips, 1996
39. *Manawatu Standard*, 25 June 2011
40. Turley, 2008; *Auckland Star*, 6 August 1886
41. Belich, 2001
42. Belich, 2001
43. Belich, 1996
44. *Star*, 21 July 1890
45. Crawford, 1999
46. Holt, 1989, p. 3
47. Swan, 1948
48. Ryan, 1996
49. Swan, 1948, p. 89
50. *Auckland Star*, 30 May 1884
51. N.Z. Rugby Football Annual 1885, cited in Hunter, 1929, p. 20
52. *Auckland Star*, 17 June 1884
53. McLean, 1975

54. Ryan, 1993
55. Ryan, 2005c
56. Hokowhitu, 2005, p. 76
57. Reeves, 1898
58. Johnson et al., 2013a
59. New Zealand Rugby Museum, 2004; Ryan, 1993
60. Palenski, 2009, 2012
61. Vincent, 2005
62. *Auckland Star*, 17 June 1884
63. *Australian Town and Country Journal*, 7 June 1884; *Sydney Morning Herald*, 2 June 1884
64. Ellison, 1902; Mackenzie, 1960
65. Ellison, 1902, p. 12
66. *Evening Post*, 15 August, 1884
67. Mackenzie, 1960
68. Mackenzie, 1960, p. 21
69. Palenski, 2012
70. Daley, 2005; Ryan, 2005b
71. Ryan, 2005b
72. Ryan, 2005a, 2005d
73. Ryan, 2005d
74. Johnson et al., 2012, 2013a, 2013b
75. McLean, 1968, p. 159
76. Veysey, 1974, p. 180
77. Ryan, 2005d
78. *Daily Telegraph*, 1921, cited in Thompson, 1975, p. 12
79. Richards, 1999; Thompson, 1975
80. Richards, 1999
81. McLean, 1975
82. Kidd, 1987; Shelford, 1990; Macdonald, 1996.
83. Chu et al., 2003
84. NZRU, 2013
85. Rashbrooke, 2013
86. Charlwood & Haynes, 2008
87. Haden, 1983; Shelford, 1990
88. New Zealand Government, 1956
89. Statistics New Zealand, 2013
90. Matheson, 2001
91. Johnson et al., 2013a, 2013b
92. Johnson et al., 2012, 2013a, 2013b

Chapter 16: Winning Black Ferns

1. *Black Ferns World Cup Media Guide*, NZRFU, 2002

Chapter 17: Winning Statistics

1. McCaw, 2012, p. 60
2. Source: stats.allblacks.com, 27 November 2013

REFERENCES

Akers, C. (1986). *Manawatu Rugby: The First 100 years*. Palmerston North, Manawatu Rugby Union and Offset Printing.

Baker, W. (1988). *Sports in the Western World*. Urbana and Chicago, University of Illinois Press.

Bartol, K.M., & Martin, D. C. (1998). *Management*. Boston, Irwin McGraw-Hill.

Belich, J. (1996). *Making Peoples: A history of the New Zealanders from Polynesian settlement to the end of the nineteenth century*. Auckland, Allen Lane.

Belich, J. (2001). *Paradise Reforged: A history of the New Zealanders from the 1880s to the year 2000*. Auckland, Auckland University Press.

Berman, S.L., Down, J., & Hill, C.W.L. (2002). Tacit knowledge as a source of competitive advantage in the National Basketball Association. *Academy of Management Journal*, 45 (1), 13–31.

Booth, D. (2000). From Allusion to Causal Explanation: The comparative method in sports history. *International Sporting Studies*, 22 (2), 5–25.

Charlwood, A., & Haynes, P. (2008). Union Membership Decline in New Zealand, 1990–2002. *Journal of Industrial Relations*, 50 (1), 87–110.

Chatman, J.A., & Cha, S.F. (2002). Leading by Leveraging Culture. In S. Chowdhury (ed.), *Next generation business series: Leadership*. New Jersey, Financial Times-Prentice Hall Publishers.

Chu, M.L., Leberman, S.I., Howe, B.L., & Bachor, D.G. (2003). The Black Ferns: The experiences of New Zealand's elite women rugby players. *Journal of Sport Behaviour*, 26 (2), 109–120.

Collins, T. (2009). *A Social History of English Rugby Union*. London and New York, Routledge.

Crawford, S. (1986). A Secular Religion: The historical iconography of New Zealand rugby. *Physical Education Review*, 8 (2), 146–158.

Crawford, S.A.G.M. (1999). Rugby and the Forging of a National Identity. In J. Nauright (ed.), *Sport, Power and Society in New Zealand: Historical and contemporary perspectives* (pp. 5–19). Sydney, ASSH Studies in Sports History, 11.

Crocombe, G., Enright, M., & Porter, M. (1991). *Upgrading New Zealand's Competitive Advantage*. Auckland, Oxford University Press. *Economic Papers*, 26 (1), 101–125.

Cushman, G. (1989). Trends in Sports in New Zealand. In T. Kamphorst & K. Roberts (eds), *Trends in Sports: A multinational perspective* (pp. 133–157). Voorthuizen, Netherlands, Giordano Bruno Culemborg.

Daley, C. (2005). The Invention of 1905. In G. Ryan (ed.), *Tackling Rugby Myths: Rugby and New Zealand Society 1854–2004* (pp. 69–87). Dunedin, Otago University Press.

De Jong, P. (1991). *Saturday's Warriors: The building of a rugby stronghold*. Palmerston North, Massey University, Department of Sociology.

Denis, J.L., Lamothe, L., & Langley, A. (2001). The dynamics of collective leadership and strategic change in pluralistic organisations. *Academy of Management Journal*, 44 (4), 809–837.

Ellison, T.R. (1902, reprinted 1997). *The Art of Rugby Football*. Christchurch, Kiwi.

Fitzpatrick, S. (2011). *Winning Matters: Being the best you can be*. London, Penguin.

Gilson, C., Pratt, M., Roberts, K., & Weymes, K. (2000). *Peak Performance*. London, HarperCollins.

Greenwood, W. (2008). Class, Conflict and the Clash of Codes: the introduction of Rugby League to New Zealand: 1908–1920. Unpublished PhD thesis. Palmerston North, Massey University.

Haden, A.M. (1983). *Boots'n all!*, Auckland, Rugby Press.

Haden, A.M. (1988). *Lock, Stock'n Barrel*, Auckland, Rugby Press.

Hermansson, G.L. (2011). *Going Mental in Sport*. Palmerston North, Inside-Out Books.

Heron, M., & Tricker, D. (2008). *Independent Review of the 2007 Rugby World Cup Campaign*. Wellington, Russell McVeagh/SPARC.

Hilton, T., & Smith, B. (1991). *An Association with Soccer: The NZFA celebrates its first 100 years*. Auckland, New Zealand Football Association.

Hokowhitu, B. (2005). Rugby and Tino Rangatiratanga: Early Maori Rugby and the formation of 'traditional' Maori masculinity. *Sporting Traditions*, 21 (2), 75–95.

Holt, R. (1989). *Sport and the British*. Oxford, Clarendon.

Howitt, R. (2012). *Graham Henry. Final Word*. Auckland, HarperCollins.

Huggins, M. (2004). *The Victorians and Sport*. London, Hambledon and London.

Hunter, I. (c. 1929). *New Zealand Rugby Football: some hints and criticisms*. Auckland, Whitcombe & Tombs.

Johnes, M. (2000). Hooligans and Barrackers: crowd disorder and soccer in South Wales, c. 1906–39. *Soccer and Society*, 1 (2), 19–35.

Johnson, T., Martin, A.J., Palmer, F.R., Watson, G.D., & Ramsey, P. (2013a). Artefacts and the All Blacks: Rites, rituals, symbols and stories. *Sporting Traditions*, 30 (1), 43–59.

Johnson, T., Martin, A.J., Palmer, F.R., Watson, G.D., & Ramsey, P. (2013b). A Core Value of Pride in Winning. The All Blacks' team culture and legacy. *The International Journal of Sport and Society*, 4 (1), 1–14.

Johnson, T., Martin, A.J., Palmer, F.R., Watson, G.D., & Ramsey, P. (2012). Collective Leadership: a case study of the All Blacks. *Asia-Pacific Management and Business Application*, 1 (1), 53–67.

Kidd, H. (1987). Rugby's Royal Return. In J. Kirwan, *John Kirwan's Rugby World* (pp. 105–110). Auckland, Rugby Press.

Kidman, L. (2001). *Developing Decision Makers: an empowerment approach to coaching*. Christchurch, Innovative Press.

Kidman, L. (2005). *Athlete-centred Coaching: developing inspired and inspiring people*. Christchurch, Innovative Press.

Kirwan, J. (2010). *All Blacks Don't Cry.* Auckland, Penguin.

Kornspan, A.S. (2009). *Fundamentals of Sport and Exercise Psychology.* Champaign, Human Kinetics.

Laidlaw, C. (2010). *Somebody Stole My Game.* Auckland, Hodder Moa.

Laidlaw, C. (1973). *Mud In Your Eye. A worm's eye view of the changing world of rugby.* Wellington, A.H. & A.W. Reed.

Lemay L. (2009). The Practice of Collective Leadership in the Public Sector. *The Public Sector Innovation Journal,* 14 (1), Article 2.

Lewin, K. (1947). Group Decision and Social Change. In E.E. Maccoby, T.M. Newcomb & E.L. Hartley (eds), *Readings in Social Psychology* (pp. 197–211). New York, Holt, Reinhart and Winston.

Lombardi, V. (2013). *Famous Quotes by Vince Lombardi.* Retrieved 1 December 2013 from www.vincelombardi.com/quotes.html.

Macdonald, C. (1999). Too Many Men and Too Few women: gender's fatal impact in nineteenth century colonies. In C. Daley & D. Montgomerie (eds), *The Gendered Kiwi* (pp. 17–35). Auckland, Auckland University Press.

Macdonald, F. (1996). *The Game of our Lives. The story of Rugby and New Zealand – and how they've shaped each other.* Penguin, Auckland.

Machiavelli, N. (1513/1950). *The Prince and the Discourses.* New York, The Modern Library Random House.

Mackenzie, J.M. (1960). *All Blacks in Chains.* Wellington, Truth.

Mangan, J.A. (1986). *The Games Ethic and Imperialism: aspects of the diffusion of an ideal.* Middlesex, Harmondsworth.

Matheson, J. (2001, October). What's the White Answer?, *NZ Rugby World,* 47, 20–38.

McCaw, R. (with McGee, G.) (2012). *The Open Side.* Auckland, Hodder Moa.

McLean, T. (1977). *Winter of Discontent.* Wellington, A.H. & A. W. Reed.

McLean, T. (1975). *All Blacks Come Back.* Wellington, A.H. & A.W. Reed.

McLean, T. (1968). *All Black Power: the story of the 1968 All Blacks in Australia and Fiji and the 1968 French team in New Zealand and Australia.* Auckland, A.H. & A.W. Reed.

McLean, T. (1964). *Willie Away: Wilson Whineray's All Blacks of 1963–64.* Wellington: A.H. & A.W. Reed.

McLintock, A.H. (1966). *An Encyclopaedia of New Zealand.* Volume 2, Wellington, Government Printer.

Miller, D. (1990). *The Icarus Paradox.* New York, HarperCollins.

Mourie, G. (with Palenski, R.) (1982). *Graham Mourie, Captain: an autobiography.* Auckland, Moa.

Murray, W. (1994). *Football: a history of the world game.* Aldershot, Scholar.

New Zealand Government. (1956). *Population Census, 1951,* Vol. 8. Wellington, Government Printer.

New Zealand Rugby Museum. (2004). 1884 – The First New Zealand Team. *New Zealand Rugby Museum Newsletter,* April 2004, Palmerston North, New Zealand Rugby Museum.

New Zealand Rugby Union. (2012). *Inspiring and Unifying New Zealand. New Zealand Rugby Union Annual Report 2012.* Wellington & Auckland, New Zealand Rugby Union.

New Zealand Rugby Union. (2013). *Black Ferns.* http://www.allblacks.com/index.cfm?layout=team_blackFerns accessed 22 October 2013.

Odendaal, A. (1988). South Africa's Black Victorians: sport and society in South Africa in the nineteenth century. In J.A. Mangan (ed.), *Pleasure, Profit, Proselytism: British culture and sport at home and abroad* (pp. 193–214). London, Frank Cass.

Olssen, E. (1992). Towards a New Society. In G.W. Rice (ed.), *The Oxford History of New Zealand* (pp. 254–284). Auckland, Oxford University Press.

Palenski, R. (2009). The Naming of the All Blacks: Unravelling the Myth. *Sporting Traditions,* 26 (1), 21–32.

Palenski, R. (2012). *The Making of New Zealanders.* Auckland, Auckland University Press.

Parrant, D., & Martin, A.J. (2010). Developing decision making in rugby. *Waikato Journal of Education,* 15 (3), 69–86.

Phillips, J. (1996). *A Man's Country? The image of the Pakeha male – a history.* Auckland, Penguin.

Rashbrooke, M. (2013). *Inequality: A New Zealand Conversation.* http://www.inequality.org.nz/understand/ accessed 29 November 2013.

Rattue, C. (2008). Why I Can No Longer Support the All Blacks. *New Zealand Herald,* 3 June 2008.

Reeves, W.P. (1898, reprinted 1973). *The Long White Cloud. Ao Tea Roa.* Auckland, Golden Press.

Richards, T. (1999). *Dancing On Our Bones: New Zealand, South Africa, rugby and racism.* Wellington, Bridget Williams.

Romanos, J. (2002). *The Judas Game: The betrayal of New Zealand rugby.* Wellington, Darius Press.

Russell, A. (1999). The New Zealand Rugby Football Union and the Springbok Tour. Unpublished Master's thesis, Palmerston North, Massey University.

Ryan, G. (1993). *Forerunners of the All Blacks: The 1888–89 New Zealand Native Football Team in Britain, Australia and New Zealand.* Christchurch, Canterbury University Press.

Ryan, G. (1996). Where the Game was Played by Decent Chaps: The Making of New Zealand Cricket 1832–1914. Unpublished PhD thesis. Christchurch, University of Canterbury.

Ryan, G. (2005a). Rural Myth and Urban Actuality: the anatomy of All Black and New Zealand Rugby 1884–1938. In G. Ryan (ed.), *Tackling Rugby Myths: Rugby and New Zealand Society 1854–2004* (pp. 33–68). Dunedin, Otago University Press.

Ryan, G. (2005b). *The Contest for Rugby Supremacy.* Christchurch, Canterbury University Press.

Ryan, G. (2005c). The Paradox of Maori Rugby 1870–1914. In G. Ryan (ed.), *Tackling Rugby Myths: Rugby and New Zealand Society 1854–2004* (pp. 89–103). Dunedin, Otago University Press.

Ryan, G. (2005d). The End of an Aura: All Black rugby and rural nostalgia in the professional era. In G. Ryan (ed.), *Tackling Rugby Myths: Rugby and New Zealand Society 1854–2004* (pp. 151–172). Dunedin, Otago University Press.

Sahlins, M. (1985). *Islands of History*. Chicago, University of Chicago Press.

Schein, E.H. (2011). *Organizational Culture and Leadership* (5th ed.). San Francisco, Jossey Bass.

Schein, E.H. (2010). *Organizational Culture and Leadership* (4th ed.). San Francisco, Jossey Bass.

Schein, E.H. (2004). *Organizational Culture and Leadership* (3rd ed.). San Francisco, Jossey Bass.

Shelford, W. (1990). *Buck. The Wayne Shelford Story*. Auckland, Moa.

Siegfried, A. (1914, reprinted 1982). *Democracy in New Zealand*. Wellington, Victoria University Press.

Sinclair, K. (1986). *A Destiny Apart: New Zealand's Search for National Indentity*, Wellington: Allen and Unwin.

Sinclair, K. (1991). *A History of New Zealand* (4th ed.). Auckland: Penguin.

Smith, D. (1981). People's Theatre – A Century of Welsh Rugby. *History Today*, 31 (3), 31–36.

Statistics New Zealand. (2013). *2013 Census QuickStats About National Highlights*. Wellington, Statistics New Zealand.

Swan, A. (1948). *History of New Zealand Rugby Football 1870–1945*. Wellington, A.H. & A.W. Reed.

Taylor, M. (1985). *All Blacks Almost*. Havelock North, TC Publications.

Thomas, P. (2003). *A Whole New Ball Game: Confronting the myths and realities of New Zealand rugby*. Auckland, Hodder Moa Beckett.

Thompson, R. (1975). *Retreat From Apartheid: New Zealand's sporting contacts with South Africa*. London, Oxford University Press.

Turley, A. (2008). *Rugby: the Pioneer Years*. Auckland, HarperCollins.

Veysey, A., Caffell, G., & Palenski, R. (1996). *Lochore: An Authorised Biography*. Auckland, Hodder Moa Beckett.

Veysey, A. (1974). *Colin Meads, All Black*. Auckland, William Collins.

Vincent, G. (2005). 'To uphold the honour of the province': Football in Canterbury c. 1854 – c. 1890. In G. Ryan (ed.), *Tackling Rugby Myths: Rugby and New Zealand Society 1854–2004* (pp. 13–30). Dunedin, Otago University Press.

Watson, G. (2003). *Aotea Sports Club: 100 Years of History 1903–2003*. Dannevirke, Te Kopara.

AUTHORS

Dr Tom Johnson, NZOM 75, recently retired, completed his doctoral thesis – *A case study of the Winning Ethos and Organisational Culture of the All Blacks (1950–2010)*, at Massey University in 2012. His background incorporates involvement with rugby, education and management. The case study years involved in Tom's dissertation closely parallel those of his own work and involvement in sport. For example, the 1950s and 1960s saw Tom as both a teacher and a rugby player. He was then an administrator at various rugby levels during the 1970s and 1980s before becoming involved in business management with New Zealand public companies. To say the least, these years collectively represent interesting times that invite reflection on a number of social and economic changes that have occurred in New Zealand and have – directly or indirectly – impacted on what we might call our rugby culture. In addition to any work history, Tom's involvement with rugby led to a range of social contacts both on and off the field which, together with his own player, coaching and administration roles, have contributed directly to Tom's experiential learning and its fundamental application to the lives of many New Zealanders.

Tom played for Hawke's Bay and was an All Blacks trialist, a leading loose forward at provincial level in the 1960s. He chaired the Hawke's Bay Rugby Union in 1972 and, upon transfer to Wellington with Europa Oil, served on the council of the New Zealand Rugby Football Union (NZRFU – renamed the New Zealand Rugby Union, NZRU, in 2006) from 1973 to 1986. During his tenure the opposition to South Africa sports tours escalated and a 1973 tour of New Zealand was scrapped. He was still there for the troubled 1981 Springbok Tour, the 1985 court-blocked plans for an All Blacks tour of South Africa and most of the top players' rebel tour as the Cavaliers of 1986. He drove a number of coaching and development initiatives that helped New Zealand maintain a pre-eminent position in the global game, leading to arguably his most important role: writing the original position paper on the need for a World Cup. In the late 1970s he also began developing international Golden Oldies rugby tournaments. In the later stages of his career he became general manager of the Hawke's Bay Racing Centre, then embarked on teaching business studies at the Eastern Institute of Technology.

Dr Andrew John Martin is an Associate Professor in the School of Sport and Exercise, Massey University. His research focus is on sport-related experiential learning settings. He was awarded a Massey University Academic Fellowship in Applied Learning in 2012. He has worked with a number of sports and corporate organisations in the development of effective training and experiential education programmes. He has also carried out a number of studies on Outward Bound, including his PhD. Andrew has followed Tom's postgraduate study with keen interest, supervising both his Master's and PhD theses. His own career began in the United Kingdom teaching mathematics and coaching football at Millfield, a top public school. Following on from his Master's degree at Loughborough University, he managed programmes and events for a leading health club facility near London. After moving to New Zealand in 1993 he worked as event manager for the Hillary Commission Big Coast Series of mountain-bike treks. In 1994 he took up his current position at Massey University and runs a successful series of children's triathlon events in Manawatu. He holds professional coaching qualifications in football and tennis, and is actively involved in coaching at both junior and senior level.

Dr Geoff Watson is a Senior Lecturer in the School of Humanities, Massey University. His research focus is sports history. He is the principal author of *Seasons of Honour: A Centennial History of New Zealand Hockey 1902–2002* and *Sporting Foundations of New Zealand Indians: A fifty-year history of the New Zealand Indian Sports Association*. He has also written a number of articles on sporting topics, including entries on hockey and on amateurism and professionalism in *Te Ara: The Encyclopedia of New Zealand*, and histories of the Aotea Sports Club and Massey University Rugby Football Club. He teaches a paper in sports history at Massey University and was one of the academic advisors for Tom's PhD thesis. He takes an interest in most sports and has been extensively involved at grassroots level, including coaching Massey University hockey teams for the past seven years. He has recently taken up running again, after a prolonged absence, and can be heard gasping for breath whilst running on the walkway alongside the Manawatu River.

Editor **Margot Butcher** is a freelance journalist known for her outstanding writing on rugby, cricket and other sports. She has been named New Zealand's Sports Journalist of the Year twice and in 2007 travelled with the All Blacks as their official biographer, gaining an inside view of the professional workings of the team. She has represented New Zealand Croatia at cricket and often reminds the otherwise male members of the team that she holds the best bowling strike rate with a winning performance of 1–0 off 0.2 overs over the Cook Islands' national women's team in 2013.

Dr Farah Rangikoepa Palmer, NZOM, is a Senior Lecturer in the School of Management, Massey University. Her research focuses on leadership and governance. Farah captained the New Zealand Black Ferns team to three consecutive Women's Rugby World Cup wins in 1998, 2002 and 2006. Whilst studying at University of Otago she joined the University club and played her first match for Otago in 1992. She first played for New Zealand on 31 August 1996 against Australia in Sydney and became captain of the Black Ferns in 1997, with a first-up 67–0 win over England. In 1998 she was awarded Women's Player of the Year by the NZRFU. In 2005 she missed her first match for the Black Ferns since 1996, due to injury. That year she was awarded International Women's Personality of the Year by the International Rugby Board (IRB). After defeating England 25–17 in the final of the 2006 Women's Rugby World Cup, Farah announced her retirement from playing. She had played 35 tests and during her time as captain the Black Ferns lost only once. Since retiring, she has continued in rugby in a variety of capacities, including a two-year stint coaching a women's club team. She has served as a member of the Women's Advisory Group for the IRB, as an independent member of the New Zealand Maori Rugby Board, helped with the personal and professional development of professional rugby players, selected national coaches and provided research and strategic planning for the NZRU and New Zealand Rugby Players' Association (NZRPA).

Dr Hugh Morton is a Professor in the School of Sport and Exercise, Massey University. He is interested in all kinds of sports data. His teaching and research focus is the application of mathematical and statistical concepts to sports performance data, and to sport and exercise more generally. All data, not only sports data, contain information and it is how to best extract it all that's important.

ACKNOWLEDGEMENTS

The authors would like to thank all the All Blacks players, captains and coaches who have participated in interviews for this work. Your insights and passion for the All Blacks have been humbling. We also acknowledge the support of the NZRU in supporting the research for this book. Thanks also to staff at Massey University who have contributed their considerable expertise in developing a number of chapters and to Peter Bush for allowing us to reproduce his photographs. This book would also not have come together without the support of our wives and families – thank you to you all. Finally, our thoughts are with the family of Dr Art Thomas, who died in October 2013 shortly after the initial thoughts for this book were being developed. Art retired to Hawke's Bay following a career as a Senior Lecturer in Marketing at both Massey University and the Eastern Institute of Technology. He was a good friend and is sadly missed.

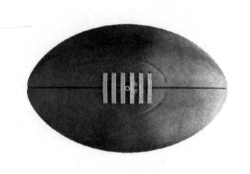